'Rather wonderful'

'A tour de force'

> Lord Rose, former CEO and Chairman of Marks & Spencer

'A breath of fresh air'   *Australian Financial Review*

'Better than Piketty'

> James K. Galbraith, author of *Welcome to the Poisoned Chalice: The Destruction of Greece and the Future of Europe*

'In *Signals* Dr Pippa Malmgren draws attention to the everyday signals – from magazine covers to shop fronts – that reveal the state of the world's economy and help us to understand recent tectonic shifts in global politics … its anecdotal, accessible and democratising approach is welcome'   Ed Jones, LSE blogs

'A fascinating read. Full of lateral insights'

> Lieutenant General Nick Pope, Deputy Chief of the General Staff

'Essential reading'

> Mahathir bin Mohamad, former Prime Minister of Malayasia

Dr Pippa Malmgren is a former presidential advisor and has served as the chief currency strategist for Bankers Trust and the deputy head of global strategy at UBS. She co-founded H Robotics, a firm which manufactures aerial robots, and DRPM, a consulting business. She serves on boards at the UK Department for International Trade, Indiana University and the Ditchley Foundation. Malmgren is a frequent guest on the BBC, including *Newsnight* and the *Today* programme, and is a popular commentator and public speaker with the *Financial Times*, the *Economist*, Intelligence Squared and others. She lives in London.

 @DrPippaM

Signals

How Everyday Signs Can
Help Us Navigate the World's
Turbulent Economy

DR PIPPA MALMGREN

WEIDENFELD & NICOLSON

First published in Great Britain in 2015
by Grosvenor House Publishing Ltd
First published in a revised edition in 2016
This updated paperback edition published in 2017
by Weidenfeld & Nicolson
an imprint of The Orion Publishing Group Ltd
Carmelite House, 50 Victoria Embankment
London EC4Y 0DZ

An Hachette UK Company

1 3 5 7 9 10 8 6 4 2

A CIP catalogue record for this book is
available from the British Library.

ISBN (paperback) 978 1 474 60352 2

Typeset by Input Data Services Ltd, Bridgwater, Somerset

Printed and bound by CPI Group (UK) Ltd, Croydon, CR0 4YY

www.orionbooks.co.uk

Contents

Introduction to the 2017 edition

It is a supreme irony that the people most adversely impacted by the world economy are typically those who are least interested in it. Meanwhile, the experts in the economics profession who claim to have the greatest interest in the world economy have been the most consistently wrong. Economists and other experts have missed every single major event of the last decade: the financial crisis in 2008, the slowdown in China, the recovery in the US, Brexit, Trump, the return of inflation and the rise of the anti-European Union or anti-Euro movement. The informed and uninformed alike have been caught out by forces beyond their understanding. Our attitude is – it's a storm. Nothing can be done.

Yet, I saw each of these events coming. I wrote and warned about them and endured ridicule at times for doing so. I assure you that I am not any smarter or even better informed than anybody else. It is simply that I opened both eyes. This sounds so childishly simple as to be ridiculous.

Let me explain how we miss the obvious all the time. During the 2016 presidential race in the US, I knew the polls said Hillary Clinton would win. But, I saw pictures of Clinton rallies with many empty seats and pictures of Trump rallies where the seats were full and people were lining up to get in. We know who won.

The experts miss these kinds of important signals for one simple reason – they insist on seeing the world half blind. They prefer to look at the world by drilling down into detail, usually mathematical detail, often deep within a narrow professional silo. They truly believe that the only legitimate answers are to be found in numbers, in data, in models, in polls and other rational mathematical approaches which are typically too boring and complex for regular people to care about or comprehend.

By looking at the world solely through a mathematical lens we also enslave ourselves to the past. After all, data is backward-looking. It only confirms what happened yesterday. Extrapolating the past into the future might sound like a good idea but it is (ironically) prohibited in the financial markets. Investment products always come with the boilerplate phrase 'past returns are not indicative of future performance'. Yet we assume the economy's past performance somehow predicates the future.

It is my contention that the style of analysis *is* the problem. When we insist on being blind in one eye, we miss all the things that cannot be calculated.

We do not like to look across the landscape and consider the signals mathematics cannot quantify – the stories, the anecdotes, the narrative or the context. But you can do both. You can notice that there are fewer crisps or chips in a bag, fewer chocolates in a packet, less cereal in a box. All signal rising input costs. So, the central banks may say that your cost of living is not rising but you can now 'see' the hints that it might well rise in the future well before the data confirms it.

Signals are hints about the future that are not yet captured in the data. By opening our eyes to both, we can achieve a more holistic view. The world is not just a mathematical theorem. 'Not everything that counts can be counted,' as Einstein reminded us.

There are many other contributing factors to our failure to understand the world economy. For example, among the educated, where there are few excuses, there is a sense of equivocacy – a notion that for every expert or indicator there is another of equal value disproving it. This has caused our interest in the facts – whether political or economic – to be increasingly supplanted by opinion. Thus, we begin a new age of post-truth and alternative facts.

Is an anecdote a fact? Perhaps not, but anecdotal evidence can still be helpful. Stories surround us which we should consider. Take fashion, for example. I open this book with a discussion of fashion signals, which sounds absurd to traditional economists. Nobody in economics looks at fashion as an indicator of the future and yet one of the most important fights in politics and economics in 2017 was between two hats. There were those wearing Donald Trump's shouty red caps with the 'Make America Great' stitching and stiff, hard peaks. Then there were those sporting the pink crocheted 'pussy hats' that have come to symbolise opposition to the former and which stand for a softer, more inclusive vision of our future. In this book, I suggest that the solution to our troubled social fabric will come from stitching together a new social contract (a new deal) between citizens and their governments. It has begun with the simple act of stitching words on and knitting caps. Show me the data point that tells us as much about the world today as those two hats.

Hard-headed professional economists and 'experts' choke at the idea that soft anecdotes can be as valuable as hard numbers. Their unwavering certainty persists despite them having been wrong almost every time. The experts say there is no inflation, despite epic efforts by central banks around the globe to generate it. When I open my eyes, I see can see the outcomes it encourages. For example, when violence broke out in Portland in the US state of Oregon, everyone was surprised. Why does no one seem to notice that rents rose there by 15 per cent in 2015 alone and continued on that path in 2016? Is there really no inflation? The people in Portland are feeling pain. We ignore that pain, and worse, we ignore the cause. In the UK, costs for heating and rail fares, school fees and housing had all risen sharply and relentlessly before the Brexit vote, yet so many failed to anticipate that people would be agitated enough to vote for Brexit.

Signals sometimes create great uproar without anybody clocking what the signal means. Witness the outrage in late 2016, when Toblerone, the firm that makes the iconic triangular chocolate bars, dared to save money by making the gaps between the pieces bigger. The iconic triangles were set wider apart which meant fewer ingredients were needed. It saved the firm money but created a firestorm of a reaction – Tobleronegate. Few registered that rising input costs at Toblerone signalled the potential for rising costs across the entire landscape of people's lives. Central banks across the industrialised world are confirming that inflation is rising. But did this need to have been such a surprise? The rising price of a chocolate bar or lipstick or some other everyday product might not seem materially important in the grander scheme of things. Yet, it is these small things that people interact with. Whatever pain or joy spills over from these small things sets the stage for the mood across the wider landscape.

Something bigger is at stake. The economists and experts who have been so wrong are still calculating the numbers and telling us what our future holds. Most of them are pretty pessimistic. So, it makes sense to ask questions. On what basis are they coming up with their projections?

Look at how central bankers compare household objects like Apples and apples. Central banks tell us that the cost of living is falling because the computing power in an Apple phone or iPad is rising so dramatically. That means the price per unit of computing power is falling. That fall in price compensates for rising prices elsewhere in our lives. The fact that the only person in your home who knows how to make use of the additional power is a fourteen-year-old is by the by. We should ask why central bankers are happy to adjust our cost of living down for an increase in computing power but they never adjust it up for a decrease in quality. Apples, as in the fruit you eat from a tree, have been grown over decades to extend their shelf life, but they have less taste than they used to. In February 2017, a genetically-modified apple that never turns brown was introduced to grocery stores. Some would say an apple that tastes worse but lasts longer represents a reduction in quality. Shouldn't any quality increase in the computing power of an

Apple computer product be offset against the decrease in the quality of an eating apple when calculating our cost of living? It's the small things, like Apples and apples, that affect people's lives and set off the irritation that evolves into bigger political movements. Yes, the leap involves a little imagination, which, as we shall see, is exactly what economists themselves say is the key to anticipating the future.

I hear economists and experts everywhere saying that they were surprised by Brexit, by Trump, by the slowdown in China. However, they are adamant that continental Europe will not vote against the EU or the Euro. Yet Europeans have begun to realise how badly broken their social contracts are. The morning after the Brexit vote in Britain, the financial markets began to attack the Italian banks, selling off their debt. After all, if Britain could walk away from the EU maybe Italy (with its epic debt problem) could too. The government responded by saying it would somehow find €5 billion for a single bank – the oldest in the world – a bank that had lost some 98 per cent of its share value. The citizens of Italy began to ask, 'How can they find that much for a dead bank when they can't find even 5 cents to deal with the under-twenty-five-year-olds who face a 39 per cent unemployment rate through no fault of their own?' Increasingly the citizens across Europe are asserting that the social contract needs to be renegotiated.

Is it really a surprise that we now hear senior officials across Europe say that a departure from the euro is 'no longer unthinkable'? It was my view when I wrote this book and it remains so that this is the right path for Greece, though it will not be easy. Leaving the euro, though not necessarily the EU, would permit Greece to devalue their new currency and grow again. Many things signal how great the pain has been. Yet the 'anti'-sentiment across the Continent catches us unaware.

No one, just to be crystal clear, can predict the future. The goal here is not to predict the uncertain future. The goal is to be better prepared for it, whatever it may bring.

So, what are the signals now? I don't have the latitude to update the paperback edition of this book with all the events that have unfolded since it first went to press. But, I can say that my arguments have been bolstered by what has happened since I crowd-funded the book in 2015 and formally published it under the wise and welcome guidance of Alan Samson at Weidenfeld and Nicolson in 2016.

The social contract

What is at stake is not just your personal situation, your job prospects, your rent, your healthcare costs, or even your children's. It is something larger – the very fabric of society is being stretche by competing forces. I explain that there is always a social contract between citizens and their states. It is being broken by the weight of the debt burden which makes it impossible for political leaders to deliver on their promises.

Sometimes the pressure on the social contract becomes so great that citizens can no longer trust the system itself. The Arab Spring resulted in a total overthrow of the system of government. Brexit is an effort to remove Britain from the supranational system called the European Union. In his inauguration speech President Trump declared that his election represented an overthrow of the system of politics as a whole: 'We are transferring power from Washington DC and giving it back to you, the people." Whatever we may think of him, or the true meaning of that statement, it is worth considering the notion that power is no longer going to be in traditional hands or wielded in the traditional way. Citizens everywhere seem to be leaning towards this idea.

Debt is the main reason that the social contract is under so much pressure. The debt burden has only grown since I wrote this book. It is estimated now that US debt doubled over the last decade and now stands on the brink of $20 trillion.

Even countries we thought were 'rich' are having to break the social contract because their governments cannot afford to keep paying out as they did in the past. Saudi Arabia, for example, in a telling signal, decided to change from the traditional lunar Hijri calendar to the solar Gregorian calendar on 1 October 2016. This might not seem a likely economic signal. But why would you change the nation's calendar? It seems the shift permitted the state to save paying civil servants some eleven days' worth of salary.* That, for me, was a more powerful signal of the state of the social contract in Saudi than any piece of data.

We thought China was 'rich' in the sense that it had almost unlimited financial reserves. How quickly things change. We once assumed China would save the world economy. Now the capital flight and erosion of reserves is so severe that the International Monetary Fund warns China constantly of imminent danger. So, they forge a new path.

It's called One Belt One Road. I explain it at length in chapter eight, but in case you think it is purely hypothetical, let me say that the Asian Infrastructure Investment Bank opened in May 2016 with a balance sheet that is larger than the World Bank's. China is already building the links. The two longest railway journeys' ever known have recently been completed: the latest running from Yiwu in eastern China all the way to London on 1–18 January 2017. The other went from Yiwu to Madrid in late 2015.

Conflicting social contracts

Perhaps the pressing issues of our time are, in essence, about conflicting social contracts as well as broken ones. Given the magnitude of the debt burden, and the lack of easy options to deal with it, we find nations set on ever more conflicting paths. Germany's social contract with its citizens precludes the use of inflation as a means of dealing with the debt problem. The social contract in Spain, Italy and probably even France seems to *require* the use of inflation to deal with the debt. Such conflicting social contracts lie at the heart of the European Union. This did not matter when inflation was low. But now, even gently rising inflation threatens to rip the Union apart.

---

* Alexandra Sims, 'Saudi Arabia switches to "Western" Gregorian calendar so it can pay workers less and save money', Independent, 3 October 2016.

The American social contract, as seen by the new President, requires that America comes 'first' in all of its relations with other nations. He has promised that jobs will move to the US and that foreign policy should first and foremost serve American interests. This arguably conflicts with China's social contract. President Xi Jinping has promised to double per capita income by 2020. Can both countries fulfil their promises simultaneously?

Can the social contracts in the US and Russia be reconciled? Are the two nations entering a period of true rapprochement? Perhaps President Putin's desire to return Russia to former greatness extends to places few are paying attention to. Russia held its first military exercises in North Africa, near El Alamein in Egypt, in October 2016.* Russian presence in the Arctic, in Kaliningrad and in the Mediterranean is increasing apace.

The American social contract is itself in flux. Technology is bringing the Uber phenomenon to politics. The new President uses technology to disintermediate, displace and disrupt traditional approaches to politics. He won and intends to govern without the pollsters, without the traditional party political fundraisers, without the 'mainstream media', without the traditional policy experts and technocrats who normally fill the political jobs. Can these power structures be reconciled? We cannot be surprised if others now bring an Uber-mentality to politics in other places.

The breakdown of the social contract is touching every life. It is worth considering why it's happening, even if that process is difficult and unpleasant. Populism is not going to be wished away. Those with opposing views are not going to be wished away either. Try as they might, the experts are not convincing anybody that the public is too stupid to understand what is at stake or what is in their own best interest.

---

* Brian Rohan, 'Russian, Egypt troops to hold drill on Mediterranean coast', *Associated Press*, 12 October 2016.

The only decent answer to today's problems is that we must build tomorrow's economy – a better, stronger economy that can deliver on its promises to a wider array of people. The innovations and advances in technology I describe at the end of this book are proving to be only the bare beginning of a truly radical transformation of the world economy. I stick to my guns on this. It is possible to grow and to innovate our way out of the problems that each person, community, company and nation faces. Innovations are happening fast, in everything from medicine to materials, from construction to chemistry, from paper money to cyber money.

If more of us can get comfortable with the idea of signals, more will be able to take advantage of change and take the calculated risks that are required to build tomorrow's economy. While others traffic in fear, my hope is to inspire the confidence required to proceed with the calculated risk-taking that each of you, my readers, is capable of. My hope is that you are about to find out that economics is engaging, fascinating, helpful, at times funny and often fun. The economy is the crucible in which the future, your future, is being forged by your choices, your views, your actions. There is always an economy of tomorrow. The only question is how you choose to engage with it. I offer Signals as a means by which to navigate with greater ease into the future, whatever it may bring.

Acknowledgements

This book is dedicated to my dad, Harald Malmgren, who taught me that there is always a difference between the story reported in the news and what actually happened. He showed me that the world economy – from textiles, to steel, to agriculture and auto parts – is absolutely fascinating. I am so grateful for the many many things he has done for me (including going beyond the bounds of duty when it came to my education). He greatly encouraged me to tell this story. As you say, Dad, 'a state that is defaulting on its citizens will obviously seek to obfuscate this, so it is the duty of good citizens to illuminate'. This book aims to throw light upon this matter. To that end, I have tried to follow the advice of your mentor Sir John Hicks, who won the Nobel Prize in 1974, and his wife, Ursula, who was one of the leading experts on public finance in the 1940s and 50s. She always said to her highly mathematical husband, 'That's all very nice, dear [referring to the extraordinary ability he had with maths and numbers], but if you can't explain it in plain English, you will never affect public policy.' To that end, I am telling the story of the world economy in plain English. How lucky I am that my mother studied with J. R. R. Tolkien and C. S. Lewis and W. H. Auden and that she passed on to me a command of language that permits me to 'tell the story' of the world economy in plain English. She would have been delighted that I managed to show that the evil Gollum from Tolkien's tales lives above the doorway in the Oval Office, which he certainly does. I saw him there myself. He may have found a new perch over at the Federal Reserve Bank as well. I will give thanks at the end to the many people who supported and advised me as I pursued this book and it relentlessly pursued me.

I also sought the advice of a few specific people who were kind and patient enough to give me the support that allowed the book to progress. I owe a special thanks to Dr Tom Hoenig for his encouragement and his gracious invitations to the annual Kansas City Federal Reserve meeting in Jackson Hole, where I built many friendships and gained many insights. Thanks go to Dr Liam Fox, who during his time as the Defence Minister in the UK encouraged me to connect the dots and weave a holistic picture that shows how economics, politics and defence are all interrelated, if not inseparable. A few have been critically supportive at particular times: Hugh Morgan, Ambassador Richard McCormack, Jacob Frenkel, Esther George, Jeffrey Lacker and Bob Jenkins. Alan Meltzer, the Federal Reserve's official historian, encouraged me to use humour to tell the story and James Galbraith deserves special thanks for taking the time to take a fine-tooth comb to the text. David Smick was also very kind to let me publish some articles on these ideas in the *International Economy*. There are many more but my book is also dedicated to my daughter, Penny. The economy of tomorrow is already being built today and she will be part of something very new and dynamic. The trick is to follow the advice of the Queen in *Alice in Wonderland*, as we shall see, and try to imagine at least six impossible things before breakfast every day because the impossible is what inevitably actually happens. If you take calculated risks based on the signals you see, as I describe here, do what you love and work pretty hard at it, everything else will follow.

1

The World Economy
Is Signalling . . .

In May 2007, I tried with all my heart to convince one of my best friends to sell her house in Ireland. She trusts me. She knows what I do for a living. My job is to figure out what is going on in the world economy and what it means for prices and investors. Nonetheless, even though I sold my own home to prove my conviction, she trusted the bank manager and the real estate agent. Both assured her that her house would be worth 'another half a million in six months'. When we come to believe that a house can be worth that much more in such a short period without even a new coat of paint, it's a signal.

Signals are everywhere. I could not help staring at the cover of British *Vogue* in June 2009 because that too was sending out an important signal. It took me a while to figure out what it was. Of course it's easy to stare at Natalia Vodianova, one of the world's leading supermodels, especially when she is completely nude and remarkably curvy for a model. But something unsettled me. 'What's wrong with this picture?' I asked myself. One of the world's leading fashion magazines had a cover with absolutely no fashion. In fact, it showed no clothes at all. It showed a mother of three who, while enviably slender, was certainly not the sort of underweight waif that had dominated magazines for so many years. Yes, that cover was an important signal. It signalled the simple fact that the fashion industry had lost its old customer base – the young who were receiving unsolicited credit cards with large borrowing balances in the mail. Once the financial crisis hit, the fashion industry became aware that it had no idea who its new customer would be. Who had money to spend on fashion? Maybe now it would be the somewhat older woman, a mother, who was a very different customer. In short, the whole industry was suddenly engaged in a massive rethink. It went back to scratch, as it were. It went back to the human form, unclothed, and started to design for a customer who could be anyone from a beautiful young supermodel to a mother of three, knowing full well that both ends of the spectrum were still cash constrained.

Natalia Vodianova on the cover of British *Vogue* in June 2009
(Mario Testino/Vogue © The Condé Nast Publications Ltd).

Years later, in 2012, I spoke about that cover with the lead fashion director at British *Vogue*, Lucinda Chambers. My sense was that she and the fashion team absolutely did not think in this way, nor did they intend to send any 'signal'. No doubt this is true, but that is the point. Often it is artists and creative people who feel and project the zeitgeist without realising they are doing so, which is one reason we should pay attention to them instead of relying so heavily on the opinions of the bankers and financial experts who dominate the business press alone. In retrospect, a *Vogue* cover with no clothes was clearly reflecting some kind of change or feeling of uncertainty.

By 2013, when the financial crisis had evolved into something much more profound, slowing economies worldwide and forcing the reinvention of business models, a traditional signal was emanating from the fashion world: the hemline. Some say hemlines go up in the good times and down in the bad. Usually, though, everyone knows exactly where the hemline is supposed to be. Yet as I write, there is no agreement whatsoever. Hemlines are all over the place. For that matter, nobody knows what the silhouette or cool shape ought to be either. Why? Perhaps it is because the fashion industry still cannot figure out who its customer really is. Because fashion can send signals about the condition of the economy.

Fashion signals

I was inspired by a conversation I had with one of the founders of the iconic British fashion store Topshop in May 2007, before the financial crisis began. It was founded in 1969 by Sir Philip Green, Richard Caring and Tony Colman and has dominated British fashion ever since. Few men know clothes better than these men.

I happened to sit next to one of them (discretion requires I don't identify him) at a lunch at Ditchley Park, an English country house in Chipping Norton, Oxfordshire, where senior policy and business people meet to discuss what's going on in the world. As I listened to his stories, I translated his fashion sense into economic signals. Coming away from the conversation, I realised that there was a powerful signal in the loud patterns and bling that had come to dominate fashion just before the financial crisis. Something was very, very wrong when every woman was wearing (and every shop was selling) loud Pucci-inspired prints. Pucci is an elegant Italian fashion label that rose to prominence in the 1950s and 1960s when Grace Kelly, Marilyn Monroe, Sophia

Loren and Jackie Onassis (who had been John F. Kennedy's wife) wore its vibrant patterned scarves and stretch-knit clothes on the Riviera. The clothing is bright and attractive, mainly on petite women. It looks pretty ridiculous on everybody else. So, why was every shop selling such bold patterns? The answer was obvious: Chinese factories were churning out clothes ever more cheaply and in higher volume. This forced designers to take greater risks with their patterns in order to differentiate their products, attract buyers away from other suppliers and make shoppers content to own something that wouldn't last long, purely because it was new and different.

By 2007 every shop was filled to the brim with poorly made, garish and eccentric copies of the Pucci look. Young women were receiving unsolicited credit cards in the mail and were delighted that Chinese factories could produce less and less expensive clothes. You could buy a blouse for a handful of loose change. In retrospect it seems clear that women were spending more than they could afford even though each item cost very little, especially since most items would only ever be worn once or twice before their fabric made them out of fashion. They were cheap and disposable. But, these customers were becoming increasingly indebted and therefore, at some point, their consumption would have to slow down. When that happened the stores would feel it.

Retailers themselves had so much access to cheap bank lending and public capital markets (IPOs)* that they had lost all their cash-flow management and inventory skills. Shops were buying too much stock and would be caught short when the economy weakened, as it was bound to do once customers hit their credit limits. After all, almost everyone was spending beyond their means. The famous singer-songwriters Eric Clapton and J. J. Cale picked up on a signal in their song 'It's Easy' from the *Road to Escondido* album, released on 7 November 2006. I thought Cale's lyrics were a signal:

---

* IPO stands for Initial Public Offering and describes the mechanism that many companies use to raise money.

> *If cash is your problem, you might regret*
> *Use that old plastic, slide two third in debt*
> *It's easy, easy you see*
> *If tomorrow never comes, everything is free*

But, tomorrow *always* comes. The music stopped in August 2007, when the financial crisis began. Suddenly, fear replaced optimism. Initially, the crisis seemed to be contained, exclusive to the financial markets and seemingly applicable only to the United States. The Federal Reserve Bank, America's central bank, announced interest-rate cuts and other policy actions, which are usually powerful signals. However, most players in the world economy did not take much notice of what was happening. It was only when Lehman Brothers failed one year later, in September 2008, that the markets and the public alike registered what was going on and a sudden collapse of confidence and economic activity ensued. Many retailers went bust, unable to borrow and unable to sell their overabundance of cheap fashion to customers who had quite a few items of clothing already, no money for any more and frankly no need for them. With the economy now shedding jobs fast, suddenly what was needed to keep a job or get a new one was a plain white shirt and a black skirt, or a good old-fashioned conservative suit. When the economy is that bad, you do not take the risk of loud clothing getting in the way of a pay cheque.

Around the same time, a clothing chain called Zara started to take off just as all the other retailers were going bust. Zara's success was a signal. What was different about Zara? For a start, this Spanish fashion firm had never manufactured much in Asia. Around three-quarters of its stock was made in Europe. It purchased fabrics from around the world, brought them back to Spain and stored them in massive refrigerated warehouses to protect the fabric until Zara's designers needed it. When the financial crisis struck they did not have the shipping time or cost that weighed down their competitors. They could get new stock into the shops three or four times a week instead of waiting every three or four months for a shipment from Asia like everybody else.

It struck me that Zara had several other reasons for its success. It's always possible to find a good black or navy skirt and a great white shirt there, which are office staples. Anyone looking for a job is going to dive into Zara confident they will find good-quality classics. Zara has also always produced good 'fashion' items that are trendier, but it usually has plenty of classic items and very few fashion items. As a result, the stock turns over very fast. People go in to check out Zara anytime they pass by because they know the stock will be new and something they like will be gone if they wait. This is partly because the goods don't come from Asia, where shipping time alone is six to eight weeks. Some 50 per cent comes from Spain and about 25 per cent from elsewhere in the European Union, so the stock in a European shop can be updated almost overnight. This speed of turnover guarantees a steady stream of returning customers who are already drawn in by the 'value for money' proposition.

Once the slowdown hit and unemployment started to rise, Zara's classic value-for-money staples combined with continuous fresh, new, trendy designs assured the company continued to do well in spite of an otherwise collapsing market for retail. It helped that Zara is a private, family-owned company. In a world where all its competitors found their share price diving and the bank calling to take back the overdraft, line of credit or inform them the IPO had been cancelled, Zara had sufficient self-generated cash flow to keep going.

So, the naked model on the cover of *Vogue* signalled that the whole business model for retail clothing needed a rethink. Zara's success at that particular time was a signal of a significant change in the world economy. Disposable fashion, where you buy a new item one day and toss it in the bin the next, died when the financial crisis stalled the economy. Zara's success, compared to so many failed companies, revealed the flaws in the traditional women's retail model, which depended heavily on a high volume of cheap, highly differentiated clothes (crazy designs) with long delivery times coming from Chinese and Bangladeshi factories, and unlimited funding from banks, private investors or the capital markets.

Glamazon and Gatsby

Looking back at that *Vogue* cover, the fact that Vodianova is a mother was also an important signal. After the athletic, 'glamazon' look of the original 1980s supermodels (Christy Turlington, Linda Evangelista and Naomi Campbell), fashion photographers favoured very skinny, very young models that looked fragile – a look epitomised by Kate Moss. It strikes me that 'skinniness' in women seems to be associated with periods of great wealth creation. One thinks of the skinny, *Great Gatsby*-style flappers of the 1920s or the Twiggy lookalikes of the 1960s. It makes sense. After all, it is very hard for a lot of women to be thin. It takes time, effort and money to be a skinny adult woman, unless you are one of the few with the DNA programming for that.

When things get rough, comfort matters more. Perhaps this is another signal in the world economy. For example, when times are hard, women will give up fashion but they won't give up make-up, especially lipstick. Estée Lauder survived the financial crisis better than anyone expected as a result of this human tendency: lipstick and lip gloss sales went up as these are affordable and indispensable items, even in a slowdown. For me, the rising sales of lipstick and lip gloss soon after the financial crisis was a signal that the world economy would carry on and not cease to exist as many then feared. It seems even war and deprivation won't dent this desire for lipstick. My publisher, Alan Samson, pointed out that Lieutenant Colonel Mervin Willett Gonin wrote about lipstick in his diary when he helped liberate some of the first of British prisoners from the German concentration camp in Bergen-Belsen in 1945. He said:

It was shortly after the British Red Cross arrived, though it may have no connection, that a very large quantity of lipstick arrived.

This was not at all what we men wanted, we were screaming for hundreds and thousands of other things and I don't know who asked for lipstick. I wish so much that I could discover who did it, it was the action of genius, sheer unadulterated brilliance. I believe nothing did more for these internees than the lipstick.*

The fashion team at *Vogue* know quite a lot about how much women care about lipstick, too, and thus signalled something important by choosing to photograph Vodianova without any fashion, but with lipstick and lip gloss. They signalled the fact that fashion could no longer survive simply by appealing to people's hopes and aspirations for the future, when we would be flush with cash and skinny again. Instead, fashion would have to appeal to real women with real income right now, regardless of their body size or shape or age. The trend to put 'plus-size' models on magazine covers and in fashion advertising has only accelerated since the beginning of the most recent economic downturn. That is a signal too.

Today, governments in the most important economies in the world – the US, the UK, Europe, Japan and China – are all sending extremely forceful signals in the world economy. Perhaps the most important signal in any economy is the price of money. Most of the industrialised countries are suppressing interest rates, which is the price of money, to historic lows. This signal has already pushed up hard asset prices like property and food, and also pushed up the value of stock markets around the world. So, it is important to understand what the economic signals are and then to consider how they might impact on our daily lives.

But most people are afraid of economics. It seems to be very complex: all mathematics and algorithms. So, I decided to write a book that will help a person with no background in economics to better understand the world economy. Rather than being a subject that you

* Extract from the diary of Lieutenant Colonel Mervin Willett Gonin DSO 1945 which now resides in the Imperial War Museum in London.

are forced to study, my goal is to help you see that it is engaging and useful in everyday life, no matter who you are or where you work, or what you do.

Everyone assumes there are smart people somewhere in the world economy who will sort it all out. When I worked in the White House I realised people looked upon me and my colleagues as those 'smart people'. When I worked on the trading floors of the world's largest investment banks, armed with a wealth of skill and technology, the public thought that we were those 'smart people'. Sadly, having been one of the 'smart' people, I fear that the public expect too much. These people are smart, but not *that* smart. They are no smarter than the collective decisions made by everyone in the economy. That being the case, our best hope of understanding the meaning and purpose of the signals being sent out by the major players in the world economy is to understand what motivates them.

Signals I have seen

Perhaps the concept of 'signals' needs further clarifying before we begin. Here are some more of the signals I saw that caused me to duck for cover and shout to my clients and friends alike: 'Sell everything!' My own family sold our primary residence and moved into rental accommodation by May 2007 in preparation for the financial crisis. Perhaps this background will help explain why I want people to notice the many signals that the world economy is sending today.

Scary china dinner sets, cabaret and mortgages

I saw many signals that the world economy was in trouble throughout 2006 and 2007, before the crisis began. For example, I accidentally wandered on to the top floor of Bloomingdale's in New York and was overwhelmed by stacks of china plates painted with gaudy Halloween designs. 'Who can afford to spend money on a china dinner plate set that will only be used once a year? Where would they keep it for the other 364 days of the year?' I wondered. If they can accommodate a rarely used Halloween dinner service, have houses become too large? How much would it cost to heat such a house? Were people spending more than they were earning? When people are spending tomorrow's income today, instead of saving some of today's income to pay for what might come, it's cause for concern. If they are willing to spend their unearned income on Halloween china plates, it's an ominous signal.

Another signal was the sense of 'affluenza' that permeated the atmosphere at that time.* The rich felt increasingly angry that they could not generate 'enough' money. Somehow, everyone felt that everybody else was even richer. Even the rich began to feel left out or left behind. My friend, Katia Hadidian, remembers going to an Eartha Kitt concert at the time, and Kitt changed the lyrics of her hit, 'Just an Old-Fashioned Girl',† from wanting to marry 'an old-fashioned millionaire' to 'an old-fashioned billionaire', winking at the audience and purring, 'inflation . . . ' The funny thing is, she was right! You have to be a millionaire to own a nothing-special, two-bedroom flat in town in many cities these days. So, only a billionaire will do.

Another signal came in September 2007 when the Hong Kong Shanghai Bank (HSBC) announced it was setting aside nearly one billion US dollars to cover losses associated with its purchase of Household Finance, a company that provided mortgages.‡ It struck me that this announcement of loan provisioning was a signal that the whole mortgage market must be in trouble. Ultimately HSBC would write off nearly $20 billion-worth of mortgages. If a big bank had made such a huge loss, what were the chances every other bank had made the same mistake? As it turned out, the banks collectively lost so much money that the losses have had to be shifted on to the taxpayers (which means you, the reader, as we shall see). The

---

* Oliver James, *Affluenza*, Vermillion Press, 2007.
† 'Just an Old-Fashioned Girl', lyrics by Marve Fisher (1958).'
‡ James Quinn, 'HSBC hit by sub-prime crisis', *Daily Telegraph*, 22 September 2007.

2007 announcement was a big signal, though few registered it at the time.

A further signal appeared around that time. I found that everything I bought that had been made in China kept breaking. This worried me, but I could not figure out what the problem was. In retrospect, China had moved so far down the value chain that even inexpensive goods were not worth the unbelievably cheap price.

Then, I detected a signal that seemed really important. Every financial trader I knew was talking about the 'inevitable financial crisis' while refusing to sell anything on the grounds that he was smarter than all the other traders and therefore he would get out (of the stock or property market) first. This was an extraordinary manifestation of hubris: traders declaring themselves smarter than the market and capable of doing something nobody has ever managed to do consistently, which is to pick the exact moment to sell.

That signal alone made me think it was time to sell the house and move my family into rental accommodation.

Handbags at dawn

Finally, and perhaps oddly, I noticed that women were spending a fortune on handbags. I have never met a straight man that was 'turned on' by a handbag (though I concede they must exist). Men, it seems to me, often get real pleasure, in contrast, from looking at women's shoes. But in a booming economy, women had enough cash to indulge in something that had no meaning to men. Could it be that handbags are designed for women to compete against other women? Rather than duelling with sabres at dawn, was I witnessing duels with oversize handbags at cocktail parties? Was this a signal of financial excess? After the financial crisis, when women became more aware of the need to look after their financial and personal future, they stopped buying so many bags and instead turned to shoes. Shoes began to outsell bags as a fashion accessory, but both the handbag duels and the shift to shoes struck me as significant signals.

For the Love of God

If we ignore or fail to register the importance of signals, it is in part because we don't want to. Think about the artwork *For the Love of God*, produced by Damien Hirst and presented to the world on 1 June 2007, just two months before the financial market crisis hit on 13 August.

This sculpture, a platinum cast of the skull of an eighteenth-century man, quite literally encrusted with diamonds, allegedly cost £14 million to produce. The *Daily Mail* headline screamed: 'Damien Hirst unveils his jewels in the crown, a £50m diamond-studded skull!' Hirst had become one of the most renowned, avant-garde, edgeworking artists of his generation. He had first shocked the world by pickling a shark in a vat of formaldehyde – *The Physical Impossibility of Death in the Mind of Someone Living* (1991). He went on to paint the horns and hooves of a dead calf in 18-carat gold and then suspend its body in a golden tank of formaldehyde (*The Golden Calf*, 2008). His ability to judge the public mood and capture the zeitgeist was well proven and well rewarded by the time he unveiled *For the Love of God*.

I confess that I missed this powerful signal at the time. With hindsight, it is so obvious that he was signalling the end of an era; that the rich had accumulated so much wealth that upon their death they could encrust their own skulls with diamonds, should they choose to do so. Hirst was reminding us that you can't take it with you. In an era of extraordinary wealth, what did you really have to show for your life? There was a biting irony to an artwork that confirmed there are limits to wealth while selling for more than any artwork ever known: $100 million. In retrospect, I now realise that the skull was hissing, 'For the love of God, how much money do you need?' Many of those who could afford to buy *For the Love of God* found their financial circumstances change for the worse only a few months after the sale took place. But the price of artwork has continued to climb. Are people really more interested in art? Or is art sending us an economic signal?

Maybe the wealthy buyers at the time could not recognise the signal for what it was, because acknowledging it would have meant making changes. They would have had to sell assets, draw down risk, sell their businesses, acknowledge that their net worth was a smaller number than they had believed. It is hard to give up a life that defines us merely because times have changed. It is so much easier to believe that the favourable circumstances we enjoyed were not the result of luck. No, we tell ourselves. We are skilled. We are smart. Therefore, we can manage any economic storm. This is why so many smart, successful people lose everything in a crisis. Confusing luck with skill is deadly.

My point is that observing signals is not enough. Action is required, and action demands having a view. To have a view of the future is to reveal our character, as Ralph Waldo Emerson observed: 'People do not seem to realise that their opinion of the world is also a confession of character.' Our view of the landscape and our perception of risk reveals our character. Our choice of what to reach for and when to reach for it, requires and reveals character.

The girl and the goat

Sometimes the economy gives us gifts wrapped in sandpaper. A serious fall in the market is an opportunity for many. When can we acquire property and a talented workforce cheaply? It's usually only during the 'bust'. Consider the audacity of the American chef Stephanie Izard who, in 2008 at the height of the financial and economic crisis, decided to open a new high-end restaurant, Girl and the Goat. No one would lend her any money, aside from friends and family, in spite of the fact that she had recently won a reality TV cooking contest. Circumstances forced her into a cheap location. She chose a part of the West Loop in Chicago that no one would ever have imagined as the home of what has now become one of the best-ranked restaurants in America. She not only created an extraordinary venue that employs more than 150 people and where the waiting list is full nine months in advance; there is a secondary market in the rights to the private dining room. As a result of her risk taking, the entire neighbourhood has now transformed into one of the hippest parts of Chicago.

Eyes wide shut

Such signals about the world economy are interesting and important, but at the same time easy to miss. Some signals are simple to receive, interpret and act upon. The child cries and we react to its distress. The traffic light turns red and we stop. The office gossip tells us colleagues are being fired so we smarten our appearance and put in extra effort to avoid the same outcome. The price of our currency versus the euro goes up or down so we schedule or cancel the trip to Europe.

Just as the smell of burning toast is a signal that makes us stand up and pay attention, so should the many signals that emanate from the world economy, which, in general, have a profound impact on our lives. Prices change and our life changes too, whether we know it or not. This is as true of the price of our mortgage, our wages and our healthcare as it is of the price of meat, lipstick and chocolate. It is equally true of the prices we may never think about but which can impact on our life, like the price of bread (the rising price of which I will argue was one of the catalysts for the Arab Spring) or credit default swaps (CDOs)* on Wall Street. Then there is the price the market will pay for our time and our skills; this changes too.

Numbers versus humans

Nonetheless, we are sometimes not very attuned to signals from the global financial markets and the world economy, in spite of their tremendous importance. The word 'economics' conjures images of complex mathematical equations and dry concepts such as 'marginal additional demand'. It is not surprising that we sometimes shy away from thinking about such things. I know from long experience that

---

* A Credit Default Swap is a complex financial investment that pools together many different grades of risky debt.

people think 'economics' is incredibly boring and mathematically challenging. Typically, economic signals are all described in the language of maths: numbers, statistics, probabilities, measurements, graphs, charts and percentages, all adjusted for things that are not easily understood, such as inflation and seasonality. This is just convention, however. Economics is not actually about numbers. Economics is about human behaviour, too. Numbers are merely a way of expressing human behaviour, though they are perhaps the least engaging way to observe economic signals. Simple events and the things we can easily observe are much more compelling.

Miami Airport and the siren

I saw a press report in the *Daily Mail* about Damon Emery and his family which caught my eye. He and his family received a very scary signal from the world economy one afternoon in Miami. I bet he was not thinking about the wider economy in the early autumn of 2008.*
Of course, the newspapers were full of headlines about the 'Global Financial Crisis', but he did not work for a bank, so he no doubt assumed it would have little to do with him. He proceeded to take his family on vacation from England to Disney World in Florida. He decided to keep his costs down by flying with a recently launched cut-price airline called XL. He and his family were shocked by the signal the world economy sent them: the wail of sirens when police cars surrounded the aircraft at Miami Airport because the airline had gone bust. The company's creditors were seizing the plane.

Did it occur to Mr Emery that he might be taking a big risk by flying with a company that had massive debt that could not be serviced from the firm's cash flow alone? Probably not. Did he understand that the only thing keeping XL in the air were bank loans? Probably not. It must have been bewildering. The credit crunch was the culprit that caused

* Michael Seamark, 'Another 30 airlines will go bust before Christmas, warns BA chief', *Daily Mail*, 13 September 2008.

XL to go bust. The signal that a credit crunch was underway was, in this case, the sound of the wailing siren.

The dog that did not bark

My neighbours got the same signal from silence. Their dog simply did not bark. They had hired a building company to construct a garage on the side of their house. One morning, the dog did not bark because the builders did not come. They never came again because the firm went bankrupt. It did not occur to my neighbours that they were at the heart of the 2007 financial crisis, which, after all, had been driven by over-investment in property, mortgages and building. Nor did they understand that many building companies would go bust. So, they hired another firm to finish the job. The new firm asked for payment up front because it was suffering from a lack of cash flow caused by the universally bad circumstances. The family paid because they really needed that garage. Once again, the dog did not bark because the new builders did not show up. Yes, the family lost their money twice.

These may seem to be small examples. But the history of wars, nation states and families are all driven by economic events. Economics usually underpins great events in history that create and destroy businesses and push and pull on private lives.

Nations and their cash woes

It is always an important signal when a nation runs out of cash. The Soviet Union collapsed in 1991 partly because it ran out of money. Its tax receipts were insufficient to finance the government's expenditure. The Suez Canal ended up in British hands in 1936 when Egypt had an economic crisis and needed cash. One of the reasons Saddam Hussein invaded Kuwait was because he ran out of cash and decided to take the oil fields next door as a means of replenishing his coffers.

Scotland ceased being an independent state and was forced into the Act of Union with England in 1707 due to a financial crisis. In the late 1600s the Scots became jealous of England's East India Company, which was generating untold wealth for England from the colonies, leaving Scotland behind. The Scots decided to create their own version of the East India Company, called the Company of Scotland. After a few failed attempts to establish Scottish colonies in what we now call New Jersey and South Carolina, an entrepreneur called William Paterson came up with an idea that the Company of Scotland decided to back: the Darien Scheme. Paterson's idea was to establish a Scottish colony in what is now Panama but was then called 'New Edinburgh', in order to tap local riches and create a base for trading with the Far East. The goal was to make the citizens of Scotland wealthy. Unfortunately, it turned out that Darien, Panama, was a swamp. The first, second and third wave of settlers all died from various waterborne diseases including malaria and cholera. The Spanish, who wanted it for the same reason that Scotland wanted it, ultimately turfed out those who survived. Only a handful of settlers made it back home.

Scottish losses amounted to roughly one-third of the nation's savings (bigger than the losses in the recent sub-prime crisis). A bailout was required to save the population from living the rest of their lives in poverty. England was the obvious saviour. The price of the bailout from the Bank of England for Scotland was the loss of Scottish independence. In exchange for the bailout, Scotland signed the Act of Union. The gain for England was that this financial accident allowed the kingdom to join forces after many years of war and strife. Thus the United Kingdom was born.

In 2007, nearly three centuries to the day later, the Royal Bank of Scotland and several other of Britain's largest banks had to be bailed out by the government with the taxpayers' money following massive losses incurred in the financial crisis. As a result, the public had to endure not only losses on their investments but also discovered that their taxes would rise and the level of services delivered by the government would fall.

By 2010, British voters were so angry about these losses that they opted to shake up conventional politics by electing a 'hung' Parliament.

This meant that the election results compelled two parties to share power. Thus the Prime Minister, David Cameron, took on Nick Clegg as his Deputy Prime Minister. They shared power and ran the nation together. The minority members of the Coalition, the Liberal Democrats, who had strong Scottish roots, immediately requested lower taxes and greater autonomy for Scotland as part of the price for their participation in the new government. This gave impetus to the Scottish independence movement, which remains a major political discussion in the United Kingdom. It is ironic that the 2007 financial crisis has provided Scotland with an opportunity for greater independence even though its largest bank was one of the principal sources of the catastrophe.

Border signals

The border between Scotland and England dissolved as a result of an economic event. Today we see borders changing everywhere. In the Middle East, the borders of Iraq and Syria are being redrawn by the fall of governments and a tide of refugees. In the South China Sea, China and its neighbours are ever more forcefully challenging where the territorial borders lie, sometimes in courts of law and sometimes through military conflict. In Eastern Europe, the borders of nations have been redefined in countries such as Ukraine, sometimes by military force. There are more new walls being erected today in Europe alone than ever existed during the Cold War.* Walls are being built, or border controls reinstated, between countries that used to have reasonably free passage, such as Germany and Austria, Denmark and Sweden, Slovenia and Croatia. In the Middle East, Saudi Arabia has built a wall on the border with Yemen. Turkey is constructing a wall with Syria.

President Trump, who we will come to later, is hardening the

---

* Dr Pippa Malmgren, 'Countries can pull up the drawbridge – but capital will pull them down again', *MoneyWeek*, 4 December 2015.

borders of the US with both physical and policy barriers. Britain, too, in the aftermath of the Brexit vote, is placing more process around immigration.

Perhaps this is not a coincidence but a signal that economic pressures are changing the cost and value of many assets. Iraq had become expensive to the US. It was costing in terms of 'blood and treasure'. But it is valuable territory for Iran, China, Russia and local political powers like DAESH / ISIS. Ukraine and Syria are (usually) large food producers and the site of Russia's only real warm-water ports, which has perhaps even greater value if food prices were to rise again. Or consider Texas. It is not surprising that many have picked up on the signals that Texas is a strong diversified economy, whether the price of oil is high or low. Silicon Valley seems to be shifting into Austin, Texas. Energy, innovation, agribusiness and property are growing apace, attracting many to move there.

Families

Family histories are often entwined with economic events. My grandmother came from Sweden to the US in 1927. She found work as a seamstress, which allowed her to make a living right through the Great Depression. She was very focused on ensuring her children would be sufficiently educated that they would not have to do manual labour. She made my father understand that he had a choice: win scholarships or get stuck in a menial job for the rest of his life. He became very attuned to a simple price signal – follow the money. Faced with the necessity to win scholarships any way he could, he won them for running and golf (which he learned only because caddying paid better than anything else available to a fourteen-year-old) and for maths, engineering and academic excellence. He ended up at Yale on a full scholarship and later at Oxford as a Henry Fellow in the late 1950s. He took the Henry Fellowship over the more famous Rhodes Scholarship in part because it paid more. He went on to be mentored by six Nobel Prize-winners, including Tom Schelling and Sir John Hicks. By following the money, he became an economic advisor to many heads of government around the world and a successful entrepreneur because he learned about prices as signals early on.

My mother dreamed of studying Middle English and Medieval French poetry. It may not be obvious that this was a useful way to spend her time, but it is part of the miracle of the world economy that someone can pursue this kind of dream, or indeed any kind of dream. The economy accommodates the wishes of the many. In her case, an economic signal permitted her to pursue that dream. Both her parents had modest incomes in Los Angeles; her mother was a public school teacher in the California state system and her father was an electrical engineer in the city of Los Angeles. So how could their child afford to go to Oxford and study with J. R. R. Tolkien, author of *The Hobbit* and *The Lord of the Rings*, and C. S. Lewis, author of *The Chronicles of Narnia*? Fortunately for my mother, the exchange rate made it possible. In the late 1950s, the exchange rate between the US dollar and British pound was such that Americans were downright rich once they arrived in England. Exchange rates are powerful signals.

My mother never understood how much the favourable exchange rate helped propel her on to that path. I only realised why years later, after becoming the Chief Currency Strategist at Bankers Trust and hearing her complain bitterly about how expensive Europe had become. I looked at a chart and saw that in 1956 the US dollar–sterling exchange rate (or 'Cable', as it is known in professional circles, because it was initially traded by cable machines) was most advantageous to Americans. My mother wasn't rich in America, but she was rich in England, which had seen its currency value collapse in the aftermath of the Second World War. So, it is not only signals of trouble that require attention. Some signals are positive and lure you towards hope, growth and opportunity.

Monks throwing bricks

Some people are overwhelmingly excited by economic signals such as price changes. Others may find their eyes glaze over at the very thought. You may say, 'I don't do economics', and 'I don't want to speculate'. The problem is, you cannot 'check out' of the world economy, not even if you are a Tibetan monk who one would imagine to be above such things. In March 2008 Tibetan monks came out of their temples and started throwing bricks, rocks and any other hard objects that were close to hand. Why? No doubt the Tibetans have long-standing frustrations about their relationship with China. No doubt there are many Tibetans who would prefer a different form of government than the one they have. But monks don't typically wake up in the middle of the night and declare: 'I have to have self-rule tomorrow.' However, they might well wake up hungry and angry that they can no longer afford rice because its price has risen so much. Global rice prices rose by 50 per cent in 2008. Once rice is beyond reach, it makes sense to pick up a brick and throw it, even for a monk. So, monks throwing bricks turned out to be a signal that the price of food was escalating and causing suffering.*

Why did the price of rice rise? Now we enter the world of economics, where supply and demand define such things. We will argue about what causes prices to move throughout this book. But the first thing is to notice that price movements are occurring and to think about what they mean for you.

No specialist equipment required

The world economy and the financial markets will influence, if not define, the direction of your life and the choices you make. Prices define how much you will pay for rice and everything else that matters.

---

* 'The China–Tibet Inflation Black Swan and Global Implications', ATCA, 19 March 2008.

How do you know when to borrow and when to buy? When to invest in skills and when to get paid for them? You form a view and act. But on what basis do you form your view? Which signals do you observe? Which signals do you miss?

The signals are always there, but the question is how to recognise and interpret them. I have spent my career working in the financial markets; advising the President of the United States on economic policy; and advising traders, investors and government officials around the world. From my seat on various trading floors to my seat in the White House, I have been paid to identify, interpret and act on these signals. At times it has been my job to send signals as well.

The world of markets and economics may seem the preserve of those insiders who are well supplied with high-tech equipment such as Bloomberg and Reuters machines, trade publications, state-of-the-art trading floors and access to privileged information via meetings with policymakers and CEOs. And yes, trading floors in banks and fund management firms are brimming with highly paid, talented personnel, cutting-edge technology, in-depth news and research, all of which seems to be essential when it comes to receiving economic and financial signals . . . except, it isn't.

When I worked on such trading floors, I had access to all the right people and all the right equipment and I learned a good deal. However I also discovered that there are many people in that privileged position who miss the signals and get it wrong. In fact, throughout history it is typically the privileged financial market experts who get it so wrong that they trigger crises, recessions and put the average taxpayer's personal future at risk. I learned, too, that many people who have no such privileges – artists and clothing retailers and editors at *Vogue*, for example – are perfectly capable of discerning, interpreting, creating and acting upon signals. Lots of people build real businesses, create jobs, innovate and make a lot of money out of catching and interpreting signals. Why not you, too?

The same questions

I have discovered over the years that whether I am talking to professional fund managers, or friends who have no clue about money, or heads of government – many of whom have no clue about finance and markets, even though they are expert in politics – I am repeatedly asked the same questions. 'Will interest rates go up / down?' 'When?' 'Will unemployment get better / worse?' 'Will my mortgage become more / less expensive to service?' 'What will happen to the value of my house / my savings / my investments / my skills / my business?' 'Will the economy grow faster / more slowly in future?' 'Will the price of oil / gold / stocks / bonds / iron ore / milk go up or down?' 'Should I expand / contract my business?' 'Should I borrow and invest or sell and take my profits?' 'Should I study more or work now?' 'Should I change jobs or stay put?'

We all want to know how to prepare for the future, how to foresee events before they occur and act well before these events are priced into the market and on the front page of the newspaper. No one can divine the future, but there are an awful lot of people who manage to make fortunes, or better protect themselves, simply by being alert to possible events and probable outcomes.

There is a conversation that goes on about what the future holds, which may be useful to know about. It is a conversation that involves traders, fund managers, pension fund trustees and sovereign wealth funds as well as entrepreneurs and people who run small businesses. Policymakers, economists and the media are constantly engaged in this conversation, but the dialogue would be richer if the general public were engaged too. And there is every reason to become a part of it, because your future depends on the actions you take, and that in turn will depend on your views and your thoughts – or lack thereof – about signals.

Today, for example, the world is divided between a vast majority who think that deflation is the greatest threat bearing down on our future and a tiny minority who think inflation is the greatest threat. There are signals for both scenarios. The debt burden keeps growing larger even though interest rates remain at historic lows, thus signalling that the debt problem will leave us with deflation or falling prices and low employment for years to come. On the other hand, there are many examples of inflation signals as the price of property and hard assets from high-grade diamonds to artwork rise to record highs. The outcome will impact on every one of us, either way. The political consequences of the pain inflation and deflation cause will be felt whichever one is contributing more to the malaise.

This book offers a version of the various conversations that I have personally been involved in during my career and, in particular, those that have taken place before and after each economic or financial crisis. It is not the definitive explanation; it is simply one of many possible explanations. But it is a place to start thinking about how the world economy works and how it will affect you.

Interpreting signals is a daunting and endless task. Signals often conflict. Some are important and others are merely noise. Signals can be overwhelming, once you start to look for them. Oscar Wilde got it right when he said, 'It is a very sad thing that nowadays there is so little useless information.'

2

Hubris and Nemesis

—

For many people, the word 'economics' is accompanied by a wave of fear and a sense of exhaustion. 'Economics' conjures images of numbers, algorithms, mathematical models and a highly technical quantitative subject. If this sounds familiar, consider a different possibility: the economy begins inside the human soul, driven by the never-ending battle between the Greek goddesses Hubris and Nemesis for possession of our psyche. The ancient Greeks described Hubris as the spirit who lights the fire of desire or greed and compels us to take risks to achieve what the ego desires. The ego wants more: more status, more money, more success, more material possessions, more recognition, more knowledge, more confidence. Hubris is a powerful force in the world economy, because it propels individuals and societies to innovate – which is always risky – and thereby generate growth, wealth and GDP.*

---

* There are many arguments about how to measure and weigh wealth versus growth versus GDP. Wealth is not the same as GDP because a government can generate GDP by taking more and more of the wealth in the economy and redistributing it. Wealth creation is really the key to success. GDP is an arguably flawed way to measure wealth creation. If anything, governments are now taking more and more private wealth in the belief that they can use it to create GDP. Wealth creation is what drives an economy forward, not wealth redistribution by governments, which is why Thomas Piketty's arguments in *Capital in the Twenty-First Century* will only lead us into infighting.

Nemesis is the goddess of retribution, targeting those who indulge in too much hubris. Nemesis douses the fire of hubris with doubt and punishes hubris with loss. Nemesis lurks at the edge of every business and every balance sheet and every job. She peers over the shoulder of every risk-taker, threatening to undermine the hope and aspiration of the endeavour. Hubris gives rise to hope and Nemesis gives rise to fear, but both are critical to the proper functioning of the world economy. It is the balancing of the two that permits people to successfully achieve their goals and contribute to a flourishing economy. An excess of either spirit is likely to end in economic catastrophe.

This balancing act within each one of us is what underpins the economy. Each time we (individually, or collectively as a society), reach for something we want, something that is a little beyond our immediate grasp, something that involves risk, growth occurs. That's where 'value added' is created. When we reach and succeed, confidence grows, along with GDP and wealth. Conviction in our abilities increases alongside productivity.

Finding a balance between Hubris and Nemesis, hope and fear, and taking risks that involve the possibility of real failure and real success has always been a popular theme for writers, poets, psychologists and other observers of the human condition. It is a quest that reveals and reinforces character. Shakespeare's enduring appeal largely rests on his ability to understand and portray the true nature of man. Macbeth cannot find a good balance between his ambition and his fear of failure: 'I have no spur / To prick the sides of my intent, but only / Vaulting ambition, which o'erleaps itself / And falls on th'other.'*

When we reach and fail, loss occurs – sometimes financial, but also loss of confidence, loss of pride, loss of dignity. Yet, even in failure, lessons are learned that serve us well when we are ready to take a risk again. Failure is thus a critical component of GDP and wealth creation. Only through failure do we become more skilled at risk-taking and

* *Macbeth*, Act I, scene 7, lines 25–28.

therefore more likely to be successful in the future, as the *Harvard Business Review* noted in April 2011 in an issue that celebrated failure.*

What is learned from mistakes can be more important than what is learned from success. The nineteenth-century American essayist and poet Ralph Waldo Emerson wrote that, 'All life is an experiment. The more experiments you make, the better.' This idea that experience is, in itself, valuable was personified by the inventor Thomas Edison, who said: 'I have not failed 1,000 times. I have successfully discovered 1,000 ways to not make a light bulb.'

The economist Joseph Schumpeter (1883–1950) concluded that the economic cycle is fundamentally driven by innovation and 'creative destruction'. He did not say innovation and destruction; he specified *creative destruction* because people learn from their mistakes. Creative destruction means the enterprise may be lost but the desire to have a successful enterprise, and the skill needed to build it, is usually not lost.

Through upturns and downturns, success and failure in the economy serve a purpose. The downturn teaches lessons and makes us more skilled at balancing and preparing for the adversity and opportunity that the future is bound to bring. Upturns and downturns alike reward those who have taken calculated, forward-looking risks and entice others to follow suit. Every time the economy changes, it emits new signals that allow us to navigate our way forward, if only we catch and interpret those signals.

Have a view

The purpose of paying attention to signals is to better inform one's view of the world. Without a view, we are adrift at sea without a North Star and perhaps even without a life raft. Without a view, navigation becomes impossible. Instead, those who have no view about the economy or its possible future direction are simply adrift in a sea of

* Amy C. Edmondson, 'Strategies for Learning from Failure', *Harvard Business Review*, April 2011.

uncertainty. Keep in mind that having no view at all is often the most dangerous position to be in, because not acting is sometimes the biggest risk of all.

To have a view, it is necessary to be able to stand against the crowd. After all, if markets and prices were always 'correct', then there would be no bets to be made. For example, the belief that your current wages are too low might encourage you to seek a higher-paying job elsewhere. Alternatively, if you think your wage is currently too high and that your employer is liable to realise this in the near future, you might opt to seek a new job or career before you get fired. By the same token, what incentive is there to start a new business venture when someone else is already providing an identical product or service at the right price?

It is the belief that the market is not supplying something, or supplying it at the wrong price, that motivates a person to build a new business. It is the conviction that the stock market or bond market is at the wrong price that causes a person to bet that the price is going to change. All investing presupposes that the price today is wrong and that the price will be better in future.

So, how can an individual learn how to have a view on the world economy? Luckily, this does not require a degree in economics. It does require that you are alert, that you use your powers of observation, and exercise common sense and character.

Common sense is not universally present (it was notably absent in financial market circles in the run-up to the financial crisis) but it can be cultivated. The tricky piece of the puzzle is character.

Character

What does character have to do with the world economy? Well, first, without risk there is no reward. Alan Greenspan put it nicely when he said, 'Risk-taking is indeed a necessary condition for the creation of wealth', or, to put it another way: 'The ultimate value of all assets rests on their ability to produce goods and services in the future. And the future, as we all know, is uncertain and hence all investments are risky.'* Although he was talking about financial investments, what he said applies to all the investments we make, including investments in ideas, aspirations, education and dreams. Risk-taking is the key to economic growth. And calculated, well-thought-through, well-directed, well-managed risk is the key to *sustained* economic growth.

Character drives all good stories, including economic ones. Character underpins all investment decisions. Consensus is already priced into the market; in other words, it is difficult to make any money out of a view that just about everyone shares. The chances that such an asset will rise in value are small because everyone already owns it. There aren't enough new buyers left to push the price up. The investment decisions that pay the best are the ones with less than best odds, where there is an element of risk. The risk is what you get paid for. Character defines the economy.

The word 'character' might imply that some people have good character and others not. On the other hand it is argued that there is no such thing as character because people change their behaviour depending on the circumstances and whom they are with. What I mean by character is this: the ability to arrive at a view of the world based on our own reasoning rather than that of the crowd; the capacity to execute and stick with that view; and the willingness to change it fluidly with circumstance in order to achieve a committed goal that is beyond our normal reach.

Most people ask me, 'What should I buy?' They rarely ask, 'What and when should I sell?' They forget that there is no such thing as profit until you take the cash off the table and put it in your pocket. Before that it may look like a profit, but it's merely hope. One of the truest tests of character, when it comes to the economy, is when we buy something like a house or stock and the price keeps going up. Most people become

* In a presentation at the annual Economic Symposium sponsored by the Federal Reserve Bank of Kansas City in Jackson Hole, Wyoming, 29 August 1997.

afraid to sell, afraid to give up the potential gains. Instead of having a clear goal, we hesitate. This illustrates the old adage: Bulls make money, bears make money, pigs get slaughtered. Selling something that is still rising in value will be met with endless derision. It takes character to stand up to that and pocket the cash while it's still on offer. Failure to sell at the right time (before everyone else is selling) leads to 'coulda, woulda, shoulda' stories about how a person 'used to have a profit' when in fact they had nothing but a possibility.

In this sense, calculated risk-taking in the world economy is a character test. To succeed in the world economy we need to be comfortable with our view. It may be that our view is the same as everyone else's, but this leaves us in danger of that all-too-human inclination to buy high and sell low. It feels comfortable going with the crowd. The problem is, by the time something is 'obvious', everyone has already done the same thing and there is usually little or no more value left in the investment. So, calculated risk-taking usually means having a different view to the majority.

This is true of all investing, including investments we make in ourselves. I studied political philosophy and military history when I was at university. Everyone said, 'You'll never get a job. Become a lawyer.' (This was partly because there was a spate of popular films and TV shows in the 1970s and 1980s, such as *Perry Mason* and *The Paper Chase*, that glamorised the legal profession.) I disregarded their advice because I wanted to make an investment in my own education in my own way. Luckily, it played out well. Now consider what's happened in recent years. By the 1990s, the degree everyone wanted was a business degree, an MBA. Again, popular films and fiction played their part in drawing a whole new generation to seek employment in the financial services sector, though Oliver Stone, the director of *Wall Street* (1987), and Michael Lewis, author of *Liar's Poker* (1989), have both expressed shock that their cautionary tales had the effect of glamorising the financial markets. The problem was, with so many people coming out of university with the same degree, the value fell and starting salaries got worse and worse. In fact an MBA no longer guarantees you either a job or a career in finance. If you have maths skills, engineering is now paying more, as we shall see.

Whether investing or choosing which sector to work in, the guiding principle should be the same. If you believe that the current price of shares in Heinz – or copper, government bonds, or breakfast cereals, for that matter – is right, then there is no point buying or selling them because you can't make a profit. In order to make a profit, you have to believe the current price is wrong and that it is going to move in the direction you expect. You might choose to work in law or mining or luxury goods. Your choice reflects a view, since it is rare that a person picks a field of endeavour that they think is a loser from the start.

Risk-taking therefore requires sufficient character, self-confidence and conviction to believe that your view is right and the view of the millions who make up the market and determine the price at any given moment is wrong. If the price is 'right' then there is no point taking a risk. There won't be any reward.

This is one reason the lessons of traditional 'free market' economics are not that useful when trying to judge the future. Too many economists assume the markets are 'perfect'. They think markets have 'priced in' or accounted for all the information about the price. In real life, however, it is fairly obvious that prices are signals that change all the time. If you want to have a view, a view that you are prepared to take a risk on, it becomes important to look for signals that support or detract from your view.

A skyline in Wuhan

Consider Hugh Hendry's videos of the Wuhan skyline in China, which he took from the window of his hotel one day in 2009. Hendry is a legendary hedge fund manager based in London. He has described the critical character qualities that define success in investing: 'First and foremost, an ability to establish a contentious premise outside the existing belief system, and have it go on and be adopted by the rest of the financial community.'* *Barron's* magazine asked Hendry in 2012, 'Where do you find yourself outside the existing belief system today?'† Hendry then described what he had seen that day from his hotel window in Wuhan. To the casual observer it was a skyline made up of multistorey buildings with huge metal cranes perched on top. To Hendry, it was a signal; observing those unfinished buildings, he realised something was amiss.

> I made a YouTube video of the empty skyscrapers . . . Goldman Sachs and others articulate a very reasonable and compelling argument of being invested in China. With the evidence of my own eyes, I concluded that China had a very robust system of creating gross domestic-product growth, but forsaking the creation of wealth.

The building boom in Wuhan and other Chinese cities had been driven in part by the belief that farmworkers would want to move to urban areas in search of a new and better life. Property developers went crazy, building for the anticipated increase in urban populations. Most people saw this activity as a sign of growth. They were convinced that China would continue to grow even though the West was in trouble, that the Chinese would be exporting manufactured goods to the rest of the world for years to come. But as Americans stopped buying imported goods, unemployment rose and the Chinese economy began to suffer.

Hendry saw buildings where work had stopped before the roofs were put on and realised that the property developers had run out of cash – proof that the financial crisis in the West was having a knock-on effect in China. As a result he took the decision to avoid what everyone else was doing – investing in China. It turned out that Hendry was right, though it wasn't immediately apparent.

* Tyler Durden, 'Hugh Hendry is Back: Full Eclectica Letter', *Zero Hedge*, 29 April 2012.
† Mark Hanna, 'Hugh Hendry's Interview with *Barron's*', *Market Montage*, 22 February 2012.

For a while, the fact that foreigners continued to invest more and more capital in China fuelled optimism. The Chinese government's response to the crisis in the property market was to throw more money in, encouraging a further wave of construction in the hope this would stop the haemorrhage. They succeeded only in creating buildings and infrastructure for which there was no need and no market.

Hendry's 'sell China' call took character. He was prepared to be laughed at and considered a crazy outlier when the majority were buying the story that China would grow. This is precisely what is required to navigate the world economy successfully – the character to come to a view of your own and the ability to know whether your particular skills and circumstances permit you to profit from your view.

Credit, credere and character

Character is itself a signal. Investors often lend on the basis of the borrower's character. The word 'credit' is derived from the Latin word *credere*, which means 'to believe'. Called to testify before a House Committee on the nation's finances in 1912, J. P. Morgan was asked to explain the basis on which he made loans. His response was the now famous maxim: 'The first thing is character, before money or property or anything else. A man I do not trust could not get money from me on all the bonds in Christendom.'*

This aligns with Warren Buffett's view: 'In evaluating people you look for three qualities: integrity, intelligence and energy. And if you don't have the first the other two will kill you.' Scientists who push beyond traditional ways of thinking and thereby invent vital solutions are engaging in the same creative, productive act of balancing between hubris and nemesis, so it should come as no surprise that Albert Einstein was another believer in the fundamental drive of character.

---

* 'The Money Trust Investigation' of the Committee on Banking and Currency, House of Representatives, 19 December 1912.

'Most people say that it is the intellect that makes a great scientist,' he said. 'They are wrong: it is character.'

The world economy produces an overwhelming number of signals. The ability to sift through those signals, recognising which have significance and correctly interpretating their meaning, takes us only so far. It's not enough to form a view, one must then have the conviction to pursue that view – taking care to balance hubris against the risk of nemesis in the process – and this is a matter of character. The world economy ensures that one's views are put to the test rather often.

Edgework

It is the business of pushing the boundary of the known that drives the world economy and creates wealth, growth and GDP. Invention, innovation and profitability all stem from this drive. The English poet Robert Browning put it simply: 'A man's reach should exceed his grasp, or what's a heaven for?'* Edgework is the business of pushing against the boundaries of the unknown. It is argued by psychologists that this is essential to life.

According to the American novelist Ernest Hemingway, 'There are only three real sports: motor racing, mountain climbing and bullfighting. All the rest are mere games.' By his measure, the others didn't sufficiently push a man to the edge. Perhaps it is the simple fact that a person has to risk his life in these sports that attracts edgeworkers. Stirling Moss, the British Formula One racing driver, has said, 'To achieve anything in this game, you must be prepared to dabble on the boundary of disaster.' The world economy may be the same. Having a view and the character to pursue it requires the same sort of 'edgework' that is usually associated with racing drivers, astronauts, experimental aircraft pilots and extreme sailors. They may all be throwing themselves at the boundary of physics, but the world

* 'Andrea del Sarto' (Called the 'Faultless Painter'), 1855.

economy compels us to confront the borders between the current state of affairs and the possible.

Think of it this way – just as sex involves pushing physical and psychological boundaries, crime challenges the boundary of the law, and music and drugs allow people to push the boundary of time and imagination, so innovation challenges the boundary of the world economy.

Boundary-pushing is not simply a matter of curiosity. It is a means of both discovering and meeting the basic needs of the human psyche. In his 1943 paper, 'A Theory of Human Motivation', the American psychologist Abraham Maslow identified boundary-pushing as an essential component of life: 'What a man *can* be, he must be . . . This need we may call self-actualisation. It refers to the desire for self-fulfilment, namely, to the tendency for him to become actualised in what he is potentially. This tendency might be phrased as the desire to become more and more what one is, to become everything that one is capable of becoming.'*

Jazz artists like Miles Davis, Charlie Parker and Dizzie Gillespie realised they would never be anything more than one-hit wonders or session musicians, paid for their time and easily replaced, unless they engaged in edgework.† Instead of playing the work of others, they wrote their own material. This allowed them to change their style and push their music beyond the accepted definition of their day, and in doing so they not only gained control of their future, they became legends. Miles Davis in particular changed his musical style quite radically every four or five years. Clearly it required a lot of conviction and character

---

* In *Man For Himself* (1947), the German social psychologist Erich Fromm wrote in agreement: 'Man's main task in life is to give birth to himself, to become what he potentially is.' A century earlier, the Irish poet Thomas Moore (1779–1852) expressed something similar: 'Nothing is more important in a person's life than to gain soul by expanding the limits of what defines him. This is transcendence, and it is an essential part of religion.'

† 50 Cent and Robert Greene, *The 50th Law*, G-Unit Books, 2009.

to move away from popular music and to keep introducing new and unfamiliar music, but as a result both Parker and Gillespie emerged as icons.

Survival and success in the world economy also depend on boundary-pushing edgework. Innovation, the single most important event that occurs in the economy, the thing that creates sustainable GDP, is edgework. For some, edgework and economics is too exhausting and endangering a combination. 'Where is the edge?' they ask nervously. 'Where is the boundary beyond which real growth is created?' The answer, provided by poet T. S. Eliot, offers little comfort to the nervous: 'Only those who risk going too far can possibly find out how far one can go.' Hunter S. Thompson, a journalist and novelist who made a living out of being on or over the edge, concurs: 'The Edge . . . there is no honest way to explain it because the only people who really know where it is are the ones who have gone over.'*

There's no getting away from it: when Nemesis gets involved, the outcome can be unpleasant. The cutting edge is a bloody place. Edgework is undeniably frightening, especially when our future is at stake. There is substance to the old cliché that business is the cutting edge of the world economy. Edgework requires care and attention because sometimes the cutting edge is clearing the path before us and speeding us on our way to success, and sometimes it is mowing us down, leaving us flailing helplessly in its wake. As the computer scientist Zalman Stern observed, 'The problem with the cutting edge is that someone has to bleed.'

So, why do it? Because there are rewards

Consider the story of chef Daniel Rose, a young man from Chicago who spoke no French but loved cooking. He moved to Paris to attend university, but instead turned to fine cuisine. In 2006, at the height of

* Hunter S. Thompson, *Hell's Angels: The Strange and Terrible Saga of the Outlaw Motorcycle Gangs*, Random House, 1966.

the booming economy, he opened a restaurant in Paris called Spring. He is now one of the highest-ranked chef-restaurateurs in France in spite of having been forced to close, move, re-open, close, re-open and re-invent his restaurant several times due to the adverse whims of the world economy. The waiting list for a table is currently running at one year.

Think about the risks that Ross Brawn took when he launched his Formula One (F1) racing team. F1 has never been a big success in America, but worldwide it draws one of the largest audiences for any spectator sport. By the time of the financial crisis in August 2007, F1 had become a frenzy of free money being thrown at teams and technology. Firms including Vodafone and Orange were paying some $75 million annually to sponsor teams. Honda and Toyota apparently spent nearly $1.5 billion in 2008 alone. In November 2007, three months after the financial market crisis began, Honda approached Brawn – who had been credited with steering the championship-winning teams of Benetton and Ferrari to success – and offered him the top job, 'team principal', in their F1 team.

A few months after the financial crisis unfolded, it suddenly became clear that Honda's sales had collapsed and the company could not afford to remain an F1 sponsor. Some say it had already decided to get out and the financial crisis provided the excuse. Either way, Brawn suddenly found himself without a backer or a team. Undaunted, he decided to buy the team and find new backers. Brawn GP or 'Team Brawn' was launched in November 2009 and, thanks to support from Virgin and QTel (the Qatari Telecom firm) and a few others, they raised enough cash – just – to make it to the next race, which meant they had to win or fold.

There are only two prizes in F1 racing – best driver (World Drivers' Championship) and best car (Constructors' Championship). In 2009, Team Brawn won both. This had never been achieved by any F1 team in its first year of existence, let alone by a team that was operating on a shoestring. Bear in mind that, aside from being an extremely expensive pursuit, F1 racing is a technical undertaking in which the driver is only as good as his car. These races are won more in the garage than on the circuit. The technical engineers who construct these machines are pushing the boundaries of physics, constantly balancing the need to shave off another gram of weight without sacrificing the structural integrity of a car that will be driven at such speeds that a sudden need to brake would snap the neck of any untrained driver. This is expensive and arduous edgework.

Joy

If you like perfume, here is an inspiring example for you. The stock market crash of 1929 and the subsequent depression devastated the economic landscape. Jean Patou owned a couture house in Paris that had invented knitted ties and sports knitwear. They had also launched a series of fragrances in the 1920s. The crash wiped out most of his clientele. He took a dramatic decision and closed the clothing business. Patou and his head perfumer, Henri Alméras, then took a bold leap of faith. On the basis that, no matter the condition of the world economy, there would always be someone who would figure out how to make money, they decided to launch the most expensive perfume ever made: Joy. Every 30 ml contains more than ten thousand jasmine flowers and the petals from more than three hundred roses. Despite the price tag, it has been almost as successful as Chanel N°5 ever since.

Talk about an edgy decision and a leap of faith! Imagine the character it takes to launch the most expensive perfume in history in the midst of such an epic economic crisis. Thank goodness for that courage though, because it created untold jobs in the perfume industry that exist to this day, as well as offering a vision of hope that continues to inspire some eight decades later.

Hurt versus injury

Not everyone is cut out to be a big risk-taker. Not all of us are entrepreneurs. Nonetheless we are all affected by the movements of the world economy. Given the damage the world economy is capable of inflicting, it's certainly better to be hurt than injured. Sportsmen know the difference between being hurt and being injured.* We can still play if we are hurt, but injuries preclude playing in the game. In world economy terms, 'hurt' is when we lose our job to a competitor, but we are still in the game and have the option of going for a similar job or changing profession or strategy. In contrast, to be 'injured' by the world economy is to find, as many have done over the last few years, at the age of fifty that our pension fund value has been damaged by losses, thus forcing us to work years longer for a lower standard of living than we anticipated.

A pensioner cannot, must not, take big financial risks and, as a rule, cannot afford to lose any capital. Their capacity to recover and re-enter the world economy is limited. That's an injury. If we have no skills and society has left us without the means to acquire them, then whole generations can be left permanently sidelined. That's an injury.

Today this problem plagues not only the elderly but the younger generation in the Eurozone, in less advantaged communities in America and the large poor and uneducated populations of emerging markets. It could even be worse than an injury. This constitutes a break in the fundamental contract between citizen and state: the social contract. To one degree or another, citizens are entitled to expect that their government will not leave them in such a perilous condition for very long. Naturally, hurt and injury give rise to a sense of hopelessness against the unknown forces of nature. This feeling of helplessness reminds me of something Peter Drucker wrote in 1939 in his first book, *The End of Economic Man*. On the subject of the Great Depression, he said the economic damage proved that 'irrational and incalculable forces also rule peacetime society: the threat of sudden permanent unemployment, of being thrown on the industrial scrap heap in one's

---

* Malcolm Gladwell, 'Offensive Play: How different are dogfighting and football?' *New Yorker*, 19 October 2009.

prime or even before one has started to work. Against these forces the individual finds himself as helpless, isolated, and atomised as against the forces of machine war.'

The character tests that the world economy brings are not just personal. Most of us can cope with a stock market that goes up and down, even one that moves violently. What most of us cannot tolerate is a world in which our faith and belief in the market mechanism is broken, and where prices no longer reflect normal market forces. There are terrible social consequences if we fail to learn how to navigate the ebbs and flows of the world economy. Edgework will make us better navigators.

The German social psychologist Erich Fromm, writing in 1942, explained how the psychology of being a 'senseless cog' proved fertile soil for the rise of Fascism in Germany, Italy and elsewhere in Europe after the population endured searing losses from multiple causes including war, hyperinflation, the rapid decline in savings and the destruction of normal price signals in the economy. Today we see economic pressures that are far less acute and yet those who would normally oppose the expansion of the state become quiescent, conceding that only the state has the power to address economic problems that are far beyond the comprehension or abilities of an individual member of the public. As a society, the financial crisis and its aftermath seems to have made us less tolerant and more dependent on the state rather than trusting ourselves to find solutions. The rise of the far right, of separatist movements and of protests against austerity reveal how vulnerable our society is to an economy that causes hurt and injury.

Without tools to understand or manage the process of economic change, Fromm says, freedom becomes 'an unbearable burden. It then becomes identical with doubt, with a kind of life which lacks meaning and direction.' The tendency is to run from such freedom, preferring to give up the rewards of calculated risk-taking for the security of known outcomes, even if such certainty requires handing power over to

Fascists and dictators or even to the friendlier faces of central bankers. Anyone will do, as long as they can restore order. Perhaps this explains something about the public's recent inclination to turn to political outsiders who can shake up the establishment.

The cutting edge is a bloody place

Failure to calculate our risks, failure to test and strengthen our resolve, failure to test our character comes at a cost. If the cutting edge of the world economy can make you bleed, then, given a choice, I have to believe that most of us would choose to bleed a little rather than to bleed a lot. We could choose to have the world economy work with us instead of against us. That requires reading signals, balancing hubris and nemesis, and taking calculated risks.

But the specifics can be small. We might start to pay more attention to the fact that the price of property is rising and that the size of flat or house one can afford to buy is shrinking. This may spur decisions to move to a less expensive part of town or even a less expensive part of the country. It will help save on grocery bills to pay a little more attention to the price per weight now that companies seem to be shrinking the size of many products while keeping the price the same as before.

There are other reasons to look for signals and to engage in edgework. Think of what we'd miss otherwise. Wayne Gretzky, the famed Canadian ice-hockey player, was right when he said, 'You miss 100 per cent of the shots you never take.' And as Woody Allen once said, edgework is required because, 'If you don't fail now and again, it's a sign you're playing it safe.' You can't build an economy or grow GDP by playing it safe.

Stop the world economy, I want to get off!

Still, there are always those who long to 'check out' of the world economy. They don't want to have a view or pay attention to signals. This instinct underpins those who rail against globalisation and the market economy. But to opt out is impossible, as acknowledged by the Tibetan monks with their empty rice bowls and flying bricks. Standing still is not an option because, as the now legendary management consultant Peter Drucker noted, 'defending yesterday – that is, not innovating – is far more risky than making tomorrow.'* After all, we will always have competition. Someone else is always innovating, even if we are not. Faced with a competitor who keeps resetting the bar higher and higher, we can either get focused or get left behind. The only constant in life is change. Change alone can throw us off balance; more so if we have no means of anticipating change.

We could take our chances and let the world economy push our lives along willy-nilly, but what would be the consequences of such an approach? As US President Calvin Coolidge observed, 'Those who trust to chance must abide by the results of chance.' Or as Jack Welch, former CEO of General Electric, put it: 'Control your destiny or someone else will!'†

Adapting to change

Sadly, we cannot outlaw change, the economic cycle, fraud, bad judgement or even plain old mistakes. Happily, human beings are pretty good at adapting to change even if they don't like it. We do it, even though we may be unaware we are adapting in response to signals. Charles Darwin is interminably misquoted on this point. He did not say 'only the strong survive'. The thrust of his argument *On the Origin of Species* is that only the *adaptable* survive. In general, we manage the small changes in the world economy very effectively. We can adjust to a life with higher or lower oil prices, and higher or lower growth rates or interest rates. We often adapt without even realising it.

Still, we'd like to think that somebody can protect us from the

* Peter Drucker, *Innovation and Entrepreneurship*, Elsevier, 1985.
† Quoted in Noel M. Tichy and Stratford Sherman, *Control Your Destiny or Someone Else Will*, HarperCollins, 1993.

world economy. Many want to believe that the world's central banks can make all the losses go away by engaging in 'quantitative easing' (the policy of flooding the markets with low interest rates and super-cheap money). But, in the end, managing the risks in the markets cannot be devolved to some third party, like the state, in the hope that they can insulate us from the future. Risk and opportunity are our own responsibility. This is an uncomfortable thought and a lot of people won't like it.

How many of us live life and make important decisions without taking account of the condition of the world economy because it seems 'beyond our control'? My central purpose in writing this book is to give people the ability to notice signals and thereby proceed into the future with a greater sense of the context that will influence any individual choices that we might make.

It isn't an easy task. We have a tendency to see signals clearly only in retrospect. The nineteenth-century novelist Mark Twain complained, 'I was seldom able to see an opportunity until it had ceased to be one.' The reality is that anybody can learn how to pick up on economic signals. The rest of this book will address that. Interpreting and acting on signals is another matter. That takes character. You have to assess not only the signals out there, but your own ability to make use of them. Of course, you might be wrong. But being prepared for change, gaining skill at edgework and still getting it wrong is not the same as being completely unskilled and unprepared.

3

A Letter to the Queen

On 9 November 2008, I imagine that Queen Elizabeth II woke up thinking about the state of the world economy given that she was opening the new £71-million lecture theatre at the London School of Economics that day. In my mind's eye, I can see her sitting quite upright in bed, no doubt ramrod straight, given what we have seen from photographs and paintings of her character and her poise, as she asked herself the question that lurked in everyone's mind, but which nobody had posed: 'Why did no one see the crisis coming?'

She posed her question to LSE economist Luis Garicano that day. After all, one would have expected economists to warn us of impending danger. Shouldn't they, of all people, have seen all the signals? The academics at LSE and indeed the members of the British Academy responded to her query many months later on 22 July 2009 in a letter in the *Financial Times*:

> When Your Majesty visited the London School of Economics last November, you quite rightly asked: why had nobody noticed that the credit crunch was on its way? The British Academy convened a forum on 17 June 2009 to debate your question, with contributions from a range of experts from business, the City, its regulators, academia, and government. This letter summarises the views of the participants and the factors that they cited in our discussion, and we hope that it offers an answer to your question.

What did members of the Academy cite as the true cause?

. . . principally a failure of the collective imagination of many bright people, both in this country and internationally, to understand the risks to the system as a whole.*

Imagination does indeed lie at the heart of the matter. Economics and imagination are deeply entwined. Here is a belated reply, which I would like to have sent her, on the very timely, apt and profound question she posed:

Her Majesty the Queen
Buckingham Palace
London sw1a 1aa

Madam,†

In answer to your question, 'Why did no one see the crisis coming?' the answer is simple and unsatisfying: We can no more predict or prevent economic crises any more than we can control the advent of storms on the high seas. What follows is an explanation and a remedy.

John Kenneth Galbraith observed that financial market experts are usually very rich (financiers) or powerful (economists), and therefore held in awe, surrounded by the most skilled staff and able to access the best information. Thus the 'experts' are 'endowed with the authority that encourages acquiescence from their subordinates and applause from their acolytes and excludes adverse opinion'. This leads to an assurance of 'personal mental superiority' that 'in turn diminishes self-scrutiny'. This fact about humankind cannot be changed. The 'experts' will always lead us

---

* David Turner, 'Credit Crunch failure explained to Queen', *Financial Times*, 26 July 2009; see also www.britac.ac.uk/news/newsrelease-economy.cfm
† 'Madam' is correct according to the official Buckingham Palace website.

down the wrong path and we will always willingly follow the path, to supposed riches, because it is so brilliantly lit with genius. The rule is simple, Galbraith notes: 'Financial genius is before the fall.'*

So far, no economist has come up with a reliable theory that allows us to predict a crisis. No one even knows how to tell when the cycle will take a turn for better or for worse, as the economists confirmed when they wrote to you. The American economist Hyman Minsky got the closest to offering an insight when he said that things in the world economy tend to change very suddenly. But even he left no formula for knowing when this will happen.

So, here is a dark joke for you, ma'am. The three best jobs in the world are:

1. Designated hitter for a major league baseball team
2. Meteorologist
3. Economist

In what other profession can you fail 79 per cent of the time and still be considered good at your job? It's an old joke. 'The only function of economic forecasting is to make astrology look respectable.'† Barring some extraordinary innovation, let's forget prediction. But, even if we cannot predict, we can still prepare. Participants in the world economy can be better equipped to manage these storms when they occur. A few specific undertakings would shore up every man and woman so that they can captain their own ship in spite of the storms, instead of being subject to fate, whose turn can be apparent before action need be taken instead of only in retrospect, as has been the case for too many.

First, there can be no sustainable economic and financial innovation without financial education. We need more than the

---

* John Kenneth Galbraith, *A Short History of Financial Euphoria*, Whittle Books, 1990.
† I conferred with James Galbraith on this quote and discovered that his father, John Kenneth Galbraith, 'never said it'. 'The remark was made by some less-well-known figure, and because it was clever, the Internet decided to credit Dad.'

efforts of banks and finance ministries to help schoolchildren understand how the interest rate on a mortgage is calculated, critical as that may be. Children leave school and start their adult lives often with no knowledge of how interest rates impact on the price of a mortgage or the APR* on a credit card, let alone how the national debt compounds. In the main, schools do not teach basic financial concepts such as what percentage of income ought to be spent on shelter or set aside for a rainy day.

For example, in the last crisis we found many British pension funds had placed their savings in a bank in Iceland simply because it paid the highest rate of interest. Later many Icelandic banks went spectacularly bust. Throughout history, it has been known that a bank has to pay over the odds to attract deposits only when it suffers from a lack of trust. That means there is a risk. Interest rates are one of many signals. People need to know what these signals are and understand how to respond to them as surely as we expect a person to stop at a red light and go on a green one.

Investing in oneself, in the markets, in the future, all require risk-taking. If there is no risk, there is no reward. So, there is little point in trying to devise new rules or even institutions that can prevent bad outcomes. The SEC, the FSA and other financial regulators can never protect us from fraud. No regulator can save us from having to do our own homework. Loss is a normal part of the world economy and indeed progress cannot occur without it. More rules and regulation, in contrast, ensure higher costs and make it harder for calculated risk-taking to occur. So, we should think about managing loss and failure as much as managing success.

These problems are not so hard to fix, especially now that online education is ubiquitous.

* Annual Percentage Rate.

Second, we need more diversity in the economy. I am not referring to more diversity of investment portfolios between stocks, bonds, property, cash and other assets. No, I mean something much more significant. I mean a greater diversity of opinion and endeavour in the world economy.

I find myself in agreement with the nineteenth-century English philosopher and economist John Stuart Mill, who wrote: 'That so few now dare to be eccentric marks the chief danger of the time' and 'All good things which exist are the fruits of originality.'*

Ironically, in financial markets it is believed that the one 'free lunch' is diversification. Yet we do not encourage diversity of opinion or diversification of economic activities in our societies. Those with a contrary view from the consensus are given air time by the press only after the fact and only if they were right. Instead, a diversity of opinion ought to be expressed regardless, so that we can consider the risk that the experts might be wrong and therefore prepare for such a possibility.

Whenever the majority of the population seeks to pursue the same idea at the same time, it usually ends in tears. It is a sure sign of trouble when 85 per cent of business school graduates want a job in the financial markets. It is a sure sign of trouble when everyone buys the same investment ideas at the same time: tulips in 1637; railroad stocks in the 1800s; Internet stocks in the 1990s. What about homes and mortgages in the 2000s?

There is some wisdom in crowds, no doubt, but there may be safety in taking a road 'less travelled' as Robert Frost put it. At least that reduces the likelihood of everybody being wrong in the same way at the same time. Volatility and the economic cycle cannot be outlawed or prevented, but we can cushion against them by encouraging more eccentricity in our edgework and our life experiences.

* John Stuart Mill, *On Liberty and the Subjection of Women*, Penguin, 2006.

The greater the diversity of opinion and activity in the economy, the more cushioned we are against the inevitable ebbs and flows in the world economy. Why? Because events can be managed better if we pursue different opinions, different business models and ideas, different activities and different visions of the future, rather than all leaning the same way at once.

Moreover, if each individual were left to forge their own eccentric and edgy path, it would develop strength of character – and strength of character is vital if we are to manage the economy's inevitably changing tides. In this way, we can begin to appreciate the opportunities that fall out of the top and the bottom of the economic cycle alike. Bear in mind, it is typically when the economic cycle sinks into crisis mode that assets are shaken free from the privileged hands of their current owners and shift, at much lower prices, into the hands of aspiring owners. And it is typically at the top of the economic cycle that the opportunity to take one's profits home presents itself. But that is precisely the moment that it is hardest to sell.

It takes vision, conviction, character and preparedness to sell at the top and buy at the bottom. As the old adage says: Bulls make money, bears make money, pigs get slaughtered. 'Pigs' suffer because they lack the necessary character and judgement. 'Pigs' do not invest. They do not hold a view with any conviction. Pigs merely follow the crowd and the seemingly easy money. Luckily, we are not bulls, bears or pigs. We are humans, with the gift of imagination.

Imagination may seem to have little to do with all this. Yet it lies at the core of economics. You cannot reach for something that exceeds your grasp unless you imagine it. Therefore all innovation, growth and GDP depends on the presence of imagination. This is why we should follow the advice of the Queen of Hearts in *Alice in Wonderland*:

> *Alice laughed. 'There's no use trying,' she said: 'one can't believe impossible things.'*
>
> *'I daresay you haven't had much practice,' said the Queen. 'When I was your age, I always did it for half an hour a day. Why, sometimes I've believed as many as six impossible things before breakfast.'*

People need to imagine at least six impossible things before breakfast. Why? you may ask. Because so often the 'impossible' actually happens in economics. Also, we should learn to use our imagination because it improves preparedness.

Already I can hear Nassim Taleb, author of *The Black Swan*, and his many fans groaning. The Taleb view is that there is no point trying to second-guess the future. You might as well go to the bar and brace yourself for an unpredictable future that will be driven by what Taleb calls 'Black Swans': totally unpredictable events that we cannot even imagine. More precisely, Black Swans are events that exist outside the realm of likely statistical predictability. No doubt the occasional 'Black Swan' will appear on the horizon. But common sense tells us that some events are not only statistically likely but they tend to follow others. If interest rates go up, it tends to produce certain outcomes. If they go down it produces others.

I agree that prediction is impossible. I am guessing that even you have not found a crystal ball among your many vaults and closets.* Happily, we don't need one. We just need more diversity and more imagination.

The solutions here are simple. We must be encouraged to reach for something that is beyond our grasp because this is how we build tomorrow's economy and GDP. We need to do edgework instead of remaining comfortable so we can be better at innovating and recovering from inevitable mistakes. All this will make us

---

* And, by the way, there is no crystal ball in the White House or on a trading floor or anywhere else (I looked for it quite hard during my time in the West Wing, and I can confirm it is not there).

less vulnerable to the random upheavals that the global economy inflicts.

The solution is definitely not to meet every crisis and economic downturn by throwing unlimited amounts of capital at the problem. Capital, as with all things in the world economy, is subject to supply and demand and has a price. Sometimes capital is cheap and easy to find, sometimes it is expensive and in short supply. It is not a shortage of capital that holds back the economy during times of economic weakness; it is a shortage of good imaginative ideas and the character to pursue them. Free money alone does not generate growth. If anything, it weakens the discipline with which we apply our convictions. When circumstances pit character against capital, character usually wins.

Preparedness for possibilities is the goal we should strive for, not prediction. Greater imagination allows us to see that there are benefits to success and adversity, to boom and bust alike. Successful navigation of the world economy and its inevitable cycles requires calculated risk-taking. Our task must be to ensure that we are prepared for the inevitable storm and the interesting opportunities that spill from the highs and the lows of the economic swells, and to benefit from their diverse treasures. This means we need to be better at reading signals, debating them with the utmost robustness, and following them when we have conviction.

Sincerely,

Pippa Malmgren

4

The Algorithm Made Me Do It

—

'This is bullshit!' the motorcycle mechanic blurted out with frustration, as he glared at the coloured LED screen on the digital multimeter he was using to measure the width of an engine part that needed replacing. The screen kept flashing different numbers and would not settle on a precise measurement. In engine construction, precision matters. An imprecise measurement is dangerous because a misfitting part can cause the engine to jam, burn out, or blow up, possibly injuring someone in the process. In the old days, motorcycle mechanics used a mechanical caliper to measure the exact size of a part that needed replacing. Today, everything is computerised and mechanics have 'upgraded' to LED instruments that measure the size of components. Except, it turns out that sometimes the old-fashioned measure of reality can be more accurate. This is as true for motorcycle parts as it is for the world economy, as motorcycle mechanic and cultural commentator Matthew Crawford points out.*

We now trust computers, numbers, algorithms and mathematical models more than we trust people, qualitative inputs and human judgement. We now put more faith in standardised tests that measure a child's progress in school rather than relying on the opinion of a potentially cranky teacher the child happens to be assigned to in the classroom. Many feel more confident knowing a computer is flying

* Matthew Crawford, *Shop Class as Soulcraft*, Penguin, 2009.

the plane than a pilot whose human error could threaten lives. Yet there are some who still trust the pilot and hope he can override the computer if he has to.

This is the essential debate in modern economics: whether and when to override the system and on what basis. Should we be guided by mathematical models or common sense?

Crawford points out that the financial crisis hinged on such a 'this is bullshit' moment – the moment someone realises that the mathematical model we are relying on is directing us to do something stupid that defies common sense.

In his article 'Recipe for Disaster: the Formula That Killed Wall Street',* financial journalist Felix Salmon explained how smart people are led to do stupid things by misplaced belief in an algorithm. In short, they become wedded to the elegance of the maths at the expense of reality. Reality is messy. You can't quantify it and it does not neatly 'fit'.

The moment common sense and algorithms come into conflict warrants close attention. These days the mortgage-lending officer at the bank finds himself in the same position as the owner of a BMW who longs to be permitted to reach into the engine and measure the oil level. Neither has the freedom to override or adjust the computer-generated outcome. Modern engines tend to be encased and locked, and any attempt to override the 'safeguards' will void the manufacturer's warranty. Mathematical algorithms in the world economy are equally difficult to circumvent. For example, in 2006 the local mortgage broker might have signed off on my mother's mortgage, given the opportunity to review her financial situation. But there was no local mortgage broker. Most banks fired their lending officers in the 2000s on the basis that the algorithm could do the job better and faster.

The algorithm did not care. I explained to my mother: 'If interest rates rise, you won't be able to make the payments. And should the

* Felix Salmon, 'Recipe for Disaster: the Formula That Killed Wall Street', *Wired* magazine, 17 February 2009.

value of the house fall in the slightest, you will have negative equity: the house will be worth less than the mortgage.' The lending officer would have agreed – which is why he had to be fired. He stood in the way of 'progress', defined in this instance as more transactions leading to a higher share price for the bank. In the world of finance, a similar signal echoed on trading floors of big banks when credit officers ceased to be invited to attend meetings where important investment decisions were being made. They asked too many questions. They had too many objections. Instead they could be found in the corridors, grumbling about not being included in the decision-making process.

By dismissing bank lending officers and excluding credit officers from meetings, banks showed they trusted algorithms more than people (an important signal at the time). Moreover it showed that the volume and speed of transactions, which would have been slowed down by questions, had become the principal driver of a higher share price. I am now alert to a signal that often appears in a booming economy: if the volume of transactions drives the share price up more than the quality of transactions, something is wrong.

Perhaps there was a moment when the closing bell at the stock exchange should have been interpreted as an alarm bell; the moment that the quantity of transactions and deals supplanted quality. In answer to the Queen's question, banks, mortgage brokers and mortgage lenders can honestly say, 'The algorithm made me do it!'

Anyone who challenges the algorithm at the expense of a rising share price is bound to be batted away, removed from a position of power, or fired. In this sense, the algorithm indeed made them do it. Bankers, fund managers and the denizens of Wall Street calculate the risk and the reward in their portfolios all day long. They also calculate the risk and reward with the algorithm that pays them.

The Queen asked, 'Why didn't anybody see it coming?' The answer is, they did. The most popular topic of discussion in 2007 was the imminent disaster in the credit markets. Most of my clients spent hours hypothesising about how the inevitable would play out, and indeed how to profit from the coming debacle.

So, why did they not sell? The algorithm is the simple answer. Being right early means selling when prices are still rising. To be right early means underperforming and therefore to risk losing clients and one's job. In the UK, this is called 'the Tony Dye effect'. Tony Dye was a British Fund manager who called the crisis correctly, much to everyone's derision, earning himself the nickname 'Dr Doom'. He sold a year early, which meant he underperformed the market and his peers. He was, therefore, fired.*

He was subsequently vindicated when the market turned, but it was too late to profit from his views by then.

Dye was out of step with the prevailing mindset in the financial sector, which rewards those who defer difficult decisions: we know the stock market and asset values are going to fall apart, but at the same time we know that we cannot be blamed or fired as long as we do not underperform our peers, thus our safest option is to sit tight. We may see the price fall 30 per cent as a result, but provided everyone else suffers similar losses, we get to keep our job. Whereas if we sell too early, we get fired.

The source of the 'bullsh**' problem: algorithms and hubris

The economics profession suffers from its desire to jam all human activity into a mathematical model. There is a long history behind this tendency to believe that the entire truth lies in maths, which is something the Hungarian-British writer Arthur Koestler called 'The Cartesian Catastrophe'. Yet the origin of the problem is clear, no better phrased than by the eighteenth-century physicist Sir Isaac Newton, who said, 'I can calculate the motion of heavenly bodies, but not the madness of people.' Notably, he said this after losing all his money in a financial market catastrophe: the South Sea Bubble of 1720.

---

* 'Requiem for a Prudent Man', *Economist*, 27 March 2008.

No doubt it is hard to quantify mathematically the 'madness of people' but there is grave danger in believing that anything we cannot ascribe a number to simply does not count. It would certainly make life easier if we could eliminate all risks we cannot quantify, including politics, policy and geopolitics, not to mention hubris, ego and incentive. These factors don't neatly fit into an algorithm.

Markets would be much easier to manage if these risks could simply be removed from the landscape. And so it has become the norm to set aside, diminish or dismiss that which cannot be quantified. The Israeli-American psychologist Daniel Kahneman, who won the Nobel Prize in Economic Sciences in 2002, was named one of the world's top global thinkers by *Foreign Policy* magazine for his work on pushing back against this tendency to quantify and restoring behaviour as a driver of economic outcomes in his book, *Thinking, Fast and Slow* (2012). Nevertheless, I find that many in the world economy derive far greater comfort from data, algorithms and maths than non-quantifiable risks, in spite of the many warnings from Nobel Prize-winners.

The pretence of knowledge

When the Austrian-British economist and philosopher Friedrich Hayek took to the stage in December 1974 to deliver his Nobel lecture, 'The Pretence of Knowledge', he made the following seemingly obvious point. Scientists can measure only the things that can be measured. But many things cannot be measured, like love, someone's tolerance for pain, national pride or the difference between the drive you have when you want something versus when you need something. He thought it was ironic that the Nobel Prize was being conferred on the economics profession at the very moment that circumstances were proving that economists had been pursuing ideas in a highly unscientific way. He wrote:

> On the one hand the still recent establishment of the Nobel Memorial Prize in Economic Science marks a significant step in the

process by which, in the opinion of the general public, economics has been conceded some of the dignity and prestige of the physical sciences. On the other hand, the economists are at this moment called upon to say how to extricate the free world from the serious threat of accelerating inflation which, it must be admitted, has been brought about by policies which the majority of economists recommended and even urged governments to pursue.

Hayek was specifically railing at policymakers about the dreadful state of the world economy in 1974, when everyone was being crushed simultaneously by high inflation and high unemployment. (It is perhaps more ironic still that we find ourselves in a situation today that echoes this past, where economists have argued that we should do everything necessary to create inflation and now that the policy begins to succeed, the result is described as a 'nightmare scenario' where growth remains weak but inflation picks up.*) Hayek continued:

> . . . this failure of the economists to guide policy more successfully is closely connected with their propensity to imitate as closely as possible the procedures of the brilliantly successful physical sciences – an attempt which in our field may lead to outright error. It is an approach which has come to be described as the 'scientistic' attitude – an attitude which, as I defined it some thirty years ago, 'is decidedly unscientific in the true sense of the word, since it involves a mechanical and uncritical application of habits of thought to fields different from those in which they have been formed'. I want today to begin by explaining how some of the gravest errors of recent economic policy are a direct consequence of this scientistic error . . . as if one needed only to follow some cooking recipes to solve all social problems.

* Peter Schiff, 'The Federal Reserve's Nightmare Scenario', 23 February 2016; www.realclearmarkets.com/articles/2016/02/23/the_federal_reserves_nightmare_scenario_102022.html

A recipe for disaster

Whatever recipe we've been following, it keeps resulting in a rather unpleasant dish. The public opinion analyst and social scientist Daniel Yankelovich, who founded the original *New York Times*/CBS poll, clearly explained why the essential ingredients were missing from the recipe:

> The first step is to measure what can be easily measured. This is okay as far as it goes. The second step is to disregard that which cannot be measured, or give it an arbitrary quantitative value. This is artificial and misleading. The third step is to presume that what cannot be measured really is not very important. This is blindness. The fourth step is to say that what cannot be measured does not really exist. This is suicide.*

Peter Drucker was more blunt: 'The computer is a moron',† though a helpful moron. He came to this conclusion on the basis that 'All a computer can handle is abstractions, and abstractions can only be relied upon if they are constantly checked against concrete results. Otherwise, they are certain to mislead.'‡

Alan Greenspan echoed the sentiment:

> Models do not fully capture what I believe has been, to date, only a peripheral addendum to business-cycle and financial modelling – the innate human responses that result in swings between euphoria and fear that repeat themselves generation after generation with little evidence of a learning curve.§

* Daniel Yankelovich, *Corporate Priorities: A Continuing Study of the New Demands on Business*, 1972.
† Peter Drucker, *Technology, Management and Society*, 1970.
‡ Peter Drucker, *Classic Drucker: From the Pages of Harvard Business Review*, Harvard Business School Press, 2008.
§ Alan Greenspan, 'We will never have a perfect model of risk', *Financial Times*, 16 March 2008.

A little poetry

Beneath all the faith in models and mathematics, there is an element of convenience. After all, maths and models can obfuscate the truth as much as they reveal it. Economists can carry on talking amongst themselves without the general public being able to join in the conversation – and policymakers can hide behind the maths and push out policies without being questioned too much.

But what price do we pay for this? John Lanchester writes in the *New Yorker*, 'The language of money is a powerful tool, and it is also a tool of power. Incomprehension is a form of consent. If we allow ourselves not to understand this language, we are signing off on the way the world works today'.*

Kenneth Boulding, an economist with poetry in his heart, captured this 'obfuscation' inclination beautifully:

> *If you do some acrobatics*
> *with a little mathematics*
> *it will take you far along.*
> *If your idea's not defensible*
> *don't make it comprehensible*
> *or folks will find you out,*
> *and your work will draw attention*
> *if you only fail to mention*
> *what the whole thing is about.*

In economics and markets we 'commit suicide', by Yankelovich's definition, every few years with, as Hayek says, catastrophic consequences for the general public. Financial and economic crises occur pretty regularly. In recent years, most have arrived as 'surprises', including the Savings and Loan crisis, Long Term Capital Management crisis, the Asian financial crisis, Mexico's default and the financial crisis

---

* John Lanchester, 'Money Talks', *New Yorker*, 4 August 2014.

of 2007/8. They are often thought of as 'Black Swans', which are, as Nassim Taleb explains in his book of the same name, inherently unpredictable. A Black Swan is a highly unlikely event that comes out of the blue. It's no use, Taleb says, trying to think about the 'unknown unknowns'.* Therefore, a Black Swan leaves everyone absolved of the responsibility to anticipate. The model, the maths, the computer – all are especially absolved because the Black Swan is an Act of God.

This may not be entirely true, however. Perhaps a Black Swan serves as a comfortable fig leaf in catastrophic moments. What if we could see a signal that an event was likely to unfold? Recast in this light, it would not be a Black Swan, though it might be a 'tail event'. This means the event might occur on a normal statistical distribution, even though it might be rare. It is unlikely, but not unpredictable. We cannot 'know' it will happen, but in terms of probabilities, we know it might.

We could incorporate the simple idea that the economist Hyman Minsky put forward: 'Stability is destabilising' and look for signals that indicate changes are occurring all the time – good changes and bad changes alike. In this way, we start to muse about six impossible things before breakfast and prepare for what the future might bring. But, this would mean considering signals that cannot be quantified, in effect challenging the dominance of the mathematical approach.

The two cultures

In 1959 C. P. Snow, the chemist and novelist, stood at the podium at Cambridge University to deliver the 291st Rede Lecture, 'The Two Cultures', on exactly this point.† He caused an academic firestorm that rages to this day. He said that the humanities and the sciences had become so separated that neither camp has any ability to solve the real problems society faces. One speaks English and the other speaks mathematics. Science/maths people occupy one world and

---

* From Donald Rumsfeld's famous Department of Defence briefing, 12 February 2002.
† C. P. Snow, 'The Two Cultures', 1959.

humanities/literary people occupy another, each ignorant of the value the other brings to the game.

A good many times I have been present at gatherings of people who, by the standards of the traditional culture, are thought highly educated and who have with considerable gusto been expressing their incredulity at the illiteracy of scientists. Once or twice I have been provoked and have asked the company how many of them could describe the Second Law of Thermodynamics. The response was cold: it was also negative. Yet I was asking something which is the scientific equivalent of, 'Have you read a work of Shakespeare's?'

I now believe that if I had asked an even simpler question – such as, 'What do you mean by mass, or acceleration?', which is the scientific equivalent of saying, 'Can you read?' – not more than one in ten of the highly educated would have felt that I was speaking the same language. So the great edifice of modern physics goes up, and the majority of the cleverest people in the western world have about as much insight into it as their neolithic ancestors would have had.

As if the world economy wasn't already complicated enough with a language of mathematics and algorithms that educated people struggle to comprehend, and non-quantifiable risks that defeat even the most brilliant minds, there is a tendency on the part of policymakers to control the release of data in order to achieve the outcome they desire.

In the early 1960s my father was working in the White House. He called in to see President Lyndon Baines Johnson. President Johnson greeted him and engaged in the usual 'Relax, I'm just a regular guy' niceties that most presidents perfect to help people sufficiently overcome their awe to be able to tell them what they need to know. The President then leaned forward and asked my father for his analysis of some international trade figures. My father, having spent days preparing for the meeting and making very sure that he was right about his maths, proudly declared, 'The number is X.' The President said,

'Your numbers are wrong.' Talk about a punch to the solar plexus! My father attempted to defend his data but the President interrupted him. 'You're not hearing me. Your numbers are *wrong*.' The President then explained that he could not negotiate the international trade deal the US needed unless that particular number was a little different.

Why would politics demand that the numbers be skewed in a particular direction? Power. Politicians and policymakers want power. They want votes. They want the mathematics to show whatever will favour them in an election. If they want a different answer they simply change the assumptions or the parameters of the algorithm.

If mathematical genius comes not from solving equations but from knowing which equations to solve, then policy genius comes not from manipulation of data but from knowing which data it is useful to manipulate. Much time is spent in the policy world ensuring the models and the maths churn out the answer that policymakers want. They may not always win at this game, but the trying is formidable.

What does all this mean? It means that the conversation about the condition of the world economy involves people with varying agendas throwing a lot of mathematics – often skewed mathematics that is opaque and inaccessible – at a confused public, while ignoring the things that cannot be easily quantified. The public has common sense but cannot easily discern whether the mathematics is right or wrong. Instead the public shakes its head with a feeling that things don't make sense.

The public could read the *Financial Times* or the *Wall Street Journal* but the terminology and concepts are presented in a way that is often hard to grasp. The easier option is to believe that there is someone in a wood-panelled office somewhere in the capital who is smarter than me who is sorting this all out. We hope and believe this is true, not realising that thinking this way means devolving responsibility for our own future to the state.

The ghost of Eric Fromm smiles and nods in recognition of this all-too-human inclination to trust in the belief that someone else can take control. Someone else will sort things out. C. P. Snow warned us about this in 1960 when he wrote, 'One of the most bizarre features of our time, is that the cardinal choices have to be made . . . by a handful of men who cannot have a first-hand knowledge of what those choices depend upon or what their results may be.'*

So, to be clear: it is vital to understand the motivations. And now we stumble upon a philosophical canyon that divides the world of economics as deeply as views on religion divide others.

Freshwater and saltwater

Whatever we think about the numbers, whether we believe the numbers are 'true' or they reflect the parameters that have been chosen to arrive at the wanted answer, what really matters when it comes to assessing signals in the world economy is whether we are 'freshwater' or 'saltwater'.

The journalist and author Peter Kilborn elegantly captured the simple question that hangs over all economics in a *New York Times* editorial: 'To tinker or not to tinker?'† Should the state intervene in the economy or should the state get out of its way?

There are those who believe that tinkering by policymakers and governments causes markets to become off-balance, veer into crises and then prolong the crises. For others, insufficient or incorrect tinkering by government is what causes and prolongs economic crises.

The first camp, those who blame governments for being the cause of economic problems, are sometimes called 'freshwater' because the proponents of this view have tended to come from institutions near the Great Lakes in the American Midwest, such as the University of Chicago. 'Freshwater economists are,' as American economist Paul Krugman explains, 'essentially, neoclassical purists. They believe that

* C. P. Snow, 'Science and Government', the Godkin Lecture at Harvard University, Harvard University Press, 1960.

† Peter Kilborn, '"Fresh Water" Economists Gain', *New York Times*, 23 July 1988.

all worthwhile economic analysis starts from the premise that people are rational and markets work.'*

The second camp, those who blame governments for failing to properly contain the excesses of markets, are called 'saltwater' because their proponents tend to come from institutions that are near the Atlantic Ocean, such as Harvard and Princeton.

Krugman says, where the freshwater economists were purists, the saltwater economists were pragmatists. He writes: 'So they were willing to deviate from the assumption of perfect markets or perfect rationality, or both, adding enough imperfections to accommodate a more or less Keynesian view of recessions. And in the saltwater view, active policy to fight recessions remained desirable.'

It matters which camp you are in because this will define how you will respond to economic signals. If you believe that the only people who can fix the economy are real people engaged in calculated risk-taking, balancing hubris and nemesis as they strive to pursue a dream that creates GDP and employs people, then you are freshwater. If, in contrast, you believe that you could fix the economy by gathering a bunch of really smart people in the nation's capital and empowering them to use the power of the state, then you are saltwater.

A freshwater thinker's version of Hell is putting a lot of smart people in the nation's capital and empowering them with the public's trust and the public's money. A saltwater thinker's version of Hell is giving power to real people in the real economy because you can't trust markets and you can't trust people to figure out how to identify or protect their own best interests.

Put another way, President Bill Clinton was a freshwater Democrat. He supported business and risk-taking by individuals and felt the state should be made smaller. President Barack Obama is more of a saltwater Democrat. He wants to tax businesses more and reduce

* Paul Krugman, 'How Did Economists Get It So Wrong?' *New York Times*, 2 September 2009.

risk-taking while putting more power into the hands of an enlarging state. President George W. Bush is a freshwater Republican at heart but got corralled into saltwater intervention by events that threatened to weaken the economy. Ronald Reagan demonstrated that he was definitively freshwater when he said, 'Government is not the solution, it is the problem.' Thus all his solutions for a weak economy involved reducing the size and scope of the government's reach, though even he believed that state expenditure on nuclear weapons would bankrupt the Soviet Union, which is a rather saltwater approach.

The divide that faces the world is no longer between the left and the right or between the followers of those two titans of economics, J. M. Keynes and Milton Friedman. The divide is between the state and the citizen and between those who favour empowerment of the one versus the other. Each of us must decide for ourselves where we stand. The choices we make will define the economy we have in the future.

An old argument

The argument is very old, but as the political and cultural commentator David Brooks explained in his piece 'Bentham vs. Hume',* the character of the two sides remains unchanged despite the passage of time.

The British philosopher and reformer Jeremy Bentham (1748–1832) believed in a plan for everything. Plans, he thought, could be measured by the greatest happiness for the greatest number. The Scottish philosopher and economist David Hume (1711–76), took the opposite view. He believed individuals were best placed to sort things out. Brooks writes: 'Mr Hume's side believe government should actively tilt the playing field to promote social goods and set off decentralised networks of reform, but they don't think government knows enough to intimately organise dynamic innovation.'

* David Brooks, 'Bentham vs Hume', *New York Times*, 5 October 2009.

People like Jeremy Bentham want to assemble the smartest people in the country in a wood-panelled room and set them to work creating a plan that will inevitably succeed because they are more brilliant than anybody else. People like Hume have no idea how to fix the economic mess, know that no 'plan' will work, and conclude that you have to trust the market to sort out a solution because the efforts of the many pursing their self-interest will always produce better results than 'bright' people locked away in a room.

This was the debate that raged between J. M. Keynes and Friederich Hayek and later Milton Friedman. It continues today when central bankers like Mario Draghi, the President of the European Central Bank say, 'We will do whatever it takes' to prevent large institutions from failing, and in response Tom Hoenig, the Vice Chairman of the Federal Deposit Insurance Corporation, says we should not protect those who have failed. It happens when we hear the Left and the Right argue about whether the solution is bigger government or smaller government, more benefits or fewer benefits, more regulation or less regulation, higher taxation or lower taxation.

Regardless of whether you are freshwater or saltwater, or whether you believe that the algorithms are right or wrong, it is important to know that both camps invoke algorithms and mathematics as proof that they are right. It is nigh on impossible for ordinary citizens to quibble with sophisticated models that neither side make readily available to the general public. Those who are skilled at mathematics have made a nice little cottage industry out of spouting criticism and insight about the models that drive policymakers, but their output is well over the head of the average person who simply wants to know what is the right thing to do.

The answer lies in something that I will shortly explore in depth: the social contract. This refers to the 'deal' that exists between the citizen and the state. Citizens and their states will decide where the line ought to be drawn between the state versus the market. That line is bound to be in a different place in France than it is in China or the US.

There is no 'right' or most efficient answer. It all depends on the views of the citizens and their leaders. That is where human qualities begin to influence the outcome.

Goalkeeper science

All policymakers, freshwater and saltwater alike, want to intervene in the economy when pain, volatility and uncertainty begin. The Canadian science and technology writer Clive Thompson wrote an insightful article for the *New York Times* in 2008 that explains why. He took as his starting point a 2005 study carried out by Israeli academics entitled 'Action Bias Among Elite Soccer Goalkeepers: The Case of Penalty Kicks'. Thompson reported:

> The academics analysed 286 penalty kicks and found that 94 per cent of the time the goalies dived to the right or the left – even though the chances of stopping the ball were highest when the goalie stayed in the centre.
>
> If that's true, why do goalies almost always dive off to one side? Because, the academics theorised, the goalies are afraid of looking as if they're doing nothing – and then missing the ball. Diving to one side, even if it decreases the chance of them catching the ball, makes them appear decisive. 'They want to show that they're doing something,' says Michael Bar-Eli, one of the study's authors. 'Otherwise they look helpless, like they don't know what to do.'*

Much policymaking is driven by the need to jump in order to avoid the appearance that the policymakers do not know what they are doing. This is the easiest course of action when we are tired or don't know what to do. Policymakers are often tired and without a quick answer; they want to appear to be in control. I know. I used to be one.

* Clive Thompson, 'Goalkeeper Science', *New York Times*, 12 December 2008.

How the algorithm made me do it

As one of six people serving on the National Economic Council, I served as a Special Assistant to the President of the United States, I have had first-hand experience of being one of the so-called 'best and the brightest' locked up in a wood-panelled room trying to solve an 'impossible' economic problem. During my time in office, America experienced seven of the nine largest bankruptcies in American history, including Enron, Tyco and Worldcom. This was just two years after the Dot.com bubble had burst, leaving the national economy, indeed the world economy, reeling.

After 9/11 we had a much bigger and more specific problem. Two thirds of the global trading capability in US government bonds had been destroyed. The New York Stock Exchange shut down after the first plane hit the World Trade Center because the power station supplying all of lower Manhattan was underneath the building. Initially it was on fire. Afterwards, the fire department flooded it. Obviously fire and water are not good for the electricity supply. The biggest practical problem to solve was how to restore the electricity supply to the Stock Exchange so that data could be forwarded to another location where the markets could be opened again.

Far from being a 'policy' issue, the problems were entirely practical. Where could a power generator be found? How could it be transported up the main highway, I-95, and across the river into lower Manhattan? How could the few critical New York Stock Exchange personnel travel down to the site so they could flip the switch to forward the data so the stock market could reopen? This last point proved especially difficult. When I was put through on the phone to police officers on the 14th Street barrier, I tried to give them the names of the NYSE staff who should be issued Bio-Suits and permitted to walk down to the World Trade Center. The officer I was speaking to clearly thought it was a prank call. 'Sure you're calling from the White House, lady.' Click. They had hung up. I had to get Governor Pataki on the line because they would recognise his voice and his authority and would not hang up on him. It is sometimes said that policymaking, especially when it involves close proximity to the head of government, is like 'drinking from a fire hydrant'. In my experience, this is true. Problems are not always philosophical; they are often practical. But the algorithm is clear: problems that rise to the level of the White House or its counterparts around the world must be resolved, and resolved in a timely way.

The simple fact is that the only issues that arrive in the White House are the ones that are too difficult, complex, or important to be successfully tackled elsewhere in government. By definition, such issues and the subsequent decisions that need to be made involve sacrificing the interests of one part of the community in order to benefit the interests of another.

Usually decisions have to be made without sufficient time or information to make the decision comfortably. They have to be made, often at great speed, because history, the public and the press corps all require an answer to the question at hand.

This situation is a permanent state of affairs. My father experienced it working for four presidents and I experienced it working for two. Perhaps the best preparation manual for a job at this level of government remains *Thinking in Time: The Uses of History for Decision Makers* (1986) by Richard E. Neustadt and Ernest R. May, which grew out of a lifetime of writing and consulting on this subject from the 1950s onwards, and from coursework they set at Harvard's John F. Kennedy School of Government. The best primer on the practical matters of managing the best and the brightest is still the unpublished paper that virtually every president has consulted: 'Some Thoughts for Newly Assigned Senior Political Appointees on the Management of Bureaucracy'* written by Richard McCormack, a long-time presidential advisor. He explains how we have to take human factors into consideration, like the fact that the staff are not

* 20 June 1970, updated 20 January 1992.

getting enough sleep at any given time – especially in emergencies.

Pilots would never be allowed to fly a plane on so little sleep, but we are content to let White House staff navigate the nation's future in this condition.

The algorithm for a politician is simple: you must win to have power. They need policies that are popular and potent in order to win. Usually this means responding to events rather than pursuing an agenda of their own choice. So, the political algorithm demands that policymakers jump to the left or jump to the right. It demands that they are seen to be doing something. It demands that they announce something to the press corps, which is always waiting for an announcement.

Ward Three morality

We cannot quantify the human factor, but we can understand that it exists. If we continue looking at the US (though the same applies to every government), the drivers for all those who set or advise on policy are easily discernable.

In an article for the *New York Times*,* David Brooks describes the 'morality' of the people who live in Ward Three of Washington DC and why it plays an important role in the making of public policy in America. It happens that I grew up in Ward Three, which is the northwest quadrant of Washington DC and centres on Chevy Chase. I speak with the confidence of a local when I say his article, 'Ward Three Morality', rings true. The residents there are, by day, senior officials who run agencies, command the military, run the intelligence agencies and can move the markets with their words and by the flourish of a pen. By weekend, they are the neighbours I grew up with: the Deputy Head of the CIA, the Senator, the head of various Congressional Committees and the like. These people always looked pale and exhausted from their labours, yet had no alternative but to mow the lawn themselves as they lacked the income to pay someone else to do it.

* David Brooks, 'Ward Three Morality', *New York Times,* 2 February 2009.

Sublimated liquidity rage

I remember one senator who always looked perplexed when he could not get the pullstring starter on the lawnmower to work on a Saturday morning. The cash flow problem is especially severe for this powerful group, who arrived in the neighbourhood due to their extensive education or exceptional brilliance. Ward Three residents inevitably have ambitions for the education of their children. Unfortunately, private school fees are extremely expensive in the neighbourhood, as are house prices, as are the people who can be hired to mow the lawn. As a result, the residents suffer from what Brooks calls 'Status-Income Disequilibrium' and 'Sublimated Liquidity Rage'.

The algorithm, the mathematical calculation that can be applied to them, is clear: work for free now to get paid a lot later. This formula holds true even among the countries that have a permanent civil service. Brussels, Washington, London, Tokyo, New Delhi and Beijing have a thriving community of ex-officials who are paid a good deal to explain policy and influence policymakers.

Who will be chosen for the lucrative post-office jobs? The most influential are first to be selected. The second consideration boils down to simpatico. Is the person left or right, saltwater or freshwater? The philosophy and principles we hold define who our employer will be. It's not very likely that a policymaker who opposes bank bailouts will end up employed by a very large bank. It is very likely that a policymaker who forcefully pursued the bank bailout will be rewarded with a significant contract, even if not visible to the public, and possibly a serious role.

Taking a bullet for the president

As members of staff, we all make risk-reward calculations. Part of our job is to take a bullet for the president or the institution we serve, should that become necessary. A Secret Service officer might have to jump in front of a real bullet but, as a staffer, we are supposed to jump in front of a political bullet when events might damage the president or presidency. Such bullets can cut our career short or even terminate it.

For me, a bullet whistled close by when Enron hit the headlines. This large energy company went bust as the result of fraud. At the time, Senator Lieberman was a leading potential presidential candidate. He issued the White House with a subpoena and a simple request for a record of any and all contacts between White House staff and Enron. I thought I had none, but it turned out that one of my former contacts in the financial markets had become the Head of Enron in Japan. We'd met for a single drink (I paid for my own) to discuss the abysmal state of the Japanese economy. I sent in the record of the meeting.

At the same time I asked White House Counsel to enquire whether Senator Lieberman felt the problem was that we in the White House had done too much to help Enron or not enough to help Enron. The answer came back: 'Yes'. In other words, whichever outcome would prove more useful for Senator Lieberman would be the correct answer. This is how politics works. Senator Lieberman was right to pursue the matter and to leave his options as open as possible. I was right to accept that my job was to tell the truth, regardless of personal consequences – even if it meant taking a bullet for the president. Luckily for me, the fact was that I had not spent any time discussing Enron with anyone at the company and so I was exonerated by the process. But such events make us realise that the longer one stays in the job, the more likely one is to be hit by a bullet sooner or later.

The 'revolving door' in Washington DC and other capitals serves a good purpose. It permits talent and experience from the real world to influence policymaking in a positive way. But it would be naïve to think that people do this work for charitable purposes, especially when the bullets start flying the moment that Congress begins investigating one's background. It is sometimes said that even Jesus Christ could not successfully pass through the Senate confirmation process. We would do well to consider the unintended consequences of a confirmation process that excludes many good people. As the Pulitzer Prize-winner Charles Krauthammer memorably wrote in his weekly column for *The Washington Post*:

> If we insist that public life be reserved for those whose personal history is pristine, we are not going to get paragons of virtue running our affairs. We will get the very rich, who contract out the messy things in life, the very dull, who have nothing to hide and nothing to show, and the very devious, expert at covering their tracks and ambitious enough to risk their discovery.*

J. R. R. Tolkien vs J. M. Keynes

Another calculation takes place whenever anyone passes through the doorway of the Oval office or its equivalents around the world. It has to do with the overwhelming surge of ego that inevitably takes place when people find themselves in close proximity to power. It was not Lord Keynes who came to my aid in the West Wing, or even the great American economist Milton Friedman. It was J. R. R. Tolkien, author of *Lord of the Rings*. During her time at Oxford, where she studied Middle English (medieval English), my mother spent hours with Tolkien and his friend, C. S. Lewis, author of *The Chronicles of Narnia*. They loved discussing imaginary other worlds that initially might seem distant from our own worldly experience, but on closer examination the characters who inhabit those worlds are driven by very human desires – foremost among them the quest for power. The same is true of the *Harry Potter* novels; as Lord Voldemort says, 'There is no good or evil, only power and those who are too weak to seek it.'†

At times it seemed to me that Gollum, the character from *Lord of the Rings*, resided above the door of the Oval Office, waiting to hop on to the shoulder of those who sought an audience with the President.

---

* Charles Krauthammer, *Washington Post*, 29 December 1989.
† J. K. Rowling, *Harry Potter and the Philosopher's Stone*, Bloomsbury, 1997.

What else could explain the sudden transformation in the men and women I ushered through that door?

A typical example was the CEO of a major firm who came into my office in preparation for his meeting with the President. As I escorted him through the corridors to the Oval Office he ranted and raved about how the President's people and policies were all wrong. 'The Secretary of the Treasury should be fired!' he told me. 'Great!' I said. 'Tell him. He needs to know what you think.' But his demeanour changed dramatically the moment we crossed the threshold of the Oval Office. 'Mr President, I am so delighted to meet you!' he gushed, launching into a flood of compliments that left me astonished. As I observed what followed, I realised that here was a man entertaining visions of being asked to join the President on Air Force One as a prelude to being appointed US Ambassador to his country of choice.

In a flash it became clear to me that the Oval Office is in fact a ring, like the one in Tolkien's stories. The shape is significant. How many rooms are round or oval? Very few. Parliaments often have rotundas. Churches and cathedrals often centre on circular structures. Temples, sepulchres and monuments are often round, like the Jefferson Memorial in Washington DC. The unusual shape is a means of conveying the power of a place. As in Tolkien's *Lord of the Rings*, in the presence of the Ring, few can resist becoming overwhelmed by the desire to wield its power.

Before my eyes this visiting CEO morphed into Gollum – the character who started out as a nice little Hobbit until the thirst for power transformed him into an ugly, evil being. In Tolkien's books we see Gollum turn into an obsequious liar who will do whatever it takes to remain close to power. He acquires his name as a result of the 'horrible swallowing noise in his throat' – a side-effect of holding his tongue rather than speaking the truth, much like the CEO, who said what he thought the President wanted to hear in anticipation of invitations and political appointments that would never come. I remember that John Maynard Keynes sometimes liked to write about the personalities that he encountered. Now I know why he cared about personalities. Character matters in the conduct of economic policy.

M&Ms and tchotchkes

After this alarming episode, I started to take closer note of my colleagues and asked my father and others about their experiences. They all said the same. Keep an eye on those who have their eye on the toys, such as Air Force One, Marine One, Camp David, presidential trips, titles, assignments, or time in the Oval Office. Sometimes the prizes were much smaller but nonetheless carried high value, such as the cheap cufflinks with the White House seal that inevitably break when the slightest strain is applied to them, or the cute boxes of M&M candies embossed with the Presidential Seal that people keep for years beyond their use-by date. Who would say or do anything to gain access to these toys, these tchotchkes and knick-knacks? The answer is: a lot of people. I'll include myself because I seem to have kept the M&Ms with the Presidential Seal. I am eyeing the box as I write, too terrified to open them now because they are thirteen years old. Would people in policy and politics steal ideas from their colleagues in order to increase the chances of being seen to be indispensable to the president? Of course!

There's a saying in politics: your worst opponents are on your own team. The main driver is this simple fact: people want access to power, they like to wield power and they will 'kill' anyone who gets in their way as sure as Gollum would kill his best friend and anyone else to secure possession of 'My precious' – the Ring. This is one reason why the greatest challenge heads of government face is surrounding themselves with those who will tell them the truth.

Once in possession of such power, it is hard for a normal human being to believe that he or she might not be doing the right thing with that power. Look at Robert McNamara, the former Head of Ford Motors, who was brought into the US government as Secretary of Defense from 1961–68. John F. Kennedy's express purpose in bringing McNamara in, and others who he called 'the best and the brightest', was to capture the mathematical, computer-based analytics that had permitted McNamara to turn Ford around. He had been named CEO of Ford in an effort to save the company, which was on the brink of bankruptcy. Under his leadership, Ford became the most successful firm in America. Kennedy hoped that this mastery of algorithms would facilitate more efficient government.

Towards the end of his life, McNamara wrote a heart-wrenching memoir* in which he describes how the infatuation with numbers and models overwhelmed his ability to see or tell the truth about the real situation during the war in Vietnam. In the end, the models did not lead to a more efficient conduct of war but a less efficient, less truthful one. McNamara's self-belief prevented him from acknowledging this until his later years; his self-belief precluded self-doubt.

Potomac Fever

The US Congressman Huey Long used to say that every senator thinks they should have been president only for some slight accident of history, and every congressman believes they will be president and it is only a question of time before this happens, barring unforeseen accidents. MPs, too, harbour the belief that the job of prime minister could be theirs, or would have been theirs, except for some small thing that went awry. To this I will add my own observation: every president has one great fear that drives him – that he will become an accident of history before or after leaving office.

There is a name for this syndrome: Potomac Fever. The Potomac is the river that runs through Washington DC and which historically carried waterborne diseases that cause the brain to swell. Does Potomac Fever play a part in the making of public policy? I dare anyone in political circles to honestly argue that it doesn't. But how do you add Potomac Fever to the mathematical model?

* Robert S. McNamara, *In Retrospect: The Tragedy and Lessons of Vietnam*, Times Books, 1995.

The algorithm made me write it

The media also indulge in calculation. Their algorithm is clear: cash flow is driven by stories, especially stories that sell, because that's what drives advertising. In order to get stories that sell they need to have sources. In the political arena, there are only two kinds of people in politics, as far as the media are concerned: sources and targets. Failure to divulge stories makes you a target. In general, targets get bad press and sources get good press.

Policymakers and politicians know that they have the power to deny access to the media. So, those who write stories that policymakers don't like find that they cannot get a meeting. Their names are dropped from the inner circle. They may gain admission to the press conference, but they won't get invited to the drinks party where all the real conversations happen. For those in the inner circle it is perfectly obvious who is in the inner circle and who is a mouthpiece for that circle. For the general public, it is sometimes nigh on impossible to distinguish between objective reporting and posturing.

When you think about it, the purpose of the news is not to educate the public. The purpose is to generate revenue and income. This is why all print media increasingly use algorithms to write news stories. *Wired* magazine reminds us, 'Every 30 seconds or so, the algorithmic bull pen of Narrative Science, a 30-person company occupying a large room on the fringes of the Chicago Loop, extrudes a story whose very byline is a question of philosophical inquiry.'* Some three minutes after an earthquake occurred in California on 17 March 2014, the first article the *Los Angeles Times* published on the story was generated by a robot. The *LA Times* writer Ken Schwencke had programmed the algorithm. All he had to do was hit the 'publish' button, according to the *Huffington Post*, which reacted to this event in an article called, 'It's

---

* Steven Levy, 'Can an Algorithm Write a Better News Story Than a Human Reporter?' *Wired*, April 2012.

All Over: Robots Are Now Writing News Stories, and Doing a Good Job'.*

Algorithms are cheaper. Can the media reconcile the various competing objectives? Can they generate revenue, provide genuinely useful content quality and serve to educate the public simultaneously? This is a constant topic of discussion among those in the media.

Perhaps more is driving the media. Michael Lewis, author of several bestselling novels including *Liar's Poker*, had a huge success with his non-fiction account of the build-up to the credit bubble, *The Big Short* – hailed by Reuters as 'probably the best single piece of financial journalism ever written'. In an interview to promote the book he posed the question: 'Why were *The Big Short* and *Flashboys* available to me to be written? These stories should have been gobbled up by newspaper and magazine journalists.' In answering this question, Lewis draws a chilling parallel between the dilemmas facing regulators and financial writers: 'Journalists are often financially insecure, just as politicians and regulators are often financially insecure – and I'm talking about personally financially insecure. It seems journalists feel they have to, one way or another, accommodate the existing financial interests in their work – and that's wrong.'†

The algorithm that makes the Fed do it

The purpose of this chapter has been to help us understand why policymakers behave the way they do. Having laid the groundwork, it's time to address a specific case: the decisions made by policymakers in response to the record debt burden and the financial crisis. The markets are quick to turn, making the story hard to follow. In January 2016, the markets had become uneasy yet again. The media used the word crisis with abandon. Famous market experts like George Soros said, 'It's the

---

* Catherine Taibi, 'It's All Over: Robots Are Now Writing News Stories, And Doing A Good Job', *Huffington Post*, 18 March 2014.

† Liam Halligan, 'The Low Tricks of High Finance: a Conversation with Michael Lewis', *Spectator*, 22 January 2016.

2008 crisis all over again!'* While Nouriel Roubini countered, 'This is not another global financial crisis.'† But, by January 2017, the Dow Jones hit an all-time record high of 20,000. One is therefore justified in asking what happened during the last crisis and might we have to face the same problems again. And, if so, who are we relying on and what algorithm motivates them?

Perhaps the models policymakers are relying on are very good multimeters, or perhaps not, to harken back to the start of this chapter. One thing is sure: in the end 'everything is reducible to the motivation of self-interest'.‡ That is the algorithm that makes everybody in public policy 'do it'.

Central banks and their choices

The Federal Reserve Bank has played a major role in defining the solutions for dealing with the crisis. In fact, the story of our economic future hinges on the arguments and motivations behind the policy choices the Fed and other central banks are making on our behalf.

Consider the situation we face today. The financial crisis of 2007/8 threatened to bankrupt the entire global banking system. The problem was not that one large bank went bust, but that virtually every large bank went bust simultaneously. Central banks in the world's industrialised countries were compelled to step in because that is the role of a central bank – to be the lender of last resort. Their job is to restore order when markets become disorderly. On this occasion, however, they were further compelled to act because most countries were so deeply indebted that fiscal policy was no longer an option. Monetary policy therefore had to bear a greater burden than usual.§

* CNBC interview on 7 January 2016 as reported by Matt Clinch.

† 'No, it isn't 2008 all over again – Roubini', Reuters, 22 January 2016.

‡ François de La Rochefoucauld, *Maxims*, 1665.

§ Fiscal policy refers to the government's budget and the capacity to spend or cut spending to quicken or slow the pace of economic activity and growth. Monetary policy refers to the central bank's control over interest rates and the volume and

This led to the historic experiment in which major central banks resorted to unconventional measures such as quantitative easing (QE) to push interest rates down and asset prices up in an effort to ward off deflation by pushing inflation higher.

This was an extraordinary undertaking. Central bankers do not as a rule try to encourage inflation.* When they switched from treating inflation as a target and instead began treating it as a tool, the central banks took a revolutionary step. They went from merely providing liquidity and instead began judging success by the level of certain asset prices, like the stock market and property values.

Even the inflation target itself is now being questioned. Many central banks think 2 per cent, the usual target number, is too low. By the way, why do we have a 2 per cent target? It could be argued that this is a level at which you can take money away from the citizens without their noticing it. Inflation is a tax, if not an expropriation of private wealth.

It is impossible to overemphasise the importance of the Fed and other central banks now that they have emerged as the market maker rather than merely a lender of last resort. Whatever they do or announce has profound consequences on prices and markets. Some say the market now entirely depends on the continuing promise that the Fed and other central banks will find ways to put in more cash and continue to support prices.

Econometricians: on tap or on top?

Who are the people at the Federal Reserve? Perhaps the best answer is provided by a conversation that occurred between US Ambassador Richard McCormack and William McChesney Martin, Chairman of the Federal Reserve Board of Governors. McCormack, who had been

---

speed of the money that is circulating in the economy.

* In spite of their historic efforts to create more inflation, the experts at the Federal Reserve and other central banks tell us that there is no inflation and no risk of it – which begs the question: in that case, why bother with QE and low interest rates?

charged with recommending candidates for the newly formed Council on International Economic Policy, could think of no one better to turn to for advice on the subject, given that Martin had been in office since April 1951, serving under five presidents (Truman, Eisenhower, Kennedy, Johnson and Nixon). The two men met on 31 January 1970, Martin's last day in office. When asked what sort of person should be recruited to head up the new council, Martin responded: 'If you want this new office to be relevant, do not appoint an academic economist, and particularly avoid econometricians.' Instead, he recommended that we recruit someone who 'had broad personal reach in the American and global economy, who understood how markets operated, and who was able through a network of personal contacts to anticipate developments before they were finally reported in the official statistics.' He went on to say:

> We have fifty econometricians working for us at the Fed. They are all located in the basement of this building, and there is a reason why they are there. Their main value to me is to pose questions that I then pass on to my own network of contacts throughout the American economy. The danger with these econometricians is that they don't know their own limitations, and they have a far greater sense of confidence in their analyses than I have found to be warranted. Such people are not dangerous to me because I understand their limitations. They are, however, dangerous to people like you and the politicians because you don't know their limitations, and you are impressed and confused by the elaborate models and mathematics. The flaws in these analyses are almost always imbedded in the assumptions upon which they are based. And that is where broader wisdom is required, a wisdom that these mathematicians generally do not have. You always want such technical experts on tap in positions like this, but never on top.
>
> Let me give you an example of what I mean. When I have a monetary policy decision to make, I get on the telephone and spend

four or five days calling informed people around the country to seek their views of supply, demand, wage, and inflation trends. I speak with labor leaders, grain dealers, manufacturers, individuals I respect in the regional Federal Reserve Banks, and others who have their fingers on the pulse of the US economy. Then I go up to New York City and spend two days visiting bankers and corporate leaders and others I trust to seek their advice. The eventual results of these discussions form the basis for my monetary policy decisions.*

It happens that I met with Ben Bernanke on 31 January 2006, the day he was confirmed by Congress in his role as Chairman of the Fed. We laughed about the fact that, whatever he had been through that day testifying before Congress, it wasn't economics, at least not the economics that we learned at school. I said, 'No, sir, it is political theatre. That's your new job.' Central banking is not a purely technical mathematical exercise where one can rely on algorithms or models to answer the many profound questions that a central bank now has to face. A human element must be factored into the calculation.

Having grabbed the steering wheel from a reckless financial market, drunk with hubris, central bankers are understandably reluctant to relinquish control. There remains a distinct air of disdain and a palpable disregard for 'the market', but it is possible that policymakers have themselves become punch-drunk with a sense of empowerment. Failing to cede control back to the market empowers the policymakers. It empowers central bankers. It empowers the staff. It is quite something to have the entire world economy hanging on your words and your mathematical models. One can understand the seduction of such power.

The question before us now is this: Who should be driving prices in the market? Should it be the Chairman of the Federal Reserve, as advised by the econometricians in the basement? Or should it be the

* Henry E. Mattox, *A Conversation with Ambassador Richard T. McCormack* (www. xlibris.com, 2013).

market mechanism that simultaneously reconciles the rapidly changing and often conflicting views of all the large and small actors in the world economy? No doubt the markets make mistakes, but policymakers can make mistakes too. It would be a shocking and tragic irony if, in the end, the Federal Reserve were to fall prey to the exact same error that the financial markets made in trusting models and algorithms that turn out to be wrong.

Perhaps the Federal Reserve's models are very good multimeters. Even so, it can't hurt to consider some common-sense signals as well. Perhaps it makes sense to look for signals that algorithms leave out. Why? Because, if their models are wrong and if these policymakers fail in generating inflation, or if they succeed, it will have a profound impact on the fabric of our society. It will touch every one of us, either way.

5

The Social Contract

___

The debt burden damages the hopes, aspirations and beliefs of people everywhere. The simple fact is that taxing 100 per cent of citizens 100 per cent of their income would be insufficient to solve the debt problem in most of the indebted countries around the world today. As a result, the social contract that exists between citizens and their states is falling apart.

What is the social contract?

It can be argued that the social contract is a very bad idea written by a very bad man who abandoned his two children. The Genevan philosopher Jean Jacques Rousseau first presented the idea in 1762, in his work *The Social Contract or Principles of Political Right*. Rousseau's particular version of the social contract was unattractive, even offensive, for many reasons, but mainly because it put the needs of the many over the rights of the few.* The notion inspired reform and even encouraged the French Revolution, which ultimately destroyed the social contract that had been in place in France till then. We may not like a particular social contract, but the very fabric of society is always based on some sort of deal between citizens and their state. There are good deals and bad deals. Some social contracts are better than others.

* I am grateful to Niall Ferguson, who took this angle at a conference I held at Ditchley Park, when trying out this concept.

Some are more robust than others, no doubt. The public favours some and rejects the rest.

There is, however, *always* a social contract. The social contract is not necessarily written, but it is understood. It is a fabric woven from the threads of history, formed from the various arguments between the freshwater camp and their saltwater opponents over time, hammered out in the courts or through conflict in the streets, preserved in institutions including the executive, the legislature, the courts and the military. The burden of debt stresses the social fabric by forcing people to reconsider, if not entirely redraw, the line between the state and the market, between those who pay and those who benefit, between spending and taxation. The social contract, whether unspoken or written, lays out the rights and responsibilities of both the state and its citizens. The citizens agree to abide by the law and pay tax and participate in the protection of society, while the state agrees to provide certain community services such as a reliable legal system, a military, a heath care and education system and the right to own property.

Inevitably there are moments in history when governments go broke and default on their promises to their citizens, thus putting the social contract under severe distress, if not destroying it altogether. Perhaps we can begin with a few examples of what it looks like when the social contract is broken.

Some of the most compelling narratives in history are about the social contract. Consider why we now assume Lady Godiva rode naked through Coventry. Why do we treasure the story about William Tell who is said to have risked his son's life by shooting an apple off his head from a great distance? Why was it so compelling that Gandhi stood in protest with the salt makers of India, revealing to the world his idea of *satyagraha* (non-violent protest), which later inspired leaders from Martin Luther King to Nelson Mandela? Why does it matter to us that the citizens of Boston threw their tea into the harbour and thereby helped launch the American independence movement? The answer is the same: anger at excessive taxation and the absence of representation. In each case, these people realised that the pain of taxation had become so great, and their voice against it so weak, that it warranted challenging the authorities, even if their freedom or even their lives would be lost.

Harvard Magazine published an article by Charles Coe on Lady Godiva which offers an explanation as to what happened. In the eleventh century, Lady Godiva feared for her community when her husband Leofric, Earl of Mercia, then the local ruler, raised onerous taxes on the citizens of Coventry and Worcester. She offered to ride naked through Coventry if he would relent. He accepted but ordered that no one should look at her. Curtains were drawn, windows closed, save for one poor fellow named Tom who, in a later version of the legend, was caught 'peeping'.*

William Tell, a sharp marksman with a crossbow, objected to the onerous tax imposed by the Hapsburg king, who had invaded what we now call Switzerland. Gessler, the king's appointed representative and tax collector, was outraged by Tell's protests and threatened to imprison him unless he could shoot an apple off the head of his own son, Walter. William Tell shot the apple in two and avoided killing his son. Gessler went ahead and imprisoned him anyway when he found Tell had a second arrow stashed away and inquired what it was for. 'If my first arrow had killed my son,' Tell answered, 'I would have shot the second at you, and I would not have missed.' Tell escaped, came back to assassinate Gessler, thereby helping spur the revolution that led to the overthrow of the Hapsburgs and the creation of an independent Swiss Confederation.†

Gandhi was outraged by onerous taxes in India, particularly the British tax on a basic staple: salt. In response to the salt tax, he organised

* 'Lady Godiva: The Naked Truth', July–August 2003; see www.harvardmagazine.com/2003/07/lady-godiva-the-naked-tr.html
† See Robert Wernick, 'In Search of William Tell', *Smithsonian Magazine*, August 2004; www.smithsonianmag.com/history/in-search-of-william-tell-2198511/?all

the earliest non-violent protest that ultimately led to the expulsion of the British from India.

The Boston Tea Party remains an iconic symbol of the American independence movement, an act of defiance provoked by excessive taxation without representation imposed by the British.

Where is the line?

Taxation is inevitable. It pays for the things that serve the collective interest. Over-taxation can call people to arms, however. The line between the two, taxation and over-taxation, is embedded in the social contract between citizens and the state. It's a flexible line, one that changes with time and circumstances, but in the main there is an understanding between citizens and their state as to where the line is drawn or at least where it ought to be. Of course the French draw that line in a very different place from where Americans draw it, and both are some distance from where North Korea might draw the line. No one has a monopoly on the 'best' 'right' or 'true' social contract. Instead, it tends to represent a series of 'deals' that are forged over time, both forming and arising from the warp and weft of the social fabric.

Throughout history, citizens have abided by the law and paid taxes in exchange for promises by the state. Sometimes the promise is simply this: pay your tax and you will be allowed to live. The Ancient Greeks, Romans, Persians, some feudal kings, modern dictators and organised crime syndicates have all taken this approach at times: 'Gimme the money and I'll let you live!'

Democracies and modern forms of government tend to promise that you will be given something valuable in exchange for your loyalty and your tax payment, something beyond your individual capabilities, such as a military to defend you, a police force to protect you, a public school system, a road network, a healthcare system of some kind, a commitment that you can rely on the ballot box rather than fearing a military coup, the provision of retirement benefits at a certain age, a welfare system for the truly poor, and a promise to maintain an acceptable balance between the interests of the majority and those of the minority, among many possible examples.

But when governments demand too much of a citizen's hard-earned cash, and fail to deliver on their promises, protests arise. There are always signals that such events are unfolding.

Exit, Voice, Loyalty

The current state of the world economy is causing social contracts around the world to crumble. All around the globe, nations have spent more than they have earned and are turning to higher taxation, spending cuts and breaking promises to save themselves. This means citizens are having to pay more taxes and/or receive fewer benefits at a time of economic weakness. Naturally, this has led to protests. Protests are a signal.

People protest in different ways, as the great twentieth-century economist Albert O. Hirschman described in his seminal work, *Exit, Voice, Loyalty: Responses to Decline in Firms, Organisations, and States* (1970). Whenever people become dissatisfied with their state they can exit or they can voice their concerns.

Some choose to remove themselves from the state's reach and become independent from their government. For example, there are the folks who think the solution is to opt out. They buy large farms with upstream water supplies, far from anybody else; they stockpile supplies of tinned food and load up with ammo and weapons. This might work for a while, but in the end, as Mad Max discovered, even in a lawless, stateless place, you will always pay tax to someone. If it isn't the government it will be organised crime or the mob that will 'redistribute' the wealth from the rich to the poor by invading your home and taking what they want or extorting protection money to prevent them from doing so.

Then there are those who try to remove themselves from the clutches of the state by committing suicide. In 2012 Dimitris Christoulas, a retired pharmacist, protested against the ever-deteriorating situation in Greece by taking his life in Syntagma Square in front of parliament. In recent years there have been hundreds of citizens of indebted countries or countries which are pained by the debt burden, including some of the workers in emerging markets, who have chosen suicide as a means of protesting their increasingly difficult economic situation. As we shall see, a young Tunisian, Mohamed Bouazizi, sparked the Arab Spring by choosing self-immolation as his protest and exit.

The most extreme example of a broken social contract occurs when a state ceases to exist or erupts in conflict, leading to mass exodus – as has happened in Syria. Moving abroad is an option pursued by thousands of people every year in an effort to escape the hand of government or abandoning their debt-ridden (or war-ridden) homeland in the hope of building a new life elsewhere in the world. But it's not only the poor who look for a way out; many wealthy citizens take advantage of their ability to move their assets, if not themselves, abroad. In Britain in the 1970s the 90 per cent tax rate forced the emigration of many of the most talented and productive members of society, who only returned when the conditions were more hospitable. More recently, in the US, people have protested the breakdown of the social contract by leaving one jurisdiction for another within their own country. When California retrospectively raised personal income tax rates to 13.5 per cent, many residents opted to move themselves or their businesses to lower-tax states such as Texas and Colorado, where the state still has the capacity to deliver paved roads and other public services but is less likely to demand ever higher tax dollars in return.*

There have been instances, as in Catalonia, Andalucía, Scotland and the Ukraine, where whole communities or ethnic groups have started to push for independence from their state, asking, 'Why should I share the wealth if the state will not deliver a better future?' Even some

---

* Adam Nagourney, 'Two-Tax Rise Tests Wealthy in California', *New York Times*, 6 February 2013.

states in America have seen separatist petitions filed by members of the public. My own home state, Maryland, consists of two large territories connected by a very thin bridge of land that barely holds the two sides together on the map. Now that money is in short supply, it is easy to see why East Maryland and West Maryland no longer want the other side to share in spending. Hence the 'Western Maryland Initiative' led by Scott Strzelczyk, which seeks to allow the West to secede from the East.

All these options involve great personal sacrifice. Breaking away from a state always comes at a price. The toughest form of secession is suicide; there is no higher price an individual can pay. But exile and immigration have costs too, because both mean losing access to one's extended family and home, as well as the institutions, traditions, culture and shared history that provide cohesion in a community.

Given the cost of departure, it would be so much easier for all concerned if the state to which allegiances had been pledged would simply deliver on its promises – providing retirement and healthcare benefits, social security payments, collecting refuse and ensuring that the mail will continue to be delivered six days a week. It would be nice to believe that the social contract is sound, but there are signals everywhere that it has broken. They are simple signals like the announcement that the US Postal Service is considering cutting mail deliveries to five days a week in order to reduce costs. Or, in another signal, the British National Health Service has announced that it is considering permitting people to pay a fee to jump the queue.* This violates the long-standing social contract that everybody pays in and gets equal treatment, but it allows the state to gain revenue at a time when it has insufficient funds to meet the healthcare promises it made.

---

* Stephen Adams and Michael Powell, 'NHS charges patients £14,000 to jump queue for crucial ops: Hospitals are letting those in need of knee and hip surgery pay to skip the queue', *Mail on Sunday*, 30 May 2015.

We see the social contract break every time a state announces that the retirement age will be raised (again). This was a bad deal to begin with. Retirement benefits were put in place when it was assumed that most people would retire at age fifty-five or sixty – and die at sixty-five. Thanks to medical advances, people are now living well beyond seventy, with many reaching ninety or more. No one says, 'The social contract assumes that you will not seek or need retirement benefits after sixty-five because you should be dead.' No, we expect the state to deliver even though it is patently obvious that the funds coming into the system are insufficient to cover the long-term costs.

Is there really a debt problem?

In a word: yes. The debt problem in the industrialised world is sufficiently large that it is unravelling the social contract. How big is the debt problem? Most people have no affinity for numbers and cannot conceive the colossal size of the debt. S. J. Simon (1904–48), the British world champion bridge player, wisely observed that although most bridge players actually enjoy devoting a Friday night to playing with numbers, they are not only mathematically ignorant but mathematically oblivious: 'Mathematical apathy is one of the most fascinating sidelights in the world of cards,' he wrote.* Well, government budgets and debt problems are a similar kind of card game, only on a vastly larger scale.

The magnitude of the debt is so huge that the human brain cannot process it purely mathematically, as the mathematician John Allen Paulos explains in his book, *Innumeracy* (1998). This is one reason why I will try to explain the debt problem without using any numbers. After all, once we reach a billion or even a trillion, the human mind converts everything to 'big'. Policymakers and economic experts are no better at this than the rest of us. The Canadian monetary policy expert William White (whose warnings about the imminent financial crisis

* S. J. Simon, *Why You Lose at Bridge*, 1967.

were ignored by policymakers around the world in 2006 and 2007) once tried to aggregate the value of all derivatives contracts in the world and came up with the number $1.2 quadrillion. Even the policy experts could not mentally process that.

It is sobering when we realise that the US, the UK and many other indebted nations would still be left with a decade-long debt repayment problem, or more, even if the government taxed every citizen 100 per cent of their income. Flip the coin: even if all government spending were eliminated – other than interest payments, retirement benefits such as social security and the national healthcare system – then the debt would still take a decade or more to pay, and that's being optimistic.

If you are saltwater, you might say, 'OK, let's tax the rich more, redistribute their wealth to those with less privilege and, in this way, preserve the social contract and the standard of living as it stands.' Congressman Steny Hoyer stated this position clearly when he said, 'We don't have a spending problem. We have a taxing problem.' Of course, the very fact that the state forces the citizen to work longer on behalf of the state, bends, if not breaks, the social contract.

A tax rate of say, 91 per cent – as suggested by the very saltwater Nobel Prize-winner, economist Paul Krugman – would force Americans to hand over a much larger proportion of their income than most are comfortable with.

Larry Summers, former Chief Economic Advisor to President Obama and the former Secretary of the Treasury, advocated a revision of tax codes to eliminate the distinction between income tax and capital gains (tax on returns from investments). In other words, he wants to raise the effective tax rate on the wealthy. This alone is a deal-breaker for those who think they belong to a society that treasures and promotes freedom of the individual and his enterprise. In France, at one point President Hollande imposed a 75 per cent tax rate on earnings above €1 million. Even in a country that is far more inclined to support socialised outcomes, the French public revolted against the higher taxes combined with a state that promised to deliver less, not more, in exchange.

If you are freshwater, you might think, 'Let's drop taxes to practically nothing, reduce the size of government and encourage the citizens to work harder and be more entrepreneurial.' No doubt, entrepreneurs would rush to build new businesses. But, this takes time. Many, if not most, new ventures fail. Advances in technology and the availability of automation mean that many new businesses won't require a large workforce. As a result, employment, which is a lagging indicator anyway, begins to lag even further behind the economy, which means nobody feels that the economy is improving. Will the population as a whole be prepared to wait for the revenue and job generation that lower taxes potentially bring?

Taxation and spending

Ultimately, the world economy is balancing between two powerful forces: the power of the state to tax and redistribute wealth and GDP, and the power of an individual worker or entrepreneur (or a group of them, working as a company) to generate wealth and GDP. One might consider the financial crisis as an event that illuminated the fact that government had over-promised and would be forced to under-deliver on their promises going forward. This was the opening salvo in a new conflict between those who generate wealth and those who want to seize and redistribute it.

The social contract seems strong when there is sufficient growth, cash and wealth-creation opportunities to meet everyone's needs. Prosperity glosses over the growing imbalances between promises and the means of fulfilling such promises. The usual business of governance always requires trade-offs. Louis Brandeis (US Supreme Court Justice 1916–39) pointed out that all legislation involves the 'weighing of public needs as against private desires; and likewise a weighing of relative social values'. Prosperity diminished the need to choose and allowed everyone's needs and desires to be met.

But the historic debt burden we face today renders trade-offs much more painful, biting into lifestyles in ways that expose the fragility and vulnerability of the social fabric. When the economy is growing, people believe they will be successful. They have hope and faith that the future will deliver them a better outcome. When the economy is stagnating, they lose their hope and belief that the future will be better. They begin to question the social contract. The state begins to demand more and citizens begin to protest at having less. When the social contract breaks, when the balance of power between the state and the citizen shifts in favour of the state's interests at the expense of the citizens' interests, a new question presents itself. It is the central question dominating the global economic landscape today: 'Why is the wealth and the power in our society being distributed to some other guy and not me?'

The burden of debt is now testing many assumptions about the way we have chosen to generate and distribute wealth and power. The debt burden poses fundamental questions we thought we had answered and which now divide us. It pits those who believe capitalism failed against those who believe the state failed to regulate capitalism properly. It pits the savers against the speculators, the young against the old, and those who contribute to the state's finances against those who benefit from the state's largesse. It even pits states against one another as they seek to control cash flows and assets that would remove the pressure from their own citizens.

Allocating the blame and the pain

It has been said, 'It's not whether you win or lose but how you allocate the blame.' Today the public policy arena is entirely consumed by the need to allocate the blame and the pain. Someone has to pay for the loss. The social contract has to break. The only question is: who will bear the loss and the pain? Much depends on how the debt will be defaulted upon and therefore how the social contract will be broken. The public debate about cutting a little here and taxing a bit more there is a deep disservice to the general public because it creates the impression that something significant is being done.

At best, most governments consider any decline in the upward trajectory of public spending, however temporary, as a victory, when in fact the nation remains on an unsustainable spending path.

The economists Ken Rogoff and Carmen Reinhart put it neatly in their book *This Time Is Different*: once the ratio of debt to GDP exceeds a certain level, growth simply cannot occur.* There is loud disagreement about what that level is – 80 per cent, 90 per cent, 70 per cent – but many agree that the higher the number, the more likely it is that a nation will tip over into a default situation, like a ship that takes on too much water. It now seems that Rogoff and Reinhart made some minor and simple errors in their mathematical calculations that has given their opponents a great excuse to dismiss their premise. But, in the end, everyone understands there are limits to the debt a nation can carry without damaging its growth prospects.

Keep in mind that interest rates in the US, and most of the West, are at the lowest levels ever recorded. The chances that they stay at this historic low level for the next decade are not good. So, the cost of the debt is probably going to rise at some point, potentially worsening the problem exponentially.

If you are quite insane, you might suggest that the debt be paid off. It can be paid, of course, but at what human cost? Paying off a debt this size takes time – at least a generation and maybe two, as Spain, Portugal, Greece and others are finding out to their great dismay. There is a clear price for agreeing to pay: years of high unemployment, low growth and economic stagnation. Japan made the decision to pay in the aftermath of its stock market crash in 1991. It has yet to recover. The country has endured more than twenty years of deflation and slow growth.

* Carmen M. Reinhart and Kenneth Rogoff, *This Time is Different*, Princeton University Press, 2009.

So far, no other large democracy has been willing to suffer such pain. It is almost impossible to imagine Western democracies enduring silently for so long. Since tax cuts, spending cuts, and paying the debt all result in the loss of a decade or more, it is possible that most, if not all, of the debt in the industrialised world today is very likely to be defaulted upon because the pain of paying it back is higher than the voters in democracies are willing to withstand. In short, it is politically impossible and mathematically difficult to pay the debt now owed by the industrialised nations. Therefore, all the tax and spend discussions are misleading to the public.

In the meantime, reducing taxes would reduce the cash flow required to pay the interest on the debt, so the state would risk being thrown into default anyway. This brings us straight to the point: taxing citizens 100 per cent of their income would impoverish the public and still require many years to repay the debt burden. Even if all spending could be cut other than retirement benefits, interest payments and healthcare benefits, the debt would take a long time to pay down. This is true of every major indebted nation, including the US, the UK, Japan, the EU members and possibly even China.

Compound interest: the eighth wonder of the world

Debt grows even if you don't feed it. It gets bigger over time due to interest. Like all borrowing, it has to be repaid with interest.

It compounds. Compounding is something we only really learn about when we feel it bite. Einstein said, 'Compound interest is the eighth wonder of the world. He who understands it, earns it. He who doesn't, pays it,' which explains much of why I have written this book. Those who will pay – and that would be most of us, dear readers, unless we take care – need to be informed of this fact so we can prepare for the consequences.

So, here is a fascinating parable about compound interest, as told by the economic policy analyst Stephen Moore:

The Emperor of China was so excited about the game of chess that he offered the inventor one wish. The inventor replied that he wanted one grain of rice on the first square of the chessboard, two grains on the second square, four on the third and so on through the 64th square. The unwitting emperor immediately agreed to the seemingly modest request.*

What the Emperor did not understand was that by the 30th square, the number added up to a billion grains of rice. 'Two to the 64th power is 18 million trillion grains of rice – more than enough to cover the entire surface of the Earth,' as Moore's version of the parable points out. (In fact, if you count the chessboard itself, and all the squares made of groups of squares, there are at total of 204 squares rather than 64.) The Emperor did not have enough money to provide the rice. By then he had bankrupted his kingdom with his promise. Of course, the Emperor had a clever solution: exercising the power of the state, he had the bright inventor executed.

What is the current account deficit?

This is the problem today. We have spent more than we have earned and we have borrowed from others to make up the difference. It tends to become harder to keep borrowing once lenders are aware of the magnitude of the debt and are therefore unsure of the ability or willingness of an individual or nation pay it back, including the interest, which is compounding every moment of every day. The government can force us to pay for the debt by threatening us with 'execution' in the form of taxes and/or higher inflation, or many other methods that leave us worse off.

It is hard for people to understand the debt problem because many don't realise they have borrowed any money. When I was working

* Stephen Moore, 'Tapping the Power of Compound Interest', originally published in *The East Valley Tribune*, 24 January 1999; reproduced on the Cato Institute website (www.cato.org).

in the White House in 2001 and 2002, I remember imploring two US Congressmen not to indulge in more fiscal spending – an argument I decisively lost. The conversation went like this:

> PIPPA : If we keep spending like this, the current account deficit will get much worse.
>
> CONGRESSMAN 1 (*Frustrated*): You economists are always going on about the current account deficit. What is the current account deficit?
>
> PIPPA (*After a moment of hesitation, realising the gravity of the question. After all, how can we expect politicians to resolve a debt problem if they do not realise they have one?*): Sir, it means we have spent more than we have earned and have been borrowing money from foreigners, mainly China, to make ends meet.
>
> CONGRESSMAN 2 (*Leaning forward rather aggressively*): There's not a single member of my district borrowing any money from the Chinese.

This conversation will leave market experts incredulous, but Congressman 2 had a point. No one in America or Britain or Europe goes to a Chinese bank to get a loan. Nobody registers that when foreigners buy US government bonds, the US is 'borrowing' the money. So it's no wonder people are surprised by the magnitude of the debt problem.

The same is true for every other indebted nation, from Britain to Spain and Portugal to America, China and Japan. How can any politician tell the public that it will have to endure twenty years of pain, as Japan did, for a problem whose existence the public is oblivious to? The sums don't add up. Why would you risk the votes and your political career on something people cannot even imagine, let alone comprehend? You would not.

Add another dimension to the problem: free money from the Federal Reserve, quantitative easing and super-low interest rates have been brought into play to subsidise the government's debt problem.

President George W. Bush's economic advisor, Larry Lindsey, and the former Head of the Office of Management and Budget, David Stockman, among others, ask, 'Why would Congress do anything about the debt problem when the Federal Reserve is funding the debt so cheaply?' There is no incentive to act.

This explains why, in the face of the financial crisis, American policymakers chose to jump in the direction they did, bailing out the broken banks rather than allowing them to fail. They took the view that the consequences of failure would be vastly greater than the public could possibly comprehend. Instead they opted to manage the debt in a way that the public would only comprehend years later. Using a combination of fiscal policy, monetary policy and regulatory policy, they effectively moved the losses from the speculators to the government and then to the taxpayers.

One can debate whether or not this shift was in the public interest. No doubt it was done with the good intention of protecting taxpayers and voters from the horrific consequences of the economic downturn that might have occurred if these institutions and the financial system as a whole had been permitted to fail – although even this is debatable. I had too many clients who would have been prepared to buy the businesses, the buildings, the hotels and the stocks and bonds that the banks and other owners would have been forced to sell had the government not bailed out the banking system. They would have invested new capital, too. But at the time, in the midst of the emergency, few were prepared to trust the market. They trusted the state.

What's done is done, except that to this day many do not understand what was done: the losses were 'socialised', passing from the banking system to the government's already over-indebted balance sheet, thus pushing the losses on to us, the public.

Put another way, the global banking system was 'saved', but what was never mentioned was the price, the true cost. The price depends on the choices we make. Here are the options.

Breaking the social contract

Here are the two inescapable choices that sovereigns and citizens of indebted countries face:

1. Pay off the debt.
2. Don't pay off the debt.

There are those who believe that the debt problems in the industrialised world are not that bad and are solvable by policy measures. The main argument is that these states – the US, France, Britain, Belgium, Portugal, Greece and others – are not insolvent but merely 'illiquid'. It's just a cash flow problem. If someone would only lend them a bit more cash, or if they simply taxed the rich more, or cut spending a bit harder, then eventually the economy would recover and they would have enough cash to pay everybody back and deliver on their promises. Herein lies the crux of the problem. The debt load is so heavy that it squashes GDP and inhibits calculated risk-taking.

Here are some inescapable truths:

1. You cannot solve a debt problem by borrowing more money. You can postpone it and exacerbate it, but not solve it.
2. All sovereign defaults have the same sequence: the government denies, denies, denies and then either says, 'Bring the defibrillator – we're defaulting', or it goes on denying.
3. When a government promises more than it can afford to deliver, the government's power to tax is pitted against the citizen's power to generate a profit. If the government tries to take too much, it kills the golden goose and destroys any hope of recovery.

The inevitable defaults

In the words of E. H. Carr (1892–1982), the widely respected British historian and international relations theorist: 'Everyone defaults, calls it something else and excoriates others for doing the same.' Here are the five principal ways in which governments default on their creditors.

1. Argentine-/Russian-style default

We can wake up one day to hear a government simply announce, 'We are never going to pay you back. Ever.' This is called an Argentine-style default because that is exactly how Argentina defaulted in 2001. Such an approach is violent, sudden and involves defaulting on the foreigners who have lent money to the nation. Russia did it in 1998. The typical consequences of such a default are: currency plunges in value, making exports cheaper, thus increasing foreign sales, which reduces the need to borrow from abroad. The downside is that a devalued currency means goods from abroad become unaffordable. Worse, there is a risk that no one will ever invest in your country ever again, since lenders will be wary of extending credit to a borrower who has defaulted on them so bluntly.

2. Haircuts

A government can say, 'We are definitely going to pay you back but a little bit later or a little bit less or both.' This sounds a lot nicer. Today the *Financial Times* and *Wall Street Journal* describe this kind of default as if nothing problematic has happened. The country merely 'extended the payments' or 'restructured' the debt. But one penny late or less is still a default when it comes to debt. A 'haircut' does not sound so bad. The most recent examples of haircuts occurred in Dubai, Greece and Ireland. In each case the *Financial Times* and other media said that Dubai's leadership had decided to 'extend the payments'. Greece has 'restructured' its debt many times since this last debt crisis began. Ireland 'successfully extended the payments' with the backing of the European Central Bank. All sound perfectly OK to the untrained ear, but these extensions have enormous consequences for those who have lent the country money – the bondholders.

To be absolutely clear, we are talking about how a government defaults on its debts. It usually acquires the debt by handing out pieces of paper known as bonds in exchange for cash. These bonds are a form of IOU – the government's way of saying 'I owe you and I promise to pay the loan back at some future date, in full and with interest'. So, when we buy a government bond, or our pension fund or mutual fund does, we expect not only to get our money back but to be paid interest for taking the risk of making the loan. The interest rate is what makes these pieces of paper popular investments. The yield (the interest rate) and the price are inversely related, so the higher the interest rate rises, the lower the price, and vice versa. But no matter what, if we don't get all our money back on time, then the bond has defaulted. From an accounting point of view, a default occurs if we are paid back one minute or one penny late.

3. Austerity

Austerity occurs when a state's debt burden becomes so massive that it cannot fund the various promises it made to its citizens and therefore defaults on those promises. For example, when it cannot find the money to pay us a pension when we reach fifty-five, or sixty-five, so it asks us to work longer by increasing the retirement age. Or it can no longer provide public transport and healthcare at the same price or to the same extent, so it requires citizens to pay out of their own pocket for these things. Public transport fares – for the Tube in London, the subway in New York City, the Metro in Paris, Madrid, Milan and Brussels – rise. Airport taxes go up. Tolls on bridges become more expensive and the police write tickets for driving three miles per hour over the speed limit instead of, say, ten miles per hour over, because they need the revenue. The government raises our taxes and reduces the services it delivers to the public.

Austerity is not just when the government reduces spending. It is when the government says, 'We promised to do certain things, like collect the rubbish twice a week, deliver mail six days a week, but now we cannot pay for these things, so your rubbish will be picked up once a week and if you want more you have to pay for it yourself, and the mail is only going to be delivered on weekdays.'

4. Devaluation

A government can permit or force the value of its currency to fall against other currencies so that our nation's goods and services become cheaper. This allows the country to earn more from sales abroad, but it makes imports more expensive. When Argentina devalued its currency by 23 per cent in January 2014, Whirlpool, which makes washers and dryers, and other companies that import into Argentina immediately announced a 30 per cent increase in their prices. An increase in the price of imported goods almost always leads to a rise in inflation. Devaluation is therefore considered a sub-category of inflation.

Devaluation may or may not be in the government's control. The Americans, British, Australians and Canadians might prefer a cheaper currency, but they cannot make it happen easily because these currencies are seen as safe havens in a world troubled by the Eurozone and the low growth and rising social protests in emerging markets. Investors buy these currencies due to their fear that other nations will seek to devalue.

5. Inflation

Inflation is the most invisible and immediately painless option (the pain comes later). All the government has to do is 'print' more currency and/or more bonds, and reduce interest rates to practically nothing so that the cost of money – the interest rate – is free. Or at least 'free' to the banks. This usually causes asset prices to rise, which is the point of the exercise. This is why Chairman of the Fed Ben Bernanke and his successor Janet Yellen claim credit for the fact that the US stock market went up after the introduction of quantitative easing. The purpose of money printing is to make asset prices rise and thereby entice investors back into the market. When governments push down the cost of money to very low levels and make it practically free to the banks, they are forcing participants in the economy to speculate. If cash pays very little and costs little to borrow, then the government is able to incentivise citizens to overcome their fear of debt and begin to speculate and invest in assets again.

However, as the eminent Swedish economist Knut Wicksell repeatedly pointed out during his long career, the interest rate is a kind of democratic instrument that balances interest between the borrowers and the lenders in a society. That balance should be 'just'. Injustice is done when interest rates are artificially suppressed because it assists the borrowers at the expense of the lenders, who are the savers. It shifts the balance of power in a society because inflation is a form of taxation, if not expropriation and confiscation. It is a means by which the state steals money from the savers and the weaker members of society in order to serve its own interests and those with vested interests. When governments assist savers or borrowers at the expense of the other, they change the nature of the social contract, whether the citizens like it or not.

John Maynard Keynes reached the same conclusion in 1919. In his book *The Economic Consequences of the Peace* he wrote:

Lenin is said to have declared that the best way to destroy the Capitalist System was to debauch the currency. By a continuing process of inflation, governments can confiscate, secretly and unobserved, an important part of the wealth of their citizens. By this method they not only confiscate, but they confiscate *arbitrarily*; and, while the process impoverishes many, it actually enriches some. The sight of this arbitrary rearrangement of riches strikes not only at security, but at confidence in the equity of the existing distribution of wealth. Those to whom the system brings windfalls, beyond their deserts and even beyond their expectations or desires, become 'profiteers', who are the object of the hatred of the bourgeoisie, whom the inflationism has impoverished, not less than of the proletariat. As the inflation proceeds and the real value of the currency fluctuates wildly from month to month, all permanent relations between debtors and creditors, which form the ultimate foundation of capitalism, become so utterly disordered as to be almost meaningless; and the process of wealth-getting degenerates into a gamble and a lottery.

If anything captures the zeitgeist of the world economy today it is this sense that we are now in a lottery; we are gambling and the only known factor is that the 'house' – the government – decides the outcome.

According to the revered hedge fund manager Stanley Druckenmiller:

Part of my advantage, is that my strength is economic forecasting, but that only works in free markets, when markets are smarter than people. That's how I started. I watched the stock market, how equities reacted to change in levels of economic activity, and I could understand how price signals worked and how to forecast them. Today, all these price signals are compromised and I'm seriously questioning whether I have any competitive advantage left.*

In other words, the market no longer depends on market prices: it depends on decisions by policymakers. Druckenmiller is making us aware that governments have not only broken the social contract, they have emerged as the most important price maker and player in the market. The line between the state and the market has moved in favour of the state's interests and against those of the individual. This gives rise to a world where citizens are challenging their leaders and repeatedly asking, 'Why is the social contract being broken or changed?'

Local consequences

This is the reason why voters everywhere are leaning towards new

* Hugo Scott-Gall, 'Stanley Druckenmiller on China's Future and Investing in the New Normal', www.zerohedge.com/news/2013-06-14/stanley-druckenmiller-chinas-future-and-investing-new-normal

politicians and new parties. They don't want the old establishment leaders because they have broken more than their promises. They have broken the social contract. We no longer trust the cut of their cloth now that they have caused the social fabric to rip and tear. This helps explain the rise of extremist politicians and parties and the sudden arrival of surprising new anti-establishment political candidates around the world. Donald Trump and Bernie Sanders were both anti-establishment candidates in the US. Now elected, President Trump is atacking the 'establishment' on all sides – mainstream media, organisational structures, fundraising, geopolitical mores and more. In Europe, too, anti-establishment sentiment led to the 'No' vote in the Italian referendum of December 2016 and continues to give rise to an anti-EU stance across the continent.

The Eurozone

At the heart of the Eurozone lies a profound social contract problem. After devastating wars in 1871, 1914–18 and 1939–45, France and Germany decided to band together and collaborate on the economic resources that they had been competing over: coal and steel. In 1950, Robert Schuman, the French Foreign Minister, proposed a European Union as a means of preventing any more war:

> Franco-German production of coal and steel as a whole can be placed under a common High Authority, within the framework of an organisation open to the participation of the other countries of Europe. The pooling of coal and steel production should immediately provide for the setting up of common foundations for economic development as a first step in the federation of Europe, and will change the destinies of those regions which have long been devoted to the manufacture of munitions of war, of which they have been the most constant victims.

The Schuman Declaration provided the foundation for what has evolved into the European Union. On 1 January 1999 some members joined the effort to launch a common currency called the euro, which it was believed would further consolidate Europe. This new currency gave the poorer, weaker countries in Europe, such as Greece and Portugal, access to capital at the same interest rates as stronger and wealthier countries, such as Germany and France. With the new-found easy money, local politicians committed to spending with little incentive to pay attention to revenues and taxes. As long as the world economy was booming, the social contract could be fulfilled. The state could make or increase payouts while not demanding the citizens pay more in tax.

The 2007/8 financial crisis revealed that spending was exceeding income by such a large amount that many European nations and financial institutions were illiquid: they could not meet their cash-flow requirements. In reality, they were more than illiquid. They were insolvent and needed a bailout.

Nations in the Eurozone are thus being forced by their financial troubles to renege on their promises. Greece and Cyprus were forced to seek bailouts and to default on their debt. The European Union, with the backing of the International Monetary Fund, supported the Cypriot government when it chose to (or was forced to) take its citizens' private savings directly from some of their bank accounts to help fund the loss. The risk is that this can happen elsewhere. There can be few greater breaches of the social contract than when your government simply takes your money directly out of your bank.

In Portugal in 2011 and Poland in 2013 governments expropriated private assets by effectively nationalising private pensions. The promise was that the employees of Portugal Telecom would still get their pensions, but now the government would be paying the pension – assuming the government can make the payments. Of course the whole reason for expropriating the pension assets was to shore up the government's balance sheet and reduce the loss it faced in order to qualify for further bailout money from the EU.

There are only a few Eurozone members that have a positive cash situation: Germany, Finland and Holland. Naturally the citizens of these states do not want to write a cheque to the 'peripheral' states, which include Greece, Portugal, Cyprus, Ireland, Spain, Italy and possibly even France and Belgium. Why should those who were fiscally sound underwrite the losses of those who were not?

The social contract problem goes much deeper, though. In short, the social contract in Germany insists that no leader ever address a debt problem by using inflation. Germans are still burned by their traumatic experience with dramatic hyperinflation in the 1920s and 1930s. Many believe that the hyperinflation caused the population to turn to a new leader who promised to protect them from its ravages, which opened the door to Adolf Hitler. The central problem today is that any effort to monetise the debt (that is, to use inflation to diminish it) – such as issuing European-wide Eurobonds, printing money or having Germany write a cheque to cover the losses – would be considered an inflationary step by most Germans. It would break the German social contract. In contrast, failure to monetise the debt breaks the social contract in the other indebted Eurozone countries.

This is why we hear the Head of the European Central Bank, Mario Draghi, say, 'We will do whatever it takes' to fix the problem. Such words make the stock markets go up. But then the Germans say 'No', they have not agreed to an ECB that can simply print money to fix the problem. They have not agreed to bail out or inflate. They quote Draghi's whole sentence, which was, 'Within our mandate, the ECB is ready to do whatever it takes to preserve the euro.'* The mandate does not include permitting inflation, say the Germans.

In the meantime, bailouts in Europe have gone directly to the lenders – the banks. The defaults have left the public in Greece and Cyprus no better off. The stark choice these countries face is clear. If they stay in the euro, they must accept the rebalancing of income versus expenditure. That means losing a generation or two to unemployment

---

* Verbatim of the remarks made by Mario Draghi, President of the European Central Bank at the Global Investment Conference in London, 26 July 2012.

while taxes go up and state benefits go down. It means enduring deflation and stagnant growth while they slowly pay off their debt.

A country could leave the euro (though stay in the EU, which would put them in a similar position to the UK). In other words, they could make their currency cheaper through devaluation. Or a country like Scotland, for example, if it pursued independence, could gain greater control over its own finances by leaving the UK, even if devaluation was not possible.* As the public begins to understand the starkness of the outcomes, populists on the right and the left gain greater sway. The far right parties have acquired followers at a striking pace. In Germany the AfD, Alternative for Germany party, reached 10 per cent support in the polls for the first time in January 2016. Greece has seen the rise of the far-right Golden Dawn party, and other extremist groups thrive elsewhere in the Eurozone. They promise to restore the social contract by opting out of the euro. In Spain the separatist movements in Andalucía and Catalonia promise the same, as does Scotland in its effort to further devolve from the United Kingdom.

So far, the public in most Eurozone countries has voted decisively against any leader who promised to do what Germany wants. To be clear, Germany wants each European citizen to be more careful about public finances (meaning they want Greeks and Italians to behave more like Germans, which seems unlikely and probably undesirable). As of 2010, Germany has more or less said that it could support writing a cheque to bail out Europe if the following conditions were met:

1. Each Eurozone member hands over some of their fiscal sovereignty to a central authority in Brussels;
2. Each Eurozone member agrees to the creation of a common federation in which there will be one single Foreign Minister, which of course means there will be one single Finance Minister as well.

* Scotland can only devalue its currency if it introduces its own currency. The Eurozone has ruled out Scottish membership in the euro.

So far, every European leader who has supported this fundamental change in the social contract has been decisively thrown out of public office. It is not surprising that no one wants to vote for a system of government that involves handing over sovereign authority to unelected officials who will probably come from other nations. But EU officials believe it is only a matter of time and explanation before the public realises that the new European Federation social contract will better their interest more than the old *national* social contract.

There are those in Brussels and European capitals who believe that, unlike the old social contract which evolved around democracy, the new social contract in Europe may have to be imposed on the people. According to these elites, the public cannot grasp that this is in their best interest. As things stand, bailing out most of the Eurozone will break the social contract in Germany and failing to do so will break the social contract in the periphery. Reconciling the two may not be possible.

In my humble opinion, Germany seems to make every effort in public to extend a half-hearted helping hand to the periphery so that it can be seen to be trying. At the same time, Germany's leaders fully understand that countries such as Greece and Cyprus cannot viably remain inside the euro. The Greek public is only now waking up to the idea that a full default on its debt (and it has defaulted on 90 per cent of its debt as I write) still leaves it dead in the water for many years to come. The Greek economy cannot grow, in spite of the debt burden being relieved by default.

Within Greece, the inability of the government to enforce the law and guarantee order due to its financial constraints has forced citizens to consider alternative mechanisms for protecting themselves and their communities. Organised crime, meanwhile, stands poised to take advantage of the situation.

Immigration

The immigration problem in Europe is partly due to the financial vulnerabilities. In April 2015, the Greeks threw open the illegal immigration detention centres for one simple reason: there was no more money to pay the guards. They tried to rehouse immigrants in old hotels and state-owned buildings, but to little avail. In this way the debt burden punched a hole in the border of the EU. The EU has had to respond to this by sending in EU border support to police the Greek border with Macedonia.* Thus the failed financial position of Greece became a window of opportunity for both émigrés and the EU, with the latter beginning to take control of its borders.

One signal that has become ever more apparent is the surge of Eurozone citizens who have moved to the United Kingdom.

When I walk into Battersea Park in London, half the people there now speak French. With the threat of higher taxes, high unemployment and lower growth, many enterprising French people are moving to London. The main French school in London, the Lycée Français in South Kensington, is completely full. So a few entrepreneurs have gone to the council in the London Borough of Wandsworth and leased some large local government buildings with the intention of turning them into new French schools so the children of these émigrés can be brought up in their chosen education system. Local British state schools are quickly introducing French and offering the National Curriculum in both French and English.† This gives local government more cash because it brings jobs to the borough. At the same time it helps raise property values in the area. In addition, I'd say it is pretty likely that the neighbourhood will soon have French bakeries and restaurants, which it currently sorely lacks.

* Duncan Robertson, 'EU plans to send more border guards to Macedonia–Greece border', *Financial Times*, 6 February 2016.

† 'Third School goes Bilingual': Wandsworth Council announcement, 16 December 2011.

Spanish, Greeks and others flee to the UK too. An interesting signal is that you almost need to be multilingual to order food in a London restaurant these days due to the large number of Continental European employees. Ask for a 'California roll' and they say '*Qué?*' because they speak Spanish, not English, and don't recognise the words. London has always been a cosmopolitan city, but the appearance of Eurozone citizens in the workforce has been striking in recent years. Part of what makes Britain more attractive is that it is outside the euro, which means it still controls its own monetary policy, interest rates and, unlike Eurozone members, its own currency, tax and fiscal affairs.

Tax is an important issue. Britain, France, Germany and the US have made immense efforts to close down offshore tax havens so that they can retrieve tax payments that their citizens might otherwise be avoiding (legally or illegally). Such pressure has been imposed that Switzerland, for example, no longer protects information about who has money on deposit in Switzerland unless they are legal residents. Switzerland has concluded that it is pretty dangerous when the financial services sector dwarfs the rest of the economy, so it has taken steps to make it more difficult for foreigners to deposit their cash there or do their financial transactions there. As smart investors look around the world, they see that the UK now has the lowest tax rates relative to everywhere else, where taxes are rising. In addition, the UK offers rule of law in a world where the social contract is breaking down. Other places have separatist movements, coups, years of deflation and the like, but the UK offers a relatively safe haven.

For wealthy families in emerging markets, Britain offers a refuge where they can trust the rule of law. It's a safe place where they can escape if the social contract back home really comes unstuck. This has led to unprecedented demand for residential property in London and the rest of the UK. Real estate agents in London have hired Mandarin, Arabic and other foreign language speakers to help cope with overwhelming demand. The presence of such staff on the payrolls of property brokers is a telling signal.

So, even though the British may be angry about the breakdown of the social contract they thought they had, many foreigners are finding that the British social contract beats the one they have at home.

Brexit

Perhaps, then, it is no surprise to find the British public are leaning more heavily in favour of exiting the European Union than politicians and policymakers had expected. There is an awareness that the social contract Britain wants and the social contract which the European Union wants are not the same. I would argue that the 'deal' Britain signed up for upon entry into the EU is not the same deal that is being offered today. Today the Germans and those with cash are implicitly asking indebted countries like Spain and Italy and Portugal to hand over more of their fiscal sovereignty to Brussels in exchange for financial largesse (more bailout money). This movement towards centralisation of power does not sit well with the British public, who are averse to losing any control over their sovereignty and fiscal affairs whatsoever.

The American social contract

The social contract in the United States is changing, too, and at many levels. Local authorities such as Detroit, for example, have simply defaulted their debt. Others are trying to reduce pension benefits or the size of police departments. Nationally, tax rates are rising while benefits are falling, although austerity is not as pronounced in the US as in the United Kingdom. But this is because America is able to pursue a monetary and fiscal policy that is much riskier than most governments can.

The fact that the US dollar is a reserve currency allows America to experiment with monetary and fiscal policy. A reserve currency is one that people put their faith in regardless of the immediate condition of the economy. Whenever there is trouble in the world or in the markets, people are prepared to believe that the US will always recover, always pay back its debt, always succeed in protecting and pursuing its own national interests. America retains full control over all aspects of economic policy.

It controls interest rates, monetary policy, fiscal policy and has the ability to generate growth without much help from abroad. It's estimated that only 10 per cent of America's GDP comes from exports.

Nonetheless, there are many people in the US who are increasingly uncomfortable with the ever-greater presence of the US government in the market. The balance of power between the state and the market has shifted in favour of the state. Then again, there are others who welcome a state that provides a bigger safety net and seeks to take more taxes from the rich rather than cutting the benefits that go to the poor. The rising presence of potholes in the road and cracks in the sidewalks signal that the state can't or won't deliver what people have taken for granted.

In each case, all over the world, as the social contract breaks or changes, the public begins to ask that simple question. 'Why is the state making decisions about how to distribute wealth and power in my society in ways that don't benefit me?' This pits the government against the citizens and the citizens against each other, which is something that will affect everyone.

It sometimes shows up in unexpected ways. In 2014 the government in Ireland came up with the not so clever idea to charge citizens a tax based on their consumption of water. In a country where it rains more often than not and which has a long history of poverty, this seemed to many a deeply unfair way to refill the state's coffers. The actor Liam Neeson, an Irishman, said 'Don't f***ing insult the Irish people any more'.* That was a signal that this was one breach of the social contract the citizens would not stand for.

Global consequences

To finish here, let's consider all this from a lender's perspective. In short, why would any lender, say the Chinese government, continue

---

* Aoife Kelly, 'Liam Neeson won't move home because of water charges', *The Independent*, 26 January 2014.

to lend money to a country that is so overwhelmed by its debt* that it has to break its promises, whether to its own citizens or to the lenders?

Telling a lender that you want the inflation rate to go up is akin to saying, 'I intend to pay you back less than I borrowed.' In an attempt to counter this, the US began to raise interest rates in 2016, so that the risk of inflation is diminished . . . Or is it? Raising interest rates from almost nothing still leaves a record surplus of liquidity in the world economy. Another solution is to move the goalposts. The Chairman of the Federal Reserve has suggested that inflation must be permitted to rise above average for some time because it was below average for so long. The 2 per cent target has alrady become 2.5 per cent. Where will it stop? Three per cent? Four per cent? This level of inflation may sound like a small jump but it would have immense implications for your rent and the cost of living.

Some might say the US, and other major indebted nations, should consider themselves lucky to get back to 2 per cent let alone expect anything higher. But emerging-market officials are all too familiar with inflation. They know that Paul Volcker is right. It cannot be micromanaged. The Fed and the Bank of England may say they are capable of exercising 'optimal control', but emerging-market lenders and many other observers know that inflation cannot be precisely controlled like a temperature dial.

Perhaps the most important risk here is that the US, the UK and other industrialised but indebted nations don't care about the spillovers or consequences for the rest of the world. Emerging markets have to think about what the spillovers might be and manage that themselves. On that basis, it begins to make sense that there is quite a serious debate, if not argument, about what is actually going on in the world economy today.

---

* In a statement released 19 January 2016 the Congressional Budget Office estimates that, on the current trajectory, US debt will reach $30 trillion dollars by 2025.

6

The Vice

___

But, you say, there is no inflation. Although the US and others may be trying to create it, thus far, there is little sign. Which brings us to an impasse that will divide us all. Before delving into the details I'd like to harken back to an argument from the past. Well, it was really more of a fight. In fact, it is an example of how two of the greatest thinkers of their generation almost came to physical blows. There may be some lessons for us today.

Ludwig Wittgenstein and Karl Popper, two of the brightest philosophers in modern history, met only once, on an autumn afternoon in Oxford in 1946.* Popper delivered a lecture at the university on the question, 'Are there philosophical problems or are there just philosophical puzzles?' Wittgenstein believed there were only puzzles; Popper believed there were only problems. Within ten minutes, Wittgenstein picked up an iron poker and, according to witnesses, waved it about shouting, 'Popper, you are wrong! You are wrong!' Bertrand Russell, another of the twentieth century's greatest philosophers, had to intervene and persuade Wittgenstein to put the threatening poker down. Wittgenstein apparently stormed off in a huff. The moral of the story is that even extremely intelligent people can find themselves married to a view and no amount of facts or argument

* David Edmonds and John Eidinow, *Wittgenstein's Poker: The Story of a Ten-Minute Argument Between Two Great Philosophers*, HarperCollins, 2002.

will dissuade them. They will wave a poker at anyone who challenges their outlook.

This brings me to a signal I have heard and observed in recent years at Jackson Hole, the venue for the Federal Reserve's annual economic policy symposium. Every August the President of the Kansas City Federal Reserve invites central bank governors from all over the world to come to this valley in Wyoming, together with a handful of the chief economists from major central banks and a smaller number of independent analysts.

For the last few years, the Fed Chairman – first Ben Bernanke and then Janet Yellen – has insisted that quantitative easing policies would have no spillover effects and would not and could not create undesirable inflation or dangerous imbalances (like artificially high asset prices or resource mis-allocations) at home in the US or anywhere else in the world. Each time this is said, I have heard a distinct sound: the sound of palms being slapped against foreheads, mainly by emerging-market central bank governors. This is a signal of an especially violent disagreement. The rolling of eyeballs by supporters of these policies at those who oppose them merely confirms the seriousness of the disagreement. The hostility is so palpable that I found myself checking the location of the nearest fire pokers – fortunately they're kept in the grand lobby of the Jackson Lake Lodge, happily out of reach of these otherwise mild-mannered bankers. Instead they deliver their blows at each other through academic papers, learned journals and columns in the *Wall Street Journal* and *Financial Times*.

Let us try to understand these opposing views and why the disagreement is so severe. After all, the signals you will observe and give credence to is liable to depend on whether you agree with the Federal Reserve's view or the view of many emerging-market central banks. The breakdown in the conversation between the two camps occurs because of an impasse over philosophy. Like Wittgenstein and Popper, the Fed and many of the emerging-market central banks see the world so differently that there is little common ground for a conversation. What is a puzzle to the Federal Reserve is a problem for many other central bankers.

The Fed's view

The situation in 2007 and 2008 was so bad that, without action, the world economy would have ended up in another Great Depression. To save the US, and even the world, from such a disastrous fate, the US central bank (and others like the Bank of England and the Bank of Japan) engaged in all kinds of conventional and unconventional efforts to support and stimulate the economy. This lifted many prices: property and stock market prices especially. These efforts, which are generally referred to as quantitative easing, have brought no unwanted, let alone adverse, consequences. The resulting higher stock market values and higher property prices are positive consequences and should be welcomed. These upward price movements confirm that their efforts have been a success but reflect absolutely nothing about inflationary price pressures.

The emerging-market view

Emerging-market central bankers do not all hold the same view, but in general, they tend to think that the whole point of record low interest rates and quantitative easing is to foster higher inflation. The so-called 'hawks' on the board of the Federal Reserve concur with this view. These camps say the efforts by America, Britain, Canada, Japan, Australia and others to create inflation are certainly working. Inflation is making its way back into the world economy. This is obvious from the extraordinary rise in asset prices that occurred in response to the flood of money that the Western central banks unleashed. Stock markets hit record highs during the QE period, as did the price of property and hard assets from commodities to artwork. The industrialised world central banks may choose to exclude such asset prices from their calculations, but emerging-market officials are well aware that rising asset prices mean inflation.

The problem, from an emerging-market point of view, is that the inflation the West is trying to create is hitting the emerging markets. They've seen an obvious rise in the cost of basic needs: food, energy and raw materials. And these rising prices are sparking social unrest across many of the emerging-market countries.

The price of oil and global commodities, in the aggregate,* may be down but the actual prices paid for things that matter in individual emerging-market countries is up. For example, consider the price of wheat. After spikes in 2008 and 2012 the price of wheat has clearly fallen. And yet, in early 2016, in the aftermath of a substantial devaluation of the rouble to a record low value, Russians are paying record prices even for locally produced wheat.†

Now consider oil prices. Saudi Arabia was considered one of the richest countries in the world, and therefore capable of substantially subsidising the price of petrol and food for its citizens. After the dramatic fall in the oil price in 2015, however, the Saudis have lost a lot of their cash flow and now suffer from a record budget deficit that amounts to about 15 per cent of their GDP. They've announced that they will issue debt for the first time in history. By early 2016, it became clear that the kingdom was considering selling off its crown jewel, Saudi Aramco, thus deepening suspicions that it is having real cash problems. As a result of the cash squeeze, the leadership announced in late 2015 that fuel subsidies would be reduced by 50 per cent. Of course, petrol prices are still far below the levels paid anywhere else in the world, but for Saudi citizens the price hike has meant a substantial increase in their cost of living. Rising input costs have prompted many bakeries in Saudi to call for permission to substantially increase the price of bread.‡ Naturally, this kind of price pressure is acutely felt by the citizens. We find ourselves back at the start of the Arab Spring, when

* See the UN Food and Agriculture Organization food indices.

† Anatoly Medetsky, 'Russians stung by ruble pay near record even for local wheat', Bloomberg.com, 26 January 2016.

‡ '1,000 bakeries in EP seek hike in product prices', *Arab News*, 5 January 2016.

rising bread prices prompted protests in various parts of the Middle East.

In India, the population has seen the price of food staples skyrocket in the aftermath of quantitative easing. The most important core foodstuffs in India are onions and pulses. In 2013 the price of onions rose by more than 300 per cent, having already risen in triple digits the year before. In August 2013, the Indian Cabinet held crisis meetings to discuss the fast-rising price of this single vegetable. The cost of onions may not sound like a big deal, but in his blog post 'What is so special about onions in India?'* Mohammad Amin, a senior economist at the World Bank, beautifully explains how onion price rises can prompt social unrest and adverse electoral outcomes in India. By 2014, the Indian government had started to severely restrict the export of onions in an effort to contain the upward price pressure.† The Indians were even forced to swallow their pride and import onions from their arch nemesis, Pakistan, in an effort to reduce the risk of serious price pressures.

In late 2015, the *Financial Times* reported that India had been hit by 'Dal shock' as the price of pulses jumped by 70 per cent to all-time record highs.‡ By 2016 the Indian government felt compelled to do something to reduce the price pressure. In an important signal, they lifted a fifty-year-old ban on a type of lentil that is said to be linked to nerve damage and possible paralysis. They are also turning to genome sequencing in the hope of preventing future shortages.

Wages are rising

It is often said that inflation cannot occur unless wages are rising – but they are rising. Emerging-market workers everywhere have responded to rising costs by demanding higher pay. The more they get paid,

* Mohammad Amin, 'What is so special about onions in India?' blogs.worldbank.org, 18 January 2011.
† Minimum Export Price (MEP).
‡ Emiko Terazono and David Keohane, 'Dal shock hits India as pulse prices soar', *Financial Times*, 23 November 2015.

though, the more money is in the economy. That tends to make prices rise again. In other words, when wages go up then rents, for example, start rising too. This is called a 'wage price spiral'.

With wages across the world standing at a record low as a percentage of GDP, and corporate profits standing at an all-time high, we have to expect that wage demands will persist, especially if the cost of living keeps rising. The debate about a 'living wage' is intensifying – even in the industrialised world. I found it ironic that a week after the 2013 Jackson Hole meeting (where the talk was that wages could not and would not rise), fast-food workers around America took industrial action that shut down restaurants across sixty cities in an effort to secure a 100 per cent wage increase. Of course they didn't get 100 per cent, but they got something more than the official inflation rate.

Hot chilli pepper

It may not matter to those in the industrialised world that the price of, say, chillies had risen in Indonesia, India and elsewhere in Asia by 300 per cent in the course of 2012. However, for emerging-market workers chillies are as essential as milk is to a Westerner. So it was noticed when, in 2013, the price of chillies starting doubling across Asia in a single month. Chillies doubled in price year over year in April 2016.

The point is that many emerging-market workers have moved from two or three meals with meat every week to four or five meals a week. Others have not achieved this but still aspire to it. The rise of food prices not only blocks their aspiration, it threatens them with the prospect of having less meat protein than they had hoped for. In addition to signalling painful upward price pressure, increases in food costs signal the end or at least postponement of a dream that had become rooted in entitlement.

Emerging-market leaders know that nothing will propel the public into the streets faster than high or rising food and energy prices, especially when it impacts on the cost of those items that are held most dear to the local population, items that may seem random or irrelevant to outsiders. Whatever the West has to say about these price hikes, whether one concedes they are real or imagined, the Chinese and other emerging markets believe that it is real enough to be a genuine threat to social stability.

Marikana

The wage price spiral in South Africa culminated in the most significant outbreak of civil unrest since the end of apartheid. In August 2012, South African police fired into a crowd of miners in Marikana, a mining town in the north-west. Few could imagine that a democratically elected government would ever resort to firearms, let alone shoot at its citizens, killing thirty-four of them. This event marked a profound break in South Africa's social contract.

The miners had gone on strike demanding as much as a 100 per cent wage hike from some of the world's largest mining companies. While the assets they were risking their lives to extract from the ground were fetching record prices – gold, platinum, palladium, thermal coal, diamonds become more attractive to investors in a financial climate where paper money is in danger of devaluation and debasement – the miners had found themselves worse off financially, thanks to the spiralling cost of fuel and groceries. In the aftermath of the shootings the South African government made veiled threats to nationalise the mining industry, which led Anglo, Rio Tinto and the other mining companies to grudgingly agree to a 25 per cent wage hike. As a result, the companies claimed some mines would no longer be profitable and they would be compelled to close them and reduce their presence in South Africa. Margins in mining are often pretty thin; Rio Tinto announced its largest loss in history in 2013 due to 'emerging-market cost overruns'.* When the workers subsequently demanded a further 60 per cent wage increase and another 100 per cent increase on top of

---

* Neil Hume, 'Rio Tinto vow after its biggest loss ever', *Financial Times*, 14 February 2013.

what was granted, mines were closed and mothballed.

With mining operations around the world becoming more costly and the prices of mined assets being highly volatile, it is logical that the supply of these assets should be constrained or at least reduced. In my talks with mining companies and resource investors at that time, it seemed apparent that there were a record number of mines for sale that no one would touch even though the price was lower than the value of the proven reserves. This was because potential buyers feared expropriation. They feared volatility. They could not raise the working capital needed to bring the assets to the surface. They could not afford the costly high-tech equipment and engineers to venture deeper below ground and boost productivity enough to generate reliable profits. So, supply-side problems develop in mining just as they had in agriculture.

In the main, inflation pressures have been localised – at least until now. Inflation has begun to creep back into the world economy, undermining the efforts of emerging markets to deliver the aspirations of their people. No doubt domestic policy choices have contributed to bad economic outcomes, like inflation, in many places. But the decision by the industrialised world to deal with debt by engaging in what is for them a relatively painless policy has proved inflammatory in emerging markets where rising asset prices have threatened the social order. The higher prices go, the harder nations will have to fight for control of the critical assets needed to keep their populations stable.

It would be foolish to deny that the industrialised world is seeking to raise the inflation rate when every possible step has been taken to secure precisely this outcome. The only questions that matter now are: Will it work? And will it create unwanted or unmanageable consequences at home or abroad?

China

China has experienced upward cost of living pressures too. Wages in China quintupled in the last few years. As of 2016, Chinese wages were still rising faster than anywhere else in Asia, in spite of the seeming slowdown. Workers found that their cost of living was rising so much that the only way to manage was to ask for higher wages.

What costs went up? Property values rose dramatically, at least until the economy began to slow in 2015. Even after a substantial fall in property prices, the cost of rented accommodation in Beijing, Shanghai and other major cities continued to go up.

Food prices have been an issue for the Chinese workers as well. The single most important core foodstuff in China is pork. In January 2016 it was reported that the price of pork had jumped by 9.5 per cent in a month. This was small in comparison with the latter part of 2015 when the price jumped by 50 per cent in one quarter. When the Chinese stock market began to fall in June 2015, I found that Chinese policymakers were more worried about rising pork prices than the plummeting value of stocks. Relatively few Chinese own stocks (most of the population don't even have a bank account), so, alarming as the optics of a falling stock market might appear, it was not in itself cause for alarm. But a falling stock market in conjunction with a rising pork price (up 45 per cent in 2016)? Now *that* is a serious problem. That will further incite demands for wage hikes.

To put the recent wage hikes into perspective, the effect has been substantial enough to seriously erode Chinese competitiveness. In 2015 wages in Mexico were, on average, some 20–40 per cent cheaper than those in China.* The differential between emerging-market wages and industrialised market wages is also narrowing. The end result has been that manufacturing businesses have begun to relocate from China to other non-Asian locations, including the US and Britain.

It now costs less to manufacture steel in the US than in China, according to a recent report issued by Price Waterhouse Coopers.†

---

* 'Want cheap labour? Head to Mexico not China', *Financial Times*, 14 January 2016.
† Robert W. McCutcheon, Robert Pethick, Michael Burak, Anthony J. Scamuffa, Sean T. Hoover, Robert B. Bono, Michael Portnoy and Thomas Waller, 'A Homecoming for US manufacturing? Why a resurgence in US manufacturing may be the next big bet', www.pwc.com, September 2012.

Firms from GE to the Otis Elevator Company to Caterpillar to Brooks Brothers to Tiffany have been bringing production back to the middle of America. Even Wham-O, the company that makes the plastic toys known as Frisbees and Hula Hoops, now make more of these in the US than overseas. Mexico, Eastern Europe and parts of Asia beyond China have all been beneficiaries of the changed landscape.

Tellingly, Chinese firms are beginning to open manufacturing facilities in America. Zhu Shanqing, CEO of the Keer Group, which owns yarn-spinning factories in China, announced his intention to invest $218 million in a new yarn factory near Charlotte, North Carolina. The *Wall Street Journal* reported, 'The new plant will pay half as much as Mr Zhu does for electricity in China and get local government support.' Plus, he will lose the overseas shipping expenses.*

There is much debate about whether the reshoring or onshoring phenomenon is real.† My own experience and observation is that the Chinese leadership, in business and in politics, no longer believe that the downturn in China's competitiveness is cyclical. When the world economy picks up again, China will not necessarily pick up with it. This is because they are no longer the world's cheapest manufacturing location. What's more, they don't want to be. If China is to double national incomes it needs to move up the 'value added' ladder. In other words, they must stop making cheap things and learn to make more complex and costly items, such as cars and engineered goods. They must learn to build and manage brands, not merely globally but locally. Japan has already demonstrated that the transition is possible: the Japanese went from making plastic flowers in the 1950s to making humanoid robots today. The big concern is, will the global macro-economic landscape help or hinder Chinese efforts?

The validity of this concern is reinforced by the fact that Chinese

---

* Cameron McWhirter and Dinny McMahon, 'Spotted Again in America: Textile Jobs', *Wall Street Journal*, 22 December 2013.

† Reshoring and onshoring refers to the return of manufacturing businesses from emerging markets back to the industrialised world, especially in the US and Europe.

firms and even the Chinese government are investing in manufacturing-related businesses and regions such as the Midwest of the USA and the Midlands in the UK.

The British are often shocked at the notion that Britain's manufacturing can effectively compete with China and other emerging markets. Yet in 2015, Xi Jinping, China's President, announced the creation of a £130 million 'China Cluster' manufacturing hub in Manchester to house Chinese businesses that were gearing up to move into the region.* Chinese investors put some £800 million into Manchester Airport in 2013 in anticipation of direct flights between Manchester and China; in fact they've put substantial money into everything from regeneration schemes around Birmingham to specific manufacturing facilities.† Changan Automotive, one of the largest car manufacturers in China, has opened a production facility near Birmingham Airport, which is also scheduled to offer direct flights to China. The BBC was not wrong when they reported in 2013, 'The West Midlands is fast becoming the first port of call for Chinese investors, following several high-profile takeovers.'‡

Knight Frank and other British property agents consistently report that the Chinese have been significant buyers of property in the Midlands, far outstripping the expected demand. Chinese buyers of residential property are seemingly buying at every pricing point, often in hard cash and frequently sight unseen. New Yorkers, the residents of San Francisco, Vancouver, Sydney and many other megacities are reporting the same phenomenon.

The implications for China, and other emerging markets, is sobering. In their view, America's efforts to create inflation are

---

* 'Manchester Airports Group launches £130m "China Cluster" at Airport City', *Manchester Evening News*, 23 October 2015.

† Graeme Brown, 'Chinese investors' plan to fund major Birmingham regeneration schemes', *Birmingham Post*, 6 November 2015.

‡ Peter Plisner, 'Chinese firms drawn to West Midlands investment', BBC News, 14 October 2013.

succeeding. Inflation always hits the poorest first. The poorest today are emerging markets.

The impasse

Those readers who take the Federal Reserve's side of the argument (or at least the argument made by the majority over at the Fed) must be busting their veins by now. They will be outraged by the suggestion that there is any inflation anywhere. They will probably be even further incensed at the notion that such price pressures would have anything to do with the monetary policy of the United States. In addition, they will be seething at the suggestion it is a central bank's job to run monetary policy for the world.

No, they'll say, every country is responsible for its own monetary policy. Nothing we have done, and nothing that has been done by any of the Western governments in concert, is responsible for whatever troubles you may be having in emerging markets.

The Fed says, look, if the argument is that low interest rates and QE put 'hot money' into the US economy and somehow it 'spilled over' and made its way into your emerging-market economy, the fact is that emerging markets could have and should have taken responsibility for their own economies by raising interest rates and allowing their currencies to strengthen as a means of offsetting any unwanted 'hot money' coming in from the outside. In other words, emerging markets should have allowed their currencies to appreciate and/or raised their interest rates.

This suggestion is outrageous, as far as many emerging markets are concerned. This would have made their own products and services more expensive and thereby lowered their growth rate at a time when the world economy was already in trouble. Emerging-market leaders blame the US for having caused the financial crisis: 'The crisis was brought about by *your* mistakes and your bad management,' they argue. 'And the attendant slowdown brought us immense pain. We now have rising unemployment and a loss of faith in the future, thanks to you. And now you expect us to raise interest rates and increase the burden on an already impoverished, poor population? Seriously?'

The Fed's response might be summarised thus: It's your own fault.

Nevertheless, they are complaining. And they continue to complain no matter what the Fed does. When the Fed added cash to the system, they complained about the hot money. Then they complained when the Fed started to nominally reverse its free money stance.* As the 'hot money' began to leave the world economy (as a result of the Fed reducing the liquidity by 'tapering', or reducing, the pace at which they had been adding money to the system every month), emerging markets experienced record declines in the value of stock markets and dramatic falls in the value of their currencies. And devaluation of currency, as we have already seen, is highly inflationary.

The carry trade

One aspect of the 'hot money' concept needs a bit more explaining. From the Fed's perspective, they may have quadrupled the size of their balance sheet since the crisis; they may have pumped some $2 trillion dollars' worth of reserves into the banking system; but since the banks did not lend the money out, there was no inflationary impact in the US or anywhere else.

Bankers – by which I mean the traders whose job it is to borrow funds and bet on finding higher returns – see it differently. Those who work the trading floors of the biggest recipients of free money (i.e. banks) have a simple outlook: their job is to take risk and make profits. When central banks, like the Fed or the Bank of England, give them record low interest rates and free money, their response is to use it. After all, the money is 'free'. Having spent time on trading floors of

---

* I say 'nominally' because the Federal Reserve was still adding record levels of liquidity to the financial markets. 'Tapering' just means it was doing it less rapidly than in the past.

major banks, I know from experience that traders are obliged to punt that free money like hell. The logic is clear: since it doesn't cost you anything, you are, as a trader, practically obliged to find the riskiest venture you possibly can and use it to bet on that. When you bet on investments that are outside your own currency or country, we call that a 'carry trade'.

When the free money began to circulate, investors immediately set out to engage in 'carry trades', buying up emerging-market currencies, stocks, property, companies and debt. Why? Because, at that time, emerging markets seemed destined to outperform anything in the debt-impaired and dragging industrialised West, thus maximising profits. In this way the 'wall of money' the Fed had created began to move into emerging markets. Traders and bankers are incredulous that central bankers, whether at the Federal Reserve or the Bank of England, don't seem to comprehend this.

Throwing punches

This is more than an argument. It is a fight. Every once in a while the players in this arena come to blows in public. In April 2014, the Governor of the Reserve Bank of India, Raghuram Rajan, clashed with the former Federal Reserve Chairman Ben Bernanke on these very issues. Rajan accused Bernanke of having unleashed 'Competitive Monetary Easing' which brings adverse consequences for economies everywhere. QE may have made sense in the immediate aftermath of the initial emergency, he said, but prolonged use of it created even bigger distortions than those that gave rise to the need for it in the first place. Furthermore, prolonged use triggered unintended spillover effects such as volatility, destabilising the entire world economy.

If Bernanke thought otherwise, Rajan suggested, then an 'independent assessor' should be appointed to determine 'whether some of these other policies have effects'. He was effectively saying, *Your free money is ending up in my country and other emerging markets! You are making a terrible mistake for which the whole world will pay and we need to bring in a referee.*

Bernanke replied, 'I think a lot of what you've been talking about today just reflects the fact that you are very sceptical about unconventional monetary policy.'* In other words, *You are a backward-thinking Luddite and pretty stupid too.*

The Federal Reserve would be inclined to dismiss Rajan's arguments and those of other emerging-market officials as rubbish and hokum. In any case, they'd say, such arguments are now irrelevant because we've commenced raising interest rates. The Fed's rate hike of 25 basis points in December 2015 pushed the whole inflation issue off the table.

The Chinese and other emerging markets, and those who take a harder line inside the central banking world, would say 'Not so fast!' A fractional rise in interest rates when starting from a record low base is not exactly a 'tightening' of policy. Interest rates will still be at historically low levels and liquidity will be at extremely high levels for a long time to come, so rate hikes cannot be said to 'tighten' economic conditions. All such hikes can do is 'normalise' the situation. Only when we get back to a 'break-even' level will a hike in interest rates achieve any tightening. We are currently so far from the break even that nobody even knows where it is any more.

In fact, the current Chairman of the Federal Reserve seems to take the view that the 2 per cent inflation target is an average. We have been far below average for so long that we should encourage inflation to rise above average for a while. Thus raising the interest rate from a super-low base allows the Fed to claim credit for reducing inflation risks while setting the stage for the inflation rate to continue rising.

---

* 'Global Monetary Policy: A View from Emerging Markets. A discussion with Raghuram Rajan, Governor of the Reserve Bank Of India', 10 April 2014. Uncorrected transcript of Audience Q&A; www.brookings.edu.

Negative interest rates

There is one other element to this story: negative interest rates. Many central banks have not only followed America's lead, they have gone much further in their effort to stoke inflation. Switzerland, Denmark and Sweden, for example, have all turned to 'negative interest rates'. Investors who want to leave their money sitting in deposit accounts or lend their money to the government (buy sovereign bonds) must pay for the privilege. The purpose of negative interest rates is, in part, to actively penalise savings. Negative interest rates are considered one of the very best ways to stimulate investment and thus encourage risk-taking, higher prices and therefore inflation. Here is a telling signal: in Japan the sales of safes is rising dramatically because people know that keeping cash in the bank actually costs something.* Given a choice, they would rather hold their cash at home in a safe. Of course governments want the public to spend or invest the cash. This is one reason why monetary policy officials are increasingly pushing for electronic cash. They want a world in which the government can simply dock a penalty from anyone who tries to save. In other words, if you have $100 in your bank account and interest rates are negative 2 per cent, you will wake up to find the government took $2 and you only have $98 left. This will keep happening as long as interest rates are negative, if we have a cashless society. Frankly, governments may find ways to implement this event if we don't go cashless. They may force the banks to dock the charge on their behalf.

Charles Goodhart and Andy Haldane, both highly respected members of the British monetary policy community, have recommended that Britain should become a cashless society. This would not be for the ease and convenience of the public. No, they want a cashless society so that it would become far easier for the

* Lucinda Shen, 'Japan's Negative Interest Rates are Driving Up Sales of Safes', *Fortune Magazine*, 23 February 2016.

government to take penalty payments direct from your bank account if you were foolish enough to leave it sitting there. (In another good example of a signal, Hasbro recently announced that new versions of their Monopoly game will no longer use cash.*)

The idea of negative interest rates seems hard to understand at first glance. So, to make it easier, remember that the whole idea of low interest rates is simple: the intention is to penalise savers and encourage speculators. If you refuse to take risks with your savings, the government will simply dock your bank account, effectively punishing you for refusing to put your money to work in the economy. More people will therefore put their money into property or hard assets or the stock market, thus pushing up property values and share prices.

Whichever way you look at it, the concerted effort to encourage a higher inflation rate remains a goal of public policy among the highly indebted industrialised countries. But many central bankers would argue that it is absolutely necessary because all other efforts to create inflation are failing. In fact, when the Japanese announced their intention to move to negative interest rates on 29 January 2016, the markets initially reacted with joy, causing substantial rallies in stock markets around the world. This soon turned to anxiety as people clocked that the situation must be pretty dire if a major country like Japan was prepared to move to negative interest rates. The secondary reaction has been a vicious downturn in financial markets globally. The many negative news stories and headlines have caused people to fear deflation again. The concern is that even negative interest rates won't work.

We've seen this movie before and know how it ends

As far as China, America's largest creditor, is concerned, it will work. It's already working. In fact it's working a bit too well. China takes the

---

* Andrew Liszewski, 'Monopoly Ultimate Banking Eliminates Cash with a Tiny ATM that Scans Property Cards by', toyland.gizmodo.com, 15 February 2016.

view that the United States has a long history of defaulting through inflation. They would say the US 'paid' for the immense debt acquired during the American Revolution with inflation. The young American Continental Congress financed that war by issuing debt called 'Continentals', and individual states followed suit. The money-printing, inflation and devaluation that ensued meant that Continentals soon declined in value, hence the phrase, 'not worth a Continental', which means 'utterly worthless'.

America 'paid' for the Civil War with inflation too. It defaulted on foreign investors when over-issuance of debt led to 9,000 per cent inflation in the Confederacy. This rendered the currency, known as 'Greenbacks', utterly worthless.

More recently, in the 1960s, the Vietnam War and the 'Great Society' programme, which encouraged the integration of African Americans into mainstream economic life, led to record debt. Once again this was 'paid for' through inflation, which began in 1965 and was not choked off until 1979.

Small wonder then that China and the emerging markets are convinced the US will do as it has done so often in the past and default on its current debts through inflation.

Goldfinger and silver bullets

The Federal Reserve and other central banks may think they can control how much inflation they produce, but this is hubris. And when inflation begins to spiral, not only do the debtors lose, but the citizens themselves feel the impact of a higher cost of living. Inflation is far from being a victimless crime.

I'm reminded of the moment the villain Goldfinger turns to the mythic hero James Bond and says, 'Mr Bond, they have a saying in Chicago: "Once is happenstance. Twice is coincidence. The third time it's enemy action."' The American Revolution, the Civil War, Vietnam and now we face this mess of debt that is too big to pay off. It's the fourth time. Therefore, it really is 'enemy action'.

For China, and many other emerging-market governments, a default by the United States and other industrialised economies would be on a scale that would go beyond an economic event and become a national security issue. The problem is not simply that these investors are going to be paid back in pieces of paper that are worthless. Will China and others potentially lose money on their massive holdings of US Treasury bonds? Quite possibly. Wen Jibao, China's former premier, is said to have regularly complained that the US was 'stealing money from China's pocket every day'. But this is the least of their worries. The bigger problem is that there are consequences when large economies face a massive debt burden and start stoking inflation.

Now, before anybody reaches for a fire poker and begins to attack the logic behind this view, let's first try to understand what the world looks like if you hold this view. As the Chinese saying goes, 'Wars are fought with silver bullets.' The opening salvo in this new war has been fired, in their view, by the export of inflation from the US and other industrialised economies to emerging markets.

What is inflation?

The Federal Reserve clearly explains, 'Inflation occurs when the prices of goods and services increase over time. Inflation cannot be measured by an increase in the cost of one product or service, or even several products or services. Rather, inflation is a general increase in the overall price level of the goods and services in the economy.' By that measure, overall, prices are still falling and thus warranting a discussion of more stimuli, more QE and slowing the pace at which QE is taken away. But, as we have seen, human beings feel the impact of some price rises more than they do others. The price of food causes real pain even if the price of, say, insurance or a mobile phone is falling. So there seems to be a widening gap between the actual rate of inflation and the fact that some prices are rising, especially prices that are important to local populations. The prices that matter most to emerging markets are not only food and energy, but specific foods and specific energy.

Ultimate proof

But wait! How can that be? Surely we are in the grip of deflation, or falling prices. At this point, we find ourselves at the centre of a heated debate: is the biggest problem in the world economy the problem of falling prices or rising prices?

The ultimate proof is the bond market. Economists generally believe that the expectation of inflation, of higher prices in the future, is expressed by the bond market. As fear of inflation rises, yields rise and people buy fewer bonds. When the yield falls, or interest rate on the bonds goes up, it makes it more expensive for governments to raise capital. In fact, since QE began, government bond yields have done nothing but go down to record lows (as every pensioner living on a fixed income knows all too well). Therefore, there is no inflation risk.

We might say it is really risky lending to the government of an emerging-market country and charge a higher rate of interest than the amount we would charge the US, because we think the US is unlikely to default on its debt. Then again, some might say that many emerging markets have better cash flows and are better bets than many industrialised countries given the debt burden.

Here is the twist, according to the naysayers. The largest buyers and owners of sovereign debt are governments themselves. The Japanese are the biggest buyers of their own debt. The US Federal Reserve and the Bank of England became the biggest buyers of their government's debt. It is hard, if not impossible, for a fund manager or an investor to take on the government. You can try to sell bonds, but you'll get hurt if the biggest player in the game – the government – is buying.

In the US, the government bought approximately three-quarters of all sovereign bonds issued in the market in 2013 and 2014. In Britain the amount is less, but still at least one third. If governments are buying their own bonds then everyone else must follow their lead and buy as well, because governments are pushing up the price.

This means that the bond market is prevented from fulfilling its traditional role as an early warning mechanism that alerts everyone to a rising risk of inflation. Governments have used QE to snap off the inflation antenna, as it were.

It's a kind of nonsense when central banks insist that bond markets are not signalling inflation when the very same central bank is ensuring, through its asset-buying activities, that it *cannot* signal inflation. The central banks have cut the line that connects the inflation perception with the bond market as sure as a person can cut the line that connects the brakes with the wheels.

Another way to support the bond market, in spite of a rising rate of inflation, would be to compel pension funds to own more bonds. In reality, this is already happening. Governments are increasingly requiring that pension funds and banks hold more 'safe' assets. This is often referred to as 'financial repression'. It means the government compels you to make investments you would otherwise never make. The government's definition of 'safe' is 'our sovereign bonds'. We can be clear what this signals. It's a way of pushing interest rates down but at the same time a way of pushing potential losses on to pensioners and savers. As we shall see, the emerging markets used to own this sovereign debt. But, in the wake of the financial crisis, they are now selling Western sovereign debt at a record rate – especially since these same sovereigns are telling the world they want the inflation rate to go up!

If somebody does not buy this debt, interest rates will go up and derail any chance of recovery and growth. So it is hardly surprising that governments are finding ways to force banks and pension funds to take on more of these bonds. The end result is that the bond markets appear to be signalling deflation, but there is good cause to question whether that particular signal is an accurate one, given the circumstances.

Let them eat iPads

This brings us to the now infamous exchange on 11 March 2011 between the President of the Federal Reserve Bank of New York,

William Dudley, and an audience in Queens, New York. Mr Dudley was at pains to stress that, on average, prices were falling. 'When was the last time, sir, that you went grocery shopping?' challenged a member of the audience. Having conceded that, OK, some prices may be rising, Mr Dudley urged them to look on the bright side: an Apple iPad now cost less. 'Yes, but I can't eat an iPad!' came a voice from the crowd.* Let's just say Mr Dudley lost his audience with this argument.

He also lost the emerging markets, who point out that people in America, and elsewhere in the industrialised world, are finding that the fall in the price of a mobile phone and a computer or even energy is no longer entirely offsetting the price hikes in other categories. So many things seem to be rising. As David Stockman points out, since 2000 the price of a movie ticket in the US is up by 95.20 per cent.† Eggs have risen by 106.20 per cent. College tuition is up by 68 per cent. A postage stamp costs 48.5 per cent more. Basic staples hit record high prices. The Congressional Budget Office estimates that generic drugs cost 11 per cent more in 2015 than in 2014. Specialty drugs will cost 18 per cent more. What do we make of the fact that in 2014 fuel prices fell by 2.7 per cent, but utilities rose by 5.8 per cent? Meanwhile, the cost of a roast rose by 19 per cent. A steak costs 15.6 per cent more. Pork chops cost 13.7 per cent more. It is estimated that it now takes 13.7 hours of minimum wage work to earn a Metrocard in New York City.

In London, where I live, house prices have risen 49.9 per cent since the crisis – there was a 19 per cent increase in 2014 alone. Average rents have hit a record high of £761 a month. The cost of energy bills, electricity, healthcare, education, insurance and shipping are all rising much faster than the official inflation rate. In the UK rail fares for

---

* Kristina Cooke, 'iPad price remark gets Fed's Dudley an earful', Reuters.com, 11 March 2011.

† James Quinn, 'Why GDP Is Not All That – The 14-Year Recession', Stockman's Contra Corner, 15 May 2014.

remote parts of the country rose by between 43 per cent and as much as 162 per cent in 2014 alone.*

Hotels and car rental firms are hitting people with all kinds of sneaky charges. There is now an 18 per cent fee for restocking a mini-bar in a hotel room, 'daily fees' to cover the gym and the pool – even if you don't use them. Car rental firms charge as much as $30 in 'administrative fees' for a toll that only costs $5.

The data may show that inflation is low, flat or only marginally rising, but this does not reflect the experience of the general public. Most people feel they're in the grip of some kind of inflation, or perhaps bi-flation would be a better term: everything that is mandatory in life is rising while some non-essential items are falling.†

A boycott?

The 2013 Jackson Hole conference became a crucible for this white-hot debate. As the conference theme, the Kansas City Federal Reserve chose 'Global Consequences of Monetary Policy'. Chairman Bernanke did not attend – no one could remember the last time a Chairman had not attended this event, which had been going for thirty-eight years. His absence was perceived as a kind of boycott, since it was fairly obvious to all that, as far as the Fed is concerned, US monetary policy has no consequences and causes no spillover, so why bother discussing it? Besides, even if spillovers are real, the responsibility lies with the emerging markets themselves.

It was deeply ironic that several emerging markets experienced financial emergencies at the time of the 2013 Jackson Hole meeting. The Governor of the Central Bank of Brazil, Alexandre Tombini, cancelled his trip to Jackson in order to implement an emergency currency intervention as the real, Brazil's currency, collapsed as a result

---

* Daniel Martin, 'Fury as rail fares in the north rise by up to 162 per cent from today', *Daily Mail*, 8 September 2014.

† I am grateful to Karl Massey for this bi-flation idea.

of the Federal Reserve's announcement that they would soon begin to reduce the level of QE by 'tapering' the purchase of assets (namely government debt and mortgages). When 'tapering' began in early 2014, it triggered a torrential outflow of capital from the emerging markets that continues as I write. The currencies of these countries began to collapse. In India the new central bank governor, Raghuram Rajan, stayed home to implement emergency capital controls as his currency collapsed to its lowest value since India's 1991 balance of payments crisis. The Turks had to raise interest rates by 425 basis points or 12 per cent in one single announcement to staunch the bloody haemorrhage that caused the Turkish lira to lose 14 per cent of its value in a matter of days when tapering commenced. The situation has only worsened since the Federal Reserve hiked interest rates in December 2015; the resulting capital outflow from emerging markets has been staggering.

Hard assets

Many emerging-market central bankers argue that when governments start printing money it is easy to appreciate that each piece of paper is going to be worth less at some point simply because there are more of them. It does not matter if the piece of paper is a bond or a banknote stamped with the words 'In God We Trust' or a picture of the Queen or any other symbol that imbues it with authority. When faced with a currency debasement, or any effort to make each piece of paper worth less, smart investors and good economic historians know they need to act.

The principal refuge against the depreciation and debasement of paper money is to be found in 'hard assets' such as property and productive farmland, along with potential substitutes for fiat money (money issued by the sovereign), like precious metals (gold, silver and platinum) or diamonds and other precious stones. 'Soft' commodities – food, energy and raw materials – are also seen as 'hard assets' because there is persistent demand for them, no matter how expensive they become.

Some investors start betting that rare and irreplaceable items – art and antiques, stamps and coins – will become more valuable during inflation. Since the QE began, the work of twentieth-century artists including Basquiat, Pollock, Modigliani, Rothko, Lichtenstein and Bacon have consistently broken records for the highest prices ever paid.

Then there are specialised investors who set out to corner the market in a particular item. Antique violins, for example. Only six hundred or so of Antonio Stradivarius's seventeenth-century violins survive today. They are in great demand in Asia, where classical music lessons are popular and people pay to rent them. The value of a Stradivarius has risen from $2 million to $6 million since QE began. High-quality antique pianos have attracted a lot of investor attention too. The share price of Steinway, the piano company whose strap line is 'Making the world's finest pianos for over 160 years', hit a record high on a bid made for the company in 2013.

The price of high-grade diamonds has soared into the stratosphere. One stone, the 'Pink Star', at nearly 60-carats, sold for a record $83 million in 2013, smashing the previous record of $46 million for a comparable gem.* The 'Blue Moon' sold in 2015 for the highest 'price per carat' ever recorded, at $48.4m for 12.03 carats.† It is an old story. For some, diamonds have proved a compelling store of value, given that a massive amount of wealth can be stored in a relatively small item that cannot set off a metal detector. Rough diamond prices have increased in value by 75 per cent since the crisis and very high-quality, rare diamonds continue to reach record prices.

---

* The buyer ended up defaulting on the purchase. Isaac Wolf, a diamond-cutting expert, announced on YouTube his intention to pay for the stone with the backing of outside investors. When he defaulted, Sotheby's was obliged to stump up $60 million for the seller under the terms of the agreement. So a record price was still paid, but such a default might be an important signal too.
† 'Flawless 12 Carat Blue Moon diamond sells for world record $48.4m in Geneva', Reuters, 11 November 2015.

Diamonds, gold, beef, pork, fish, wheat, soy, platinum, property, agricultural farmland and other such 'hard assets' have achieved record prices in many parts of the world since the financial crisis. Granted, these prices are hugely volatile, but, in general, they keep rising in spite of news that global demand is actually slowing.

Cows

Across the industrialised world, from Canada to the US to Australia, dairies are closing at a record rate because the cost of producing milk and cheese, just like the cost of raising cattle, is nearly commensurate with the price that can be charged. That means there is no profit margin. Furthermore, the size of cattle herds is falling worldwide, even in the US, where the size of the cattle herd reached its lowest level since 1953. The price of dairy items may have hit record highs in recent years in the US, but so has the cost of production. Profit margins have been crushed, which explains why there is little investment or lending.

This means milk and cheese prices start to rise. Bloomberg reported in July 2014 that butter prices had risen 83 per cent in a single year in the US. Milk prices hit record highs in 2014. That year, blocks of cheddar cheese sold for record highs at auctions in the US.

As I write, I see that a crime long consigned to cowboy movies has returned: cattle rustling. Cows are disappearing in the middle of the night in California and Texas, because it's now worthwhile to steal them. What thieves choose to steal is often another good signal.

Chained CPI

On a darker note, emerging-market officials can be heard muttering that the President must know all this and that's why, for example, he has declared his desire to use 'chained CPI'* when calculating payouts to government workers. Typically, chained CPI produces a lower final

---

* CPI stands for Consumer Price Index.

number than Core CPI, for example. 'Wonkbook', a blog published by the *Washington Post*, noted that:

> 'Chaining CPI' saves money by switching the government to a slower measure of inflation. That slower measure of inflation means Social Security slows down the cost-of-living increases built into its benefits. It also increases taxes, albeit by less than it cuts spending, by moving people into higher brackets more quickly.*

The AFL-CIO, one of America's biggest unions, said, 'It's unconscionable we're asking seniors, people with disabilities and veterans to be squeezed of every last penny.'†

Keep in mind that a higher inflation rate is useful to governments because the higher asset prices that tend to ensue permit taxation at higher valuations. Milton Friedman tried to draw attention to this when he wrote:

> In addition, inflation also increases the yield of the personal and corporate income tax by pushing individuals and corporations into higher income groups, generating artificial (paper) capital gains on which taxes must be paid, and rendering permitted depreciation allowances inadequate to replace capital, so taxing a return *of* capital to shareholders as if it were a return *on* capital.‡

Obviously, all that works to the advantage of a deeply indebted government.

---

* Ezra Klein and Evan Soltas, 'Wonkbook: The trick of chained-CPI', *Washington Post*, 8 April 2013.
† Damon Silvers, 'Bad Policy: President Obama's Budget Cuts Social Security and Medicare', aflcio.org, 4 June 2013.
‡ Milton Friedman, *Monetary Correction: A Proposal for Escalator Clauses to Reduce the Costs of Ending Inflation*, Institute of Economic Affairs, Occasional Paper, no. 41, 1974.

Early inflation signals in the West

There are other signals of gathering inflation pressures that are visible if you only open your eyes. For example, the size of many goods is shrinking while the price and packaging remains the same. This 'shrinkflation' is a signal.

Cadbury's announced in 2010 that it was taking two squares of chocolate off its Dairy Milk bar but keeping the price the same. In other words, the price per weight went up. The British public took note when Cadbury's announced in 2013 that it would no longer sell six Creme Eggs in a box. It would only provide five. On closer inspection it became clear that Cadbury's had degraded the quality of the chocolate, and made the shells thinner so as to use less of it. The public became enraged. Cadbury's responded by restoring the sixth egg but making each one and the package smaller while keeping the price the same. Again, the price per weight went up.

The comments of a blogger called Carlos reflect how widespread this 'shrinkflation' has become in the US:

> I noted with interest that the Walmart I shop at had cleared the shelves of 'Great Value' brand coffee in 39oz cans for about two weeks. Today the new can appeared, with the following differences: 1) Can is now 33.9oz, down from 39oz. Also conspicuously missing is the conversion of 2lb, 7oz therefore no comparison in pounds is easily made. 2) Price for this smaller can is up from $9.88 to $10.48, by my rustic math an approximate 20 per cent increase! 3) Contents of can are no longer 'Premium Columbian' Decaffeinated. Now labelled '100 per cent 2 Classic Decaf.'

Try checking your cereal and you'll probably find there's less cereal in the box and more air than there used to be. Compressed air has a weight, so technically there are still the same number of ounces inside the package – but fewer of those ounces are cereal. Or you might find that the fine print on the package shows the amount of cereal in the box has decreased, but the packaging has remained the same size – or in some cases increased. A box of Shredded Wheat in the United Kingdom, for example, was reduced from 525 grams to 470 grams in 2014, though the price remained the same.

The actual size of tins is shrinking too. Tuna used to come in a 6oz tin but is now often found in a 4oz tin. There are fewer fish in a tin of sardines. Coca-Cola is now sold in a 250ml can, which is far more slender and short than the old 330ml cans, though the new cans cost more per ounce.

Some say that stores are describing ten items as the 'new dozen'. In March 2013 a British newspaper, the *Daily Mail*, ran a story with the headline: 'Food packet racket: The sizes are shrinking . . . but the price stays the same'. The number of potato chips – or crisps as the British call them – in a bag of Walkers crisps had fallen to eleven. One irate crisp fan wrote in to complain that when he was a kid, packets of Walkers potato chips were always full, while now there is more compressed air.*

The point is, shrinking sizes signal that input costs are rising. It's a signal that companies are facing pressure on their margins and trying to compel the consumer to 'eat' the difference in order to protect their profitability. Yes, this can be cleverly and legitimately disguised as portion control and concern over your health. But then why ask you to pay more per ounce? If health concerns alone were driving this, the price per weight would remain the same.

Zigzagging is a signal

Another way that producers try to pass on higher prices is 'zigzagging'. This means they raise the price of something, say sun lotion, and then reduce it and raise it and then offer it at 'half price'. When you compare the original price and 'half price', it often turns out that the so-called 'half price' is actually the same or higher than the original. Prices are meant to

---

* Sean Poulter, 'Food packet racket: The sizes are shrinking . . . but the price stays the same', *Daily Mail*, 20 March 2013.

move in response to supply and demand. But fast-changing prices permit producers to raise prices through a kind of 'sleight of hand' that consumers can be easily duped by. Not all 'discounts' are discounts, it seems.*

Aperture inflation is a signal

Here is another signal that pressures on profit margins are rising and inflation is creeping up on us: the apertures on bottles of powder and tubes of gel are getting bigger. A friend noticed that she could no longer gently sprinkle cinnamon powder on to her porridge or talcum powder on to her baby without a deluge of dusty powder coming out. Somehow the size of the holes on the bottles was bigger and the contents less easy to control. This is no accident. Larger apertures mean faster use of a product. It's another way to charge you more for less stuff.

The companies that manufacture powder and gels know full well that anything which makes you use the product faster will result in more profits for them. I learned this from someone who had worked for one of the world's largest personal products firms.

It is worth a company's while making the top of the toothpaste tube wider. It is also worth putting less powder and gel in the bottle or tube and weighting or 'dimpling' a perfume bottle so that it feels full even when there isn't as much inside. These are sly means of making the consumer pay more for less. Of course, over time we learn to handle the new packaging properly, but we should understand the thought process behind these size changes.

Property pressures

Shrinkflation affects property too. Rents in the US are now so steep that many Americans are paying more than 50 per cent of their income in rent† while young low-paid workers are moving into 'micro

---

* Louise Eccles, 'Uncovered . . . great sun cream swindle: Prices inflated then slashed to give the illusion of discounts', *Daily Mail*, 14 July 2014.

† Jonathan Ernst, 'Many more Americans seen spending half their income on rent', Reuters, 21 September 2015.

apartments'. The US Census Bureau reports that the median size of apartments in new buildings fell in 2013 to 1,043 square feet. This is the smallest since 2002. What used to be called a cramped studio is now a 'micro-unit'. There is an industry that builds 'transformer apartments' where a 420-square-foot micro-unit can be adapted to different uses during the day thanks to the installation of sliding walls. New York City launched the 'My Micro NY' programme in 2013. It allows the construction of buildings with apartments that range from 250 to 370 square feet.* The Actors Fund HD has supported these developments because actors, generally speaking, don't earn a lot and, given the high cost of living in New York, it makes economic sense to fit more actors into smaller living spaces. No doubt this leads to many jokes about poor actors beginning to live like sardines in a can – except the sardines have more room because there are fewer to the can.

The situation in some cities is so severe that creative solutions are being explored. In San Francisco, where the proximity of Silicon Valley pushed rents sky-high, a tent in a garden rented at $965 a month.† When riots broke out in Portland in 2016, rents had risen 15 per cent in year.

Where is the truth?

The former mayor of my city is Boris Johnson. He has never been one to toe a party line. In 2015 he announced that, by his calculations, the cost of living in London is now 40 per cent higher than it was ten years ago. Wages during that time have risen by a couple of per cent at best. I feel the pain this has caused. I hear the pain as people who live in this city complain that their children can no longer count on a job, no matter how extensive their education. They cannot afford the rent even if they are lucky enough to find a job.

* John del Signore, 'First Look Inside NYC's Tiny New "Micro-Unit" Apartments, Creepy Old Man Ghost Included', Gothamist weblog, 22 January 2013.
† Alyssa Pereira, 'Mountain View man renting small tent near Google for $965 per month', CBS, 24 January 2015.

In late January 2016, the London *Evening Standard* published a Monopoly Board image 'to illustrate rocketing rents across the capital'.* British consumers have been shocked by jumps of 10 per cent and above in the cost of energy bills, water bills and transportation. People were appalled when the Prime Minister's spokesman suggested people should cope with the cold weather by wearing 'more jumpers'.† This is not going to win many votes. In the UK, the government has had to apply pressure in order to persuade industries such as airlines and energy providers to pass on the energy cost savings that have occurred since the price of oil collapsed in 2015. Sadly, in the main, firms are choosing to hang on to that margin in order to enhance the company's profits and share price. The same is true in the US: in 2014 the cost of electricity per kilowatt hour hit a record high, even adjusted for inflation. According to the Bureau of Labor Statistics, 2014 was the most expensive year ever for electricity in the US.

It has become increasingly obvious that the oil price collapse has simply masked a lot of otherwise upward price pressure, delaying our recognition of the underlying reality. I met with one of the longest-serving board members of the Federal Reserve who said to me, 'Something is wrong with our models: I live in Washington DC and I feel the rising cost of living, but our numbers don't show this.' That person, and others at the Fed and at the Bank of England have asked me to comment on the problem. But, if they don't know, how can we know?

I cannot and do not claim that the effort to keep rising price pressure from view is deliberate (even if it is convenient, given that inflation allows a government to invisibly default on their debts). I can confidently say that aggregate prices and the price I pay, or you pay, are not the same thing. I can confidently say that people will respond to the prices they pay and the pain that they feel.

---

* Lizzie Riviera, 'New version of Monopoly map for Generation Rent reveals the spiralling cost of being a London tenant', *Evening Standard*, 28 January 2016.
† Patrick Wintour, 'No.10 says people should consider wearing jumpers to keep fuel bills down', *Guardian*, 18 October 2013.

Quantitative easing and qualitative squeezing

Social unrest around the world is prompted by price signals, and the social unrest itself signals that there is a common thread weaving itself through the fabric of the world economy. The free money and low interest rates may have held up asset prices and institutions in the industrialised world, but the success of the policy is causing socially meaningful asset prices to rise as well. These are increasingly squeezing the poor – initially in emerging markets, but now even in the industrialised world.

As meaningful prices rise, the workers in emerging markets find themselves caught in a painful vice. On the one side is the debt and deflation burden. On the other side is the rising cost of living. The two pressures bear down on every person, every family, every company and every nation.

The pressure in emerging markets is becoming even worse now that the US Federal Reserve has commenced raising interest rates. Why? Put simply, the problem is that all these emerging markets borrowed heavily when the world was pumping money their

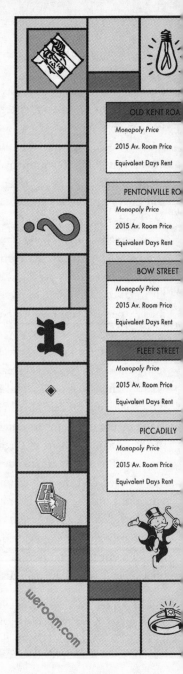

OLD KENT ROA
Monopoly Price
2015 Av. Room Price
Equivalent Days Rent

PENTONVILLE RO
Monopoly Price
2015 Av. Room Price
Equivalent Days Rent

BOW STREET
Monopoly Price
2015 Av. Room Price
Equivalent Days Rent

FLEET STREET
Monopoly Price
2015 Av. Room Price
Equivalent Days Rent

PICCADILLY
Monopoly Price
2015 Av. Room Price
Equivalent Days Rent

weroom.com

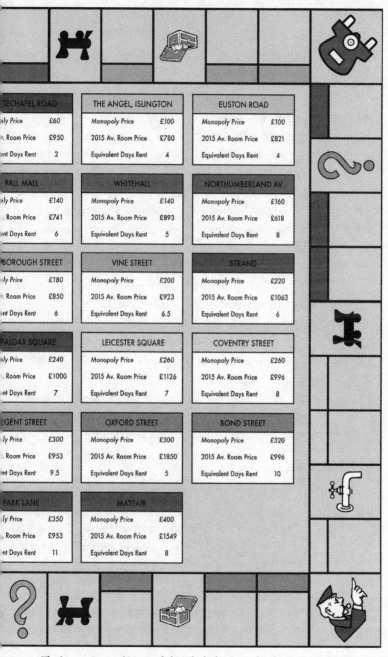

The 'generation rent' Monopoly board which appeared in the *Evening Standard* on 28 January 2016 (© Weroom).

way. They took the free/cheap money. Now that the US economy is stronger and more competitive and the Fed wants to raise interest rates, inevitably the value of emerging-market currencies will fall. This in turn will make the value of their debt expand. As a result, they now have even more debt with even less valuable currency.

But the thing that irks China and other emerging markets the most is something the industrialised nations may not yet have cottoned on to. As emerging-market workers continue to demand higher pay to meet the higher costs they face, economic activity will be driven elsewhere. Foxconn, the Chinese assembler of Apple, Kindle, PlayStation and Dell products, is the second largest employer in China; on 22 November 2013 they announced their intention to build a new $30-million production facility in Harrisburg, Pennsylvania. Apple itself has similar plans. In May 2013, Apple's CEO, Tim Cook, announced a new production facility in Texas.* In November 2013, Tim Cook announced a new manufacturing facility in Mesa, Arizona.† Markets will continue this process of moving productive assets to the most competitive locations until the West wins back jobs and competitiveness at the expense of the poor emerging markets.

The end result of the West's inflation policy could lend a new twist to Mr Dudley's 'Let them eat iPads' PR debacle: there could come a day when the price of an Apple iPad *may not* keep falling.

Our currency, but your problem

So, to reiterate, supporters of the Fed and those who believe the mathematical models are entirely correct would say, 'Even if it were true that the US and others are exporting inflation (which they would not accept), then emerging-market central bank governors could easily

* Jessica E. Lessin and James R. Hagerty, 'Apple CEO Says Mac Production Coming to US', *Wall Street Journal*, 6 December 2012.
† 'Governor Jan Brewer Welcomes Apple to Arizona: New Manufacturing Operation to Create 700-plus Quality Jobs', press release of the Office of the Governor, State of Arizona, 4 November 2013.

manage this by raising interest rates.' Emerging-market leaders would respond by saying, 'We get unemployment due to your bad mistakes and now you want us to inflict more pain on our impoverished population?'

America always reverts to its usual stance on the currency, which was best expressed in the standpoint taken by the last Secretary of the US Treasury to preside over the start of inflation – John Connally. This tall Texan senator became Treasury Secretary under President Nixon. In 1971 Connally faced a roomful of European finance ministry officials who accused the US of exporting inflation with the same conviction as emerging-market leaders have today. His reply was that the dollar 'is our currency, but your problem'.

And that, say the emerging markets, is *precisely* the problem.

7

The Perfect Circle

—

Buddhists say that suffering is what happens when you have an argument with reality. So, your perception of 'reality' matters. After an economic crisis there is bound to be nostalgia for the past. We knew how to make a living in the old economy, so we want to go back to the good old days. But an economic crisis, rather like an avalanche, does not just wipe away our savings and damage our confidence, it can permanently alter the landscape. Rather than wishing for past circumstances that cannot be recreated, we have to stop arguing with reality and instead survey the new landscape, assess the reality of the world economy as it stands today, and evaluate what it means for everyone in it. This means avoiding the human tendency that Winston Churchill so aptly described: 'Men occasionally stumble over the truth, but most of them pick themselves up and hurry off as if nothing ever happened.'

How money moved around

We used to have a kind of 'perfect circle' in the world economy. Put simply, the perfect circle was created when investment from the industrialised world went into the emerging markets, thus creating new capacity, new factories and a new supply of things. The emerging markets sold these things to the industrialised world, took the cash they earned from the sales and placed a good deal of it in the bond markets of the industrialised countries.

Why? In part because recycling that cash into the domestic economy would likely have created inflation. If governments deploy their reserves domestically, it tends to push up the price of everything, because more pieces of cash are chasing the same amount of stuff. For example, if a nation chooses to place their savings into US Treasury bonds, as most emerging markets did for many years, it lowered interest rates in the US but it did not affect the local economy. Whereas if they had spent the money at home, investing in, say, new ports and roads, it would have found its way into the money supply. More money spent locally means more money chasing the same goods and services, which means prices go up.

This is how and why China, for example, emerged as the largest buyer of US government bonds. This is also how China became the largest lender to the United States and to many other industrialised nations including the UK. China and others bought not only US government bonds but other US government debt instruments, especially Fannie Mae and Freddie Mac, the US home-loan companies. Foreigners especially loved Fannie Mae and Freddie Mac because they believed such debt was as good as Treasury bonds and effectively backed by the US government, but it paid a little more than Treasuries. More purchases of Fannie and Freddie debt lowered the mortgage rates for millions of Americans and others who could now buy more and bigger houses, which needed to be filled with more of the things that emerging-market workers were making for ever-cheaper prices. It also fuelled the housing boom that subsequently blew up. Other nations, like the UK, had no equivalent of Fannie Mae and Freddie Mac and so attracted less capital at that time.

Yes, there were some negative side-effects of the perfect circle. Jobs moved from the industrialised world to the emerging markets, from the US and the UK and Europe and Japan to China. This created friction and political pressure. The US began to demand that China revalue its currency so that Chinese goods would become more expensive and less competitive. A stronger yuan would also lessen the inflation pressures for China and reduce the flow of money into an increasingly overheated US government bond market. China complied to a degree but, in the main, the forces driving the perfect circle persisted until the financial crisis began in 2007.

This perfect circle gave rise to views that many hold today. It stands behind the idea that, 'All the jobs have moved to China, China is the future and America is finished.' This has been a popular view in recent years, taken as a given in the popular media, regularly dropped into dinner party conversations and the foundation for a good deal of investment. It's a signal when the wealthy hire Mandarin-speaking nannies for their children and people invest in Mandarin classes. And yet, if we look around, we see that manufacturing has been moving back to the US and the West very rapidly over the last few years. Hardly anyone is moving to China any more. In fact, the Chinese are leaving China and having to learn English and other languages in the process. The capital flight from China has been so severe that by early 2016 Bloomberg reported their reserves had fallen by more than $200 million in two months.* The Head of the Institute for International Finance, Charles Collyns, put it beautifully when he said, 'What is worrying is that there could be a broadening of the outflows. There has been a surge in "errors and emissions" and this is ominous. A lot of this is a capital outflow below board through inflated trade invoices and other forms of subterfuge, and some of it is ending up in the London property market.'† Yes, the capital flight is a problem for China. As the economist Ken Rogoff notes, 'If just one of every 20 Chinese citizens exercised this option, China's foreign-exchange reserves would be wiped out.'‡ It looks like more than 1 in 20 is trying. Where are they

---

* 'Holding Back China's Capital Flight "Dam" is Key', Bloomberg News, 7 February 2016.

† Ambrose Evans-Pritchard, 'Time running out for China on capital flight, warns bank chief', *Daily Telegraph*, 1 February 2016.

‡ Kenneth Rogoff, 'Can China avoid a huge, destabilising devaluation of the yuan?', MarketWatch, 2 February 2016.

placing their money? In the West. In London. In the Midwest and in the Midlands. In NYC. In San Francisco. In Vancouver. The list goes on.

Similarly, the perfect circle caused people to believe, at least in the industrialised world, that the greatest economic threat on the landscape was deflation. This is not surprising if you think that emerging markets will always drive inflation down because their workers will always do things for less money than anybody else. You cannot charge fifteen dollars an hour to make a toy if someone elsewhere will make the same toy for only one dollar an hour. The market will always buy the cheaper product and thus impose discipline on the cost of labour.

If you see the world this way, based on the perfect circle, then the risk is that we end up like Japan, with years of slow growth, falling prices for everything – from food to houses – and de-leveraging, which means banks and other financial institutions will be selling assets for which there are few buyers. To avoid such a crisis, it is argued, we must do everything possible, including relying on governments to hold up the prices of falling assets such as houses and bond markets and to spend and print money (quantitative easing).

Is the perfect circle still with us or is it broken? Is there inflation or deflation? Where does reality lie? Ben Bernanke and his successor Janet Yellen fear deflation. This is why the US central bank has been busy adopting unorthodox and historic measures to conjure forth a much-dreaded old nemesis called inflation. They see it as a strong 'animal spirit' that can pull us out of the ditch of deflation. If we should succeed in bringing this dangerous creature back to life, and it starts to threaten us again, then we will simply kill it. Central bankers believe that this is easy.

Deflation, on the other hand, is very difficult to address. There are virtually no academic theories or practical experiences of successfully reversing a deflation. Inflation is well documented; there have been many such episodes in history. The solution is simple: raise interest rates or at least stop printing new money.

Then there are those who say there's no such thing as just a little inflation. It's not like spilt milk. Stimulus, especially on this extraordinary scale, is like accelerant. You throw cash around (liquidity, it is often called) precisely because it behaves like gasoline. Its very purpose is to reignite the economy. Being flammable, we should not be surprised to find that it is not so easy to clean up. A little goes a long way and we have indulged in the largest monetary policy experiment in *history*, not just the largest in the history of the United States. Never before have so many large economies other than the US thrown record amounts of stimulus at the world economy in unorthodox ways, let alone done so simultaneously.

The man who had to kill inflation last time around was Paul Volcker, Chairman of the Federal Reserve under presidents Jimmy Carter and Ronald Reagan. In the 1980s he wrestled US inflation down and strangled it into unconsciousness principally by pushing interest rates up to 21 per cent. This landed him on the cover of *Time* magazine as the most hated man in America for administering the painful but necessary medicine at that time. He has since come to be revered as the Bruce Willis action hero of economics, the man who saved us from the ravages of inflation through sheer tough mindedness.

In May 2013 Volcker gave a stern, though subtle, warning. He told the Economic Club of New York: 'Credibility is an enormous asset. Once earned, it must not be frittered away by yielding to the notion that "a little inflation right now" is a good thing to release the animal spirits and to pep up investment.'* This would be pure hubris in light of historic experience. He says we should be wary of 'the implicit assumption behind that Siren call', which is 'that the inflation rate can be manipulated to reach the economic objectives – up today, maybe a little more tomorrow and then be pulled back on command.' To

---

* 'Central Banking at a Crossroad – Remarks by Paul Volcker Upon Receiving the Economic Club of New York Award for Leadership Excellence'; transcript at www. econclubny.com, 29 May 2013.

emphasise his point, he hammered home the message with this blunt statement: 'All experience amply demonstrates that inflation, when fairly and deliberately started, is hard to control and reverse.'

The big question is whether all this pertains to the future or whether it is an issue today. Volcker rightly hints that central bankers need to act, and indeed usually act, well before the signs and signals of inflation are apparent. The rough rule has always been that the central bank should start restraining the economy some eighteen months before the action needs to take effect. But, today the supporters of Mr Bernanke and his Federal Reserve believe that we should wait until the US economy reaches very low unemployment and achieves a certain momentum before changing course.

Around the same time that Janet Yellen was confirmed as the new Chairman of the US Federal Reserve Bank the senior staff of the institution announced the goalposts were being moved. In a paper presented to the International Monetary Fund,* the Fed gently implied that the acceptable inflation rate should no longer be 2.0 per cent but 2.5 per cent. Yellen has also implied, or the markets have inferred, that she believes inflation has been below average for so long that it should be permitted to rise above average for a while. In a Federal Reserve meeting in 1995 she was quoted as saying, 'when the goals conflict and it comes to calling for tough trade-offs, to me, a wise and humane policy is occasionally to let inflation rise even when inflation is running above target'.† In short, the Chairman is signalling that there will be no practical inflation target until all risk of deflation has firmly past. We are no longer aiming at 2 per cent. We are aiming at a number that is higher than that.

Of course, saying this out loud would terrify investors and the bond

---

* William B. English, J. David López-Salido and Robert J. Tetlow, 'The Federal Reserve's Framework For Monetary Policy – Recent Changes And New Questions', The International Monetary Fund's 14th Jacques Polak Annual Research Conference, 7–8 November 2013, transcript at www.imf.org.

† Mary Anastasia O'Grady , 'Janet Yellen's Record', *Wall Street Journal*, 6 August 2013.

market. In addition, any signs of growth require the Fed and other central banks to commence raising interest rates. By the end of 2015, it had become clear to the Fed the US growth was strong enough to undertake the first rate hike since the crisis.

Tightening versus normalising

The sleight of hand may be hard to understand. How can you aim at a higher inflation rate while raising interest rates? Well, keep in mind that interest rates are so very low that a few official increases in the rate still leaves you with near record low rates. We'll do it very slowly and warn the market well in advance. This gradual and hand-holding approach is called 'forward guidance'. But it has its detractors. In a September 2015 interview I conducted with Allan Meltzer, the official historian of the Federal Reserve, he said the fact that the Fed signalled a rate hike but dithered about doing it for fear of the market's reaction was 'shameful'.*

The real question is 'what level is an "emergency" rate and what level is normal?' We are so far away from 'normal' that nobody knows where it is any more. A central bank can raise rates and honestly argue that they are not 'tightening', they are merely 'normalising'. Of course, as long as rates are below normal, the risk of inflation remains to the upside. The free money can keep doing its work in an effort to stoke inflation and the central banks still looks like it's being responsible. But driving with the brake and the gas pedal at the same time doesn't usually work very well.

Drugs

The reluctance to act is not too surprising given that the market tends to respond violently to any suggestion that the level of liquidity might be reduced at some future date. Some liken quantitative easing to free

* Pippa Malmgren interview with Allan Meltzer Part One, Real Vision TV, 4 September 2015.

drugs. It's akin to giving morphine to a recovering heroin addict; the addict becomes agitated at the thought that his fix might be reduced. In 2013, for example, President of the Richmond Federal Reserve Jeffrey Lacker, who repeatedly dissented against continued QE, pointed out that the central bank had not even begun to talk about reducing QE. He said, 'The Committee will be reducing (liquidity) only the pace at which it is adding accommodation. In other words, the Federal Reserve is not only leaving the punch bowl in place, we're continuing to spike the punch, though at a decreasing rate over the next year.'*

This analogy derives from something once said by the longest-serving Federal Reserve Chairman ever, William McChesney Martin. He memorably said, 'The Fed's job is to take away the punchbowl before the party ends.' The central banks around the world are, in the main, still adding more free drugs to the punchbowl rather than taking them away.

The Fed attempted to reduce the flow of drugs to the market by a minuscule 25 basis points on 16 December 2015. All hell started to break loose. The list of events that illustrate this is long, but let's just say, for me, it was a signal when the security guard at the offices of my literary agent, WME in New York, asked me what I thought about the economy and whether things would get really bad. I assumed that he'd seen that I was an economist on his screen. But, no. He was asking everyone who signed in to enter the building.

He would not have been aware of all the following events, but he surely felt their reverberations.

Chinese capital flight became so severe the level of Chinese reserves fell to the bottom end of the IMF's 'safe band'. This shocked the markets. The country that everyone had expected to emerge as a 'reserve

---

* Jeffrey M. Lacker, 'Economic Outlook, June 2013', Judicial Conference of the Fourth Circuit, White Sulphur Springs, West Virginia, 28 June 2013. Transcript available at www.richmondfed.org.

currency' was now in such severe difficulty that only a substantial devaluation could fix it. In another contributing factor, the Kingdom of Saudi Arabia announced that they needed to issue sovereign bonds for the first time ever. They also announced their intention to sell off some of its best oil assets, thus proving they were broke from a low oil price and needed cash in a hurry. In other words, the 'rich' emerging markets that had been funding the overspending in the industrialised world were no longer in a position to keep doing this. Investors began to reconsider their implicit assumption that somehow governments would always bail out private sector losses.

European bank shares started collapsing. The value of shares in Credit Suisse fell by 40 per cent in the first two months of 2016. The CEO of Deutsche Bank and the German Finance Minister were compelled to issue statements saying that the banks' finances were 'rock solid' because the shares were falling like a rock. Rumours began to spread that the ECB would 'monetise the debt' or, to put it plainly, print money (thus breaking the social contract in Germany as I explained earlier).

The volatility readings on stock markets spiked to panic levels. Fears began to escalate that the losses from a low oil price would cause massive losses. This was exacerbated by a statement made by the CEO of BP at Davos. He said it was 'not impossible' for the price of oil to fall to $10. Suddenly, everyone realised that the loans to energy businesses might have to be written off. News began to surface that the natural gas frackers in the US could not sell their equipment. In fact, they had to pay people to come take it away. Therefore, the value of all the collateral in the energy industry had obviously collapsed to nothing.

The Japanese central bank, the Bank of Japan, suddenly and unexpectedly announced on 29 January 2016 that they would be moving to negative interest rates. They were the first G7 country to cross the line into negative interest. Bloomberg estimated that as much as 30 per cent of all sovereign bonds were in negative territory, but this was the first time the official central bank rate would drop into the negative zone.* Sweden, which had already slipped into a negative official interest rate, then announced it would go further and cut rates to -0.50 per cent. That raised the spectre that a little bit negative might not be enough. Everyone knew that the Fed had asked all the American banks to prepare for the possibility of negative interest rates, while insisting that this was only to test what would happen if the market pushed yields into negative territory. Yellen made it clear that this in no way presupposed the Fed would cause the official interest rate to fall below zero. Having said that, she then spooked the markets by hinting that the Fed might not have the legal authority to actually do this, even if they wanted to.†

In short, the volatility and uncertainty that was now perceptible to the security guard in New York City had been brought about by the simple question: are policymakers omnipotent or impotent? If they are omnipotent, a bailout will postpone the day of reckoning. If they are impotent the day of reckoning is going to be sooner rather than later. Given that policymakers and politicians want to remain in power, the betting is between those that think they'll come up with some new way to inject cash into the system (which would be inflationary) and those who think the last bullet has been fired (which would be deflationary).

All this merely confirmed for the deflation camp that there was no risk of inflation whatsoever. In contrast, it confirmed for the inflation camp that the inflation rate around the world would be even more likely to go up.

The fall of the Berlin Wall

Monetary policy serves a political function in our society, not just a technical one. Its role is to preserve the integrity of the currency on

---

* Tyler Durden, '$7 trillion in bonds now have negative yields', www.zerohedge.com, 9 February 2016.
† Jeff Cox, 'Fed's Janet Yellen: Not sure we can do a negative rate; rate cut unlikely', CNBC, 10 February 2016.

behalf of the citizens. Otherwise, politicians would keep on printing money to fund all their favourite and vote-winning pet projects. It also serves to balance the interests of the savers against those of the speculators. Monetary policy is considered to be a domestic phenomenon, not an international one. Citizens make their own choices about who to elect and which policies to pursue, and need to live by the consequences. No one in America or Britain ought to be held to account for Zimbabwe's decision to print so much money that hyperinflation was provoked and its currency became worthless. Imagine if the Federal Reserve or the Bank of England or the ECB said, 'We are raising interest rates because inflation in Zimbabwe is increasing.' The public would be incredulous and outraged.

And yet, common sense tells us that we live in a global economy, which functions as a single global market. Monetary policy brings international consequences. One of the global consequences over the last quarter of a century was the so-called 'Great Moderation of inflation'. It came about when Paul Volcker, when he was the Fed chairman, set the stage for lowering inflation in 1979. He raised interest rates and choked off rampant inflation in the US. But the thing that really killed inflation globally was the fall of the Berlin Wall in 1989. The weight of that event crushed inflation ten years after Volcker began to slay the beast.

Most people who are responsible for the world economy today are under the age of fifty, which means they hardly remember the Soviet Union and the Cold War. Most of them were born after 1961, when the Communist Bloc erected a vast wall that cut Berlin and indeed Germany into two disconnected parts. The wall was not only physical, it marked the psychological and ideological border between Capitalism and Communism. It was known as the 'Iron Curtain', separating East from West Germany. At the time the Communist leadership described its purpose as a means of protecting the public from anti-socialists such as Fascists and Capitalists who sought to undermine the 'will of the people' in their effort to build a socialist state. In fact it served to prevent emigration, defection and other means by which East Germans might try to escape the new social contract that Communism imposed on them. By 1989 it had become clear that the Communist approach could not fulfil the promises of its social contract. After years of economic hardship, having to line up for limited or rationed goods and food, the citizens within the Communist world began to revolt. It became 'the will of the people' to take hammers and sledges to the Berlin Wall on the night of 9 November 1989.

This event, in retrospect, marked the end of Communism not merely for East Germany, but for every other Communist state around the world. The Soviet Union morphed into Russia, or more precisely into Russia and other members of the Commonwealth of Independent States (CIS), of which Russia emerged as an equal member but with far greater influence. Soviet dependencies including Poland, Estonia, Georgia and Ukraine morphed into independent nations.

India's story

The demise of the Soviet Union forced India to move away from a state-controlled economy. India had sold the Soviets many goods, from cotton to food; when the Soviet Union ceased to exist, it defaulted on the debt it owed India. This left India with a massive financial crisis.

I went to India in 1992 to interview the then Finance Minister, Dr Manmohan Singh, who would go on to become the Prime Minister in his later years. I remember the look on his face. He was clearly caught between a sense of resignation and the flickering flames of hope. As always in a crisis, Nemesis and Hubris were both in play. I could feel the tussle in his very being and in his nation. 'We have no money,' he told me. He explained that India would have to open the economy to market forces because in the absence of cash, there were no other options.* As Margaret Thatcher once said, 'The problem with

* Pippa Malmgren, 'Singh's song: an exclusive interview with Manmohan Singh,

Socialism is that you eventually run out of other people's money.'

At the heart of it, that was the economic force that caused the Soviet Union to fail. Tax revenues were insufficient to keep up with the state's expenditure. Even in Latin America, after the Berlin Wall fell the pro-market right came to power more forcefully than ever before. With the demise of the Soviet Union, defenders of Socialism and Communism were silenced. Francis Fukuyama wrote that it was 'The End of History'. Capitalism had won the argument. The economic consequences of this were formidable.

I first heard Alan Greenspan explain the importance of the Berlin Wall at a meeting in the White House long before he wrote about it in his book, *The Age of Turbulence* (2007). He said that following the end of partition between East and West Germany, billions of new workers from China, Bangladesh, India, Africa and Latin America suddenly entered the world economy. This pushed down wages and prices all over the world. Prices could not rise because some new emerging-market worker was always around the corner, prepared to make whatever you needed for less. This brought about a 'great moderation' of inflationary forces, as economists now call it. It created a world where growth mainly went up and inflation mainly went down.

Today, the majority of people who are running businesses and managing assets grew up in a post-Berlin Wall world. We think growth mainly goes up and inflation mainly falls. We think this is normal, when in fact it was created by an exceptional set of historic and probably temporary circumstances that no longer exist.

Most emerging-market workers are now clamouring for wage hikes that render them and their nations uncompetitive. The jig is up.* They are not prepared to work for next to nothing any more. Meanwhile, the terrible pressure brought to bear by the financial crisis has given

---

Finance Minister of India', *International Economy*, 1 May 1993.

* I am grateful to my friend Elizabeth Dempsey, who summarised my long-winded explanation with this pithy sentence.

rise to great innovation in the industrialised world. People have reorganised their personal and professional business models and their activities in ways that render the industrialised world competitive with the emerging markets once again.

The perfect circle was temporary

It is hard for us to recognise that the last twenty-five years were not 'normal'. It was a very privileged period of history during which we were blessed with an especially favourable set of circumstances. This exceptional situation is highly unlikely to be repeated.

Some will take issue with this, arguing that there have been many bumps in the road during this period. No doubt this is true. The landscape of the last twenty-five years is rife with economic catastrophes. There was the US Savings and Loan Crisis of the 1980s and 1990s, which was kicked off when Volcker raised interest rates and more than seven hundred Saving and Loan companies went bust. There was the Scandinavian banking crisis of the early 1990s and the Mexican Peso crisis in 1994. Few remember the former but the latter caused a firestorm when Mexico required a bailout. The Asian financial crisis ensued in 1997, which culminated in a default by Russia in 1998. Argentina defaulted in 1999. Financial institutions including the Connecticut hedge fund, Long-Term Capital Management, got caught up in the price movements caused by these events and began to threaten the stability of the world economy. The recent financial crisis began in September 2007 but became visible to the public when Lehman Brothers defaulted in 2008.

From such a list one might expect that people would assume the world economy is a volatile and dangerous place that forces one to prepare for the worst at all times. But no, this seems not to be the case. Perhaps because each of these episodes of economic distress and crisis were met with policy responses (government bailouts), each trauma passed and all were followed by a return to happy growing conditions. People seem to think about the last twenty-five years as good times with brief interruptions instead of as bad times with brief moments of growth.

It may be that for someone who is now fifty years old the economic circumstances have been volatile and unpredictable, but there is no doubt that many people seem to believe growth is usually dependable and prices generally fall. They believe that they can plan for the future based on their experience of the past.

The end of Communism

People still want to believe that the stock market and the bond market will deliver their retirement intact. They are still quick to borrow tomorrow's income and spend it now, as is evidenced by the record personal and sovereign debt levels in the world today.

It is an irony that in the financial markets we are required (by law) to repeatedly explain that 'past returns are no guarantee of future performance' and yet many people assume their past experience will continue to define their future. Therefore, it is worth describing the economic forces that many now believe to be 'normal'. These things may seem blindingly obvious to well-informed economists and historians but, in twenty years of speaking to audiences around the world, I have found that it makes sense to explain the 'bleedin' obvious', as the Brits call it, because it usually turns out that not everybody understands what happened in the past or what it means for them. Let's face it, libraries are filled with books with competing views about what happened in history, so let's spend a moment reviewing some of what happened and why, so that at least a few more of us can be ready to join the spirited punch-up about why the argument is right or wrong, relevant or irrelevant.

The fall of the Berlin Wall triggered forces that contributed to the perfect circle. These forces moderated inflation and enhanced growth: the end of centralised state control and the end of the Cold War. It is hard for young people today to imagine, and hard for older people to remember, a 'command economy' world in which

Communist leaders decided how much steel would be made and how much milk would be available in Moscow or St Petersburg. It is almost impossible to imagine or even remember that the Communist style of asset allocation put all the power in the hands of bureaucrats who chose where things would be made, who would be allowed to buy them, and what the price would be for everything, from a pencil to a steel beam to a potato. Under Communism, the state decided who got what. It determined what subjects you would be allowed to study, which job you would be allocated, and how much bread you could buy.

The peace dividend

The demise of the Soviet Union and the end of Communism brought another significant deflationary economic force: the peace dividend. Again, it is hard for many people today to remember the zeitgeist of the Cold War period. As a child growing up in Washington DC in the 1960s, I had to participate in the nuclear alarm that took place once a month or so at Chevy Chase Elementary School. This was not like a fire alarm when we children had to exit the building as quickly as possible. With a nuclear alarm, the trick was to dive under your desk as quickly as possible. I still don't know why anyone thought being under a desk at the moment of a ground-zero nuclear event would have made the slightest bit of difference, but it certainly instilled a deep fear of a nuclear exchange in me and my generation. For a long time I aspired to be a nuclear weapons negotiator – an ambition that lasted until I realised, at about age seventeen, that you actually need to be a nuclear physicist to do that job. Anyway, SALT* came along under Jimmy Carter and there was no need for nuclear weapons negotiators any more, which was when I became interested in the world economy

---

* Strategic Arms Limitations Talks, which commenced in 1969 and culminated in an agreement in 1979, in SALT II. SALT led to START – the Strategic Arms Limitations Treaties – which put the issue to bed until recently.

instead. So I know exactly why my generation was more than prepared to spend on nuclear deterrence – Mutual Assured Destruction as it came to be known – and more than delighted when such spending was no longer required.

From the end of the Second World War, the United States and the Soviet Union were locked in a contest for power and deeply entrenched in an arms race. Put simply, a good deal of GDP was diverted into the prevention of and preparation for war. The spending that was channelled towards unproductive resources such as nuclear arsenals, border guards at Checkpoint Charlie on the Berlin Wall and wars against Communism in various parts of the world such as Vietnam, was now free to be redeployed into more productive use in the real economy.

In America, President Johnson and President Kennedy had tried to have both 'guns and butter'. Kennedy paid what was required to beat the Russians in the arms race, but he wanted funds to lift millions of Americans out of poverty, including African Americans who had hitherto been denied access to the fruits of citizenship. After Kennedy's untimely death, his successor President Lyndon B. Johnson pursued the 'Great Society' programme which cemented the road for African Americans to achieve civil rights and begin integrating into American society.

While it was obviously necessary, it proved an expensive approach to deploy defence money on wars while at the same time funding expanding social safety nets such as Medicare and Medicaid and welfare payments for the poor. In fact it was so expensive that it was decided to simply print and then spend money. This was when America's debt problem began to compound. The Federal Reserve estimates that the great inflation of that era, the one that Paul Volcker had to finally kill in 1979, actually started in 1965. Once it was dead, around the time that Ronald Reagan came to power, policymakers everywhere remained respectful of inflation.

When the Berlin Wall finally came down, the memory of inflation began to fade. As the great moderation of inflation and the peace dividend together progressed, it created a belief that growth mainly went up and inflation mainly went down while defence issues mainly receded and social benefits could mainly be expanded. This gave people everywhere a belief that the system would not only supply everyone's needs, it would serve every individual and every nation's interest to support this.

The baby boom

Demographics played a large part in creating the foundation for the perfect circle. In the West, the appearance of the 'baby boomers' (the children of the sudden population increase that occurred at the end of the Second World War in the US and Europe) meant that the young far outnumbered those that retired ahead of them. This meant that the amount of money coming into government, from taxes, social security and other state programme payments, was larger than the amount that needed to be paid out. Demographics from the late 1940s onward created the illusion that the amount of cash coming into government coffers would continue rising and therefore governments could continue increasing the pay-out of benefits to their citizens. In addition, it created the belief that growth could be relied upon and that one could spend tomorrow's tax receipts today. The perfect circle caused an important signal to become more pronounced – debts rose as people became more and more confident that they could safely stop saving for tomorrow. Indeed they could even spend money they expected to earn in future. Usually it makes sense to save for tomorrow in preparation for uncertainty. Instead, belief in the perfect circle gave rise to a benign landscape that provided a clear vision of the future. This 'clarity' caused governments and individuals alike to assume that they could indulge in leverage (borrowing) and borrow from the future to pay for the present.

We built our national and personal budgets, our corporate and family balance sheets and our personal lives on this false and ephemeral foundation: the perfect circle.

The financial crisis of 2007/2008

At first, it was assumed the losses were in the banks alone and that they could be saved from certain demise through government bailouts of various sorts – low interest rates, cash, government support for certain assets such as mortgage-backed securities and European sovereign debt and semi-nationalisation, among other things. But these efforts proved insufficient. In the early years of the 2007/8 financial crisis a series of decisions were taken that effectively moved the losses from the banking system to the taxpayers.

This in turn exposed the fact that governments themselves were broke. When the economy stalled, tax receipts collapsed (it did not help that the baby boomer era was coming to an end), and it became clear that governments had been using the same flawed business model – agreeing to pay out to citizens today based on tomorrow's expected income. Suddenly, all the promises the government made to pay out to citizens could not be kept because there simply wasn't enough money coming into government coffers.

Luck vs skill

As always, when times are good, hubris returns to centre stage. It is a signal when we confuse good luck with skill. Such a signal is amplified when we begin to presume that any particular state of affairs is permanent. Everyone did this in the perfect circle world. The West and the East, America and China, the industrialised world and the emerging markets all expressed their hubris in different ways, but hubris nonetheless pushed the perfect circle on to a mutually destructive trajectory. Instead of binding economies together, it began to pull them apart.

The American expression of hubris took many forms. In the West, especially the US, people bought houses with no thought as to the budget that would be required to heat them or maintain them or to continue to own them if they happened to lose their job. Banks lent more and more to less and less qualified borrowers, assuming that all would benefit from the rising tide of national growth and income.

The Chinese did exactly the same thing, but in a different way. Rural workers left their homes to find a job in the big cities without knowing where they would live or how much they would be paid. Employers provided housing, food and necessities for living, but working and living conditions tended to be horrible, and wages were often paid as much as several years in arrears. These itinerant and migrant workers did not spend tomorrow's income today but they did work in the hope that today's income would be paid tomorrow. In other words, they took a big risk too.

Their bosses, the factory owners, displayed the same behaviour as Americans. Instead of borrowing, mortgaging and leaning on credit, this group built their businesses on the assumption that the value of the business was in the market share, the future growth, and not in today's cash flow. In fact, Chinese businesses often had negative cash flows. Contrary to the popular image that China was a land of unlimited profits, private equity returns in China were broadly negative from 2000–2007, the supposed boom years. Like the Internet bubble, and frankly all other speculative bubbles, people began to believe that performance would come in the future even though profits had not yet appeared. China's economy has now softened and confidence in it has weakened.

More risk for less return

Luckily, Western investors continued to provide never-ending Foreign Direct Investment by buying shares in Chinese businesses, mainly through the Hong Kong and Shanghai stock exchanges or buying equity in Chinese firms. This new investment filled the gap between the losses and the lack of profits. The focus of Chinese business owners was not on today's cash flow but on tomorrow's exit strategy – the IPO, the sale to a larger firm, the rising share price. In fact, this preoccupation with the future led to an ever-greater willingness to cut costs and skimp on quality. Chinese businesses seemed to become less concerned with quality and more concerned with quantity. This is exactly what happened in the Western financial markets. People and businesses became so preoccupied with the idea of an IPO or the sale of a company to a competitor, a rising share price and other ways of exiting the business and taking cash off the table, that they cared less and less about the quality of transactions and more and more about the quantity of transactions.

The financial community was sufficiently confident that the future would be reliably bright that it started to take increasingly risky bets. In short, investors took ever-greater risks. But the returns on the risk fell as more money chased these returns. When everybody is buying Bangladeshi stocks because China's assets already seem expensive, it makes Bangladeshi shares and bonds rally and become more valuable and seemingly less risky. When the yield on risky emerging-market debt, such as African bonds, is nearly the same as the yield on a US or European company, then the market is no longer distinguishing between one risk asset and another. That is what happened as a result of QE and the carry trade. Everything went up in value. But this also meant the yields on the debt, even on African and Bangladeshi debt went down.

The only way to improve the performance on that debt was to leverage up the investment, which meant borrowing to make financial bets. In the same way that Americans put less and less money down to buy a house that was larger and more expensive than they ever imagined it possible to own, financial speculators did the same. They put less and less money down to take bigger and bigger financial bets on deals, on equities, on bonds, on foreign exchange markets, on commodities, on everything that would enable them to get 'positions' and trades that were larger than the actual cash they happened to have on hand. This became a signal that the markets were no longer afraid of risk.

Quantity vs quality

In another signal, we saw that Western asset management firms and financial institutions stopped concentrating on stewardship of assets and instead focused on increasing the volume of assets under management. They became less concerned about profitability and more focused on size. More assets under management and more transactions meant more fees and a higher share price or a higher future value of the business. In other words, just as Chinese firms became less concerned with profitability and more concerned with market share, so asset management firms became less concerned with quality of management and focused on the quantity they managed.

In yet another signal, business models began to change as management came to believe that the flow of cash and a rising GDP were permanent and sustainable. In a world where capital was endlessly available, it seemed smart to outsource production to the least expensive locations around the world, no matter the distance. Manufacturing shifted the location of production to the lowest-cost places on the planet. We failed to build in redundancy because we assumed that there would always be enough capital to move goods from such faraway places back home. We moved a good deal of the world's production to places that were neither geographically nor socially stable on the grounds that there was always going to be enough capital to throw at fixing any problem.

In a final example of a signal, it could be seen that many state and local governments, as well as national governments, had begun to build their budgets on the assumption that tomorrow's cash flows would be stronger and higher than today's. They continued to promise increased benefits to citizens and considered it a victory when the value of the benefits (like food stamps or pension benefits) went up less than the expected income. Then, unfortunately, the expected income dried up when the financial crisis occurred. Business transactions fell. Business income and the tax take from business was reduced. More and more people became unemployed, thus reducing their ability to pay personal income tax. As tax receipts fell, the state ran out of the cash required to pay out the promised benefits and services to its citizens and was therefore compelled to borrow.

Steve Malanga explains how this happened in his article, 'How States Hid their Budget Deficits'.* In 2001 the state of New Jersey made a decision 'to borrow $2.8 billion and stick it in its own pension funds in lieu of making contributions from tax revenues. To make the gambit seem reasonable, Trenton, a city in New Jersey, projected unrealistic annual investment returns – between 8 per cent and 12 per cent per year – on the borrowed money.' Malanga explains that by 2004 the state's budget fell short by $2 billion, so it borrowed more money, which, as Malanga so neatly puts it, 'is like borrowing on your credit card to pay off your mortgage'. If you borrow to fund a pension, you can technically report, as Malanga reminds us, 'We have X amount of dollars in that pension, so everything is fine, and we don't need to make any further contributions'. But the fact is that the funds have to be paid back with interest and the state will have to pay in whatever is required to cover the cost of the benefits that will need to be paid out to citizens.

All these events signalled that the perfect circle was under pressure.

Reversing the perfect circle

In retrospect, it is obvious that the perfect circle caused us to collectively bet on a linear projection of the future. When we lost the perfect circle, it bankrupted the entire system – banks, governments, enterprises and individuals, thus requiring a government response.

The perfect circle began to reverse to such an extent that investors no longer cared about the return *on* their assets. They just wanted the return *of* their assets. People no longer cared about buying a bigger

* Steve Malanga, 'How States Hide Their Budget Deficits', *Wall Street Journal*, 23 August 2010.

house, they wanted the one they owned to retain some vestige of equity (many didn't and some found themselves with negative equity instead). Bankers no longer cared about their deferred stocks and options, they wanted to simply keep their jobs. Governments no longer focused on the promises that would be made in the future, they instead started to tax their citizens more aggressively and to reduce their commitments to the citizens in order to protect the government from bankruptcy. Many governments became effectively bankrupt anyway. At a minimum, they wholly depend on the kindness of foreigners who bought their debt in order to allow the gap between saving and spending to be financed. Many prefer not to refer to such a situation as 'bankrupt' but as 'dependent'.

What now?

Cracked open by the crushing weight of the debt and exposed by the financial crisis, we find the perfect circle now reveals the most important problems of our generation: the conflict between the productive and the unproductive, between the rich and the poor, between the state and the market, between the industrialised world and the emerging markets, between deflation and inflation. The question still hangs: who is right? Mr Bernanke or Mr Volcker?

The question has been passed on to the next generation as well. Esther George, the President of the Kansas City Federal Reserve, had dissented at just about every single FOMC* meeting since she was appointed in 2011 until hikes began in 2016. She has demonstrated a spirited defence of Volcker's legacy. Janet Yellen has taken up Bernanke's ideological role but with an even greater willingness to take risks in favour of growth over inflation. Who is right? Esther George or Janet Yellen? Are there signals we should pay attention to, which will help us in this debate? My view is yes. It is an important signal when members of the establishment start to turn away from the

* Federal Open Market Committee.

consensus view. When Paul Volcker began to warn about inflation in the aftermath of QE, it was easy for Federal Reserve staff to dismiss him as an 'old man' who was no longer 'in the game' or worthy of our attention. I wonder if we should not be listening to the Bruce Willis character in this movie, even if he has aged a bit.

In May 2014 Martin Feldstein, another high priest of the economics profession in the US, wrote an editorial* in which he warned: 'Inflation is rising in the United States and could become a serious problem sooner than the Federal Reserve and many others now recognise.' In October 2015, I interviewed John Taylor, who is perhaps one of the most revered high priests of the economics profession. He invented the so-called 'Taylor Rule' which helps us know when a central bank should be raising or lowering interest rates. His view was that we were not that far away from 2 per cent; and he implied that things would become very tricky indeed once inflation's stealthy undercurrent of pressure began to become visible in the models.†

By early March 2016, it had begun to show. The Vice Chairman of the Federal Reserve, Stanley Fischer, said, 'We may well be seeing the first stirrings of an increase in the inflation rate – something that we'd like to happen.'‡ By January, most banks forecast that inflation would rise across the US and Europe.

But there is no need to rely on the words of experts. Instead, I ask that you open your eyes and ask yourself what you see. You can and should observe for yourself the signals that the world economy is sending. Then you can make your own decisions and choose what to do about such signals based on your own risk-taking capability and skill.

---

* Martin Feldstein, 'Warning: Inflation is running above 2 per cent: research suggests that unemployment may not restrain wages. If so, real trouble may be ahead', *Wall Street Journal*, 9 June 2014.

† Interview on Real Vision TV with John Taylor, released 23 October 2015.

‡ Shawn Donnan, 'Fed's Fischer sees "first stirrings" of rising inflation', *Financial Times*, 7 March 2016.

8

Can the Circle Be Unbroken?

—

China's Ministry of Foreign Affairs would not confirm it until days after the event, but on 11 January 2007, the Second Artillery Battalion of the People's Liberation Army launched an exo-atmospheric kinetic kill vehicle. The ground-launched object hurtled into space, bearing down on its target: China's own ageing weather satellite, which was orbiting some 535 miles above the Earth. The satellite disintegrated on impact. Afterwards, the Russians and Americans complained about the dangerous debris China had left floating in space that now threatened other travelling satellites. Most of the international press focused on the technological feat: China had just become only the third country, after the US and Russia, to aim at a target in space and actually hit it.

For many in the US defence and foreign policy establishment, the event was perceived as the 'Sputnik' of our time. Sputnik was the first Earth satellite and its launch from Kazakhstan in 1957 signalled that the Soviet Union, America's then rival, was ahead in the space race. The Chinese Anti-Satellite Test (ASAT) event signalled that the US defence stance could possibly be rendered useless by new technology.* After all, if you destroy America's satellites you can potentially render the US Navy dead in the water. Few can pilot an aircraft carrier with a compass

---

* Some US capabilities can navigate and operate without satellite guidance, but, in the main, all modern military equipment is pretty heavily dependent on electronics one way or another.

or a sextant. Without satellite guidance, nothing happens: you can't navigate and weapons systems won't work. This has special meaning, given China's fears about America's endlessly increasing naval presence around its shores in the East and South China Seas and the Pacific. It is interesting that the Chinese military consistently train without access to electricity, Wi-Fi, satellites and other high-tech electronic support systems. This is done elsewhere, but perhaps not so consistently. It is a telling signal that in late 2015 the United States Navy announced its intention to reintroduce celestial navigation training.*

To informed observers, the event signalled something new: China's growing fear of its own economic vulnerabilities. It signalled China's realisation that the logistics of delivering food, energy and raw materials at the right price to its population could easily be constrained by the US and its allies. From a Chinese perspective, the landscape is clear: It cannot feed itself. China's vastly depleted water tables and polluted water supply are a threat to the population. It has limited arable land. The country lacks sufficient copper, iron ore, gas, oil and other raw materials to keep the population housed, working and building. China is extremely dependent on bringing these things home from elsewhere.

As a result, China has become increasingly uneasy about the formidable presence of the US, which could potentially disrupt China's freedom to fulfil its basic needs. A glance across the South China Sea and the Pacific reveals the ever-increasing presence of the US Navy and those of America's allies. The US has steadily added to its forward capabilities in the Pacific since the Second World War, but during the last decade the acceleration has been rapid.

As in China, American policies are often revealed slowly in a series of speeches and public comments. Secretary of State Clinton revealed that the US intended to redeploy military assets from the Middle East

---

* The US Navy stopped teaching celestial navigation in 1998, three years after GPS was introduced. In 2011 celestial navigation was reintroduced for ship navigators. The Naval Academy Class of 2017 will be tested on their ability to use a sextant.

to the Pacific and around China. In an article in *Foreign Policy* magazine she wrote: 'One of the most important tasks of American statecraft over the next decade will therefore be to lock in a substantially increased investment – diplomatic, economic, strategic, and otherwise – in the Asia-Pacific region.'*

Shortly afterwards, in November 2011, President Obama gave a speech in Australia in which he said, 'As President, I have, therefore, made a deliberate and strategic decision . . . the United States has been, and always will be, a Pacific nation.'†

Friction

The problem is that China does not necessarily view the US and its allies as friends. They may be 'frenemies'.‡ In fact, China fears that the purpose of placing more aircraft carriers and weapons systems closer to its shores is to make threats with them or actually use them. The US Department of Defense Strategic Guidance issued in January 2012 made clear that the burden was on China to prove it was not a threat: ' . . . the growth of China's military power must be accompanied by greater clarity of its strategic intentions in order to avoid causing friction in the region' it stated.

There *is* friction, however. It comes from the simple fact that the US and China have many competing interests. China wants security of supply and the US wants to remain close enough to China to disrupt that security if it feels it needs to. China wants to secure control over critical food and energy channels in the region, which the US and its allies contend do not belong to China.

Philosophically, the US and China are at odds. In the post-War period

---

* Hillary Rodham Clinton, 'America's Pacific Century: The future of politics will be decided in Asia, not Afghanistan or Iraq, and the United States will be right at the centre of the action', *Foreign Policy* magazine, 11 October 2011.
† 'Remarks by President Obama to the Australian Parliament', from the White House Office of the Press Secretary, 17 November 2011.
‡ A 'frenemy' is a friend who is also an enemy.

the US has championed a world in which the distribution of wealth and power in the global economy is determined by market mechanisms. The promise was that the US dollar-based system of global trade and the institutions which support that, like the IMF and the World Bank, would serve everyone's best interests.

China's leadership finds it ironic and disturbing to hear the US claim to support markets as the best means of managing economies, growth and power. The debt burden that is owed to China and others is proving so onerous that America is prepared to default on its debt through inflation, and to control market prices through QE and asset purchases. A series of questions arise: Who has more state control over the economy now, the US or China? Which is a more 'autarchic' economy? Who is a bigger supporter of the global system of rules that regulate commerce and the world economy, China or the US?* It can be argued that the US now has even more state intervention than China and Russia. As a result, the US has forfeited the ability to claim that China and others should be more 'market-oriented' and emerging-market leaders are less inclined to answer America's questions about the way they use state power.

America's decision to bail out the financial system has consequences for China, as far as the Chinese are concerned, whether the US authorities concede this or not. So, not only is America trying hard to default on its debt to China, which means the Chinese public must ultimately incur a loss, but inflationary policies are driving up the price of food and energy (locally), which jeopardises China's political stability.

In this sense, one can understand why some Chinese policymakers view US economic and defence policy as 'enemy action'. There are

* Professor Michael Ignatieff, 'The post-Ukraine world order', 50th Annual Lecture at the Ditchley Foundation, 12 July 2014. He describes the differences between capitalism and capitalist autarchies, which are authoritarian in nature and involve a high degree of state control and intervention. Ignatieff calls them 'capitalist in economics and nationalist in ideology'.

more than enough Chinese policymakers who understand that US economic policy is usually made without any consideration for its impact abroad. This subject can be argued over endlessly, and is. But it is impossible to argue about the purpose and presence of weapons that are within striking distance. Their presence requires a response, especially given the way technology has rendered weapons ever faster and more accurate.

China has responded to these pressures in various ways: some military, some policy, some involving the creation of new institutions.

Military response

China's military response has been to focus on achieving dominance in space (the realm of satellites, GPS and communications); to focus on the high seas, where above-water capabilities (ships to satellites) can be challenged by China's focus on below-water capabilities (submarines to cables); and to gain strength in cyberspace, on which all military capabilities depend.

Meanwhile, most US and Western policymakers emphasise the commonality of US and Chinese interests, arguing that the two countries have far more in common than in opposition. But there is a substantial group, especially in the US defence community, that see China's position as fundamentally hostile. There are those who fear that China will become more aggressive, given its increasingly precarious economic position, its rapidly ageing and predominantly male population, and the fact that the export-led business model is now sufficiently damaged that the Chinese public may not remain as quiet as in the past.

Shipping lanes

The only practical way that China can bring raw materials home is on ships travelling across the high seas and through the major shipping lanes that feed into its limited coastline. Some 90 per cent of global commerce moves on ships, which is one of China's weak spots. It is dependent on shipping, lacking the infrastructure to rely on railways or airports, even though it fully intends to build some four hundred and fifty new airports over the next decade and roughly six times the railway infrastructure of Switzerland every single year over the same period (within China). Even so, air cargo and railways are expensive and logistically difficult. In the end, ships and shipping lanes are essential to China's survival and stability.

Anyone surveying the Chinese coastline can plainly see the overwhelming presence of the US Navy and the naval vessels of America's regional allies. Since the Second World War, the US Navy has maintained a formidable physical presence, from Guam and Diego Garcia to Honolulu and Okinawa to Darwin in Australia. This presence has escalated in recent years. President Obama announced the 'pivot strategy' in 2012, in which military assets would be diverted from the Middle East and Afghanistan to be redeployed in the Pacific. The strategy involved 'strengthening bilateral security alliances; deepening our working relationships with emerging powers, including with China; engaging with regional multilateral institutions; expanding trade and investment; forging a broad-based military presence; and advancing democracy and human rights.'*

All this is seen as potentially, or actually, hostile to China. It marks the continuation of an evermore aggressive US stance in the region. The US has deployed its Navy in the Pacific under every US President since Japan bombed Pearl Harbor. After the Second World War the US chose Qingdao in China, then Subic Bay in the Philippines, and later Asoka in Japan as the home of the Seventh Fleet, America's permanent forward-deployed naval capability in the region. All other carrier strike groups are based in the US. The purpose of having a forward presence in Asia has always been described by America as a means of protecting the region from anything that would disrupt the free movement of traffic along the many shipping lanes. In a statement to Congress by the

* Hillary Clinton, 'America's Pacific Century', *Foreign Policy*, 11 October 2011.

Chief of Naval Operations in March 2012, Admiral Jonathan Greenert stated the position clearly: 'Operating globally at the front line of our nation's efforts in war and peace, our Fleet protects the interconnected systems of trade, information, and security that underpin our own economy and those of our friends and allies.'*

Who's protecting who?

The US and China are well aware that both countries share this common interest. But, while the Americans may say they are there to protect the shipping lanes for the benefit of all, including China, the suspicion is that the US is trying to protect the shipping lanes *from* China rather than *for* China. Similarly, China may say it shares this common interest, but the US and its regional allies fear that China seeks to challenge America's presence on the high seas, space and cyberspace as a means of serving China's interests and not those of the broader community.

When the perfect circle was in play, common interests between the US and China were constantly reinforced by mutual benefits. Sales from China led to cash flows that the Chinese redeployed into the US bond market, thus lowering interest rates for Americans and further enabling American consumption of Chinese-made goods. In the perfect circle scenario, China had easy access to raw materials because it had the cash to pay whatever the market demanded. The US had no incentive to disrupt China's shipping because it served the interests of the US for the goods to arrive. The noise and pushback around job losses in the US was never enough to truly jeopardise the perfect circle, given the benefits that came to both countries.

Now that the perfect circle is broken, conflicting interests are far more apparent. China feels much more vulnerable to any possible disruption of the shipping lanes, especially in a post-Arab Spring world

* Chief of Naval Operations Admiral Jonathan Greenert's Statement before Congress on FY2013 Department of Navy Posture, March 2012.

where it is clear that higher food and energy prices are a catalyst for social unrest. The fact that the US and its allies dominate space, cyberspace and the ocean waves creates the impression that the US could disrupt or interdict that traffic. This is a crucial practical problem when a lack of food stocks renders China highly sensitive to any supply disruption.

It also happens that natural gas finds in the South China Sea have ignited a new issue in the region. Modern technology now allows the profitable harvesting of the energy, food and mineral assets in the seabed underneath the seemingly insignificant rocks that form the territories that many Asian nations claim as their own. Oil and gas are more valuable than ever to both energy-starved China and its energy-starved neighbours. The oil price may have fallen but access to a local supply is still valuable.

Further inflaming these disputes is the rise of nationalism and populism in the region. As Asian workers begin to realise they might not get rich before they get old, they start to question why the wealth in their societies is being distributed to someone else and not to them. Citizens are asking, 'Why are the rich so rich and the poor so poor?' 'Why is corruption permitted?' 'Why should the current leaders be in charge if they are not serving my best interests?' These political pressures necessarily require the leadership in these countries to demonstrate that they can protect the national interest from a strategic security point of view. They have to show they can avoid food and energy-supply problems that would hurt the population. After all, the leadership have made a social contract with the Chinese public. They have promised to double per capita income by 2020.

Fish

Let us not forget the fact that some 10 per cent of the world's fish supply comes from these seas. The price of fish hit an all-time-record high in 2013, and is doing so again in 2015/2016, so China and its neighbours are justifiably concerned about who controls that critical source of protein.* Arguments over fish are therefore intensifying, especially as the price of other proteins such as beef, pork, poultry and even soy keep rising. There have been an increasing number of confrontations between Chinese fishing and military vessels and those of other nations.

All 'fishing vessels' in China now come under the auspices of the People's Liberation Army.† Today these vessels are often painted in People's Liberation Army Navy grey and, though they might at first glance appear to be equipped with fishing gear, they also carry intelligence-gathering equipment. This is how and why a Chinese vessel managed to take a US underwater drone from the Bowditch, a US civilian 'research' vessel, soon after President Trump was elected. These fishing vessels are called 'phantoms' or 'little blue men'. One US Naval War College Professor has said, 'While Russia's little green men in Crimea are widely known, insufficient attention has been paid to China's little blue men in the South China Sea.'‡ Meanwhile, the US uses oceanographic 'research vessels' in a very similar way.

Cabbage strategy

Fishing and fish are not the only drivers of conflict; physical presence is another. *The New York Times* described China's 'Cabbage Strategy' in the South China Sea by quoting one of China's most senior generals:

> 'Since [the standoff], we have begun to take measures to seal and control the areas around the Huangyan Island,' Major General Zhang Zhaozhong, of China's People's Liberation Army, said in a television interview in May, using the Chinese term for

* Emiko Terazono, 'Global fish prices leap to an all-time high', *Financial Times*, 18 June 2013.
† Lucio Blanco Pitlo III, 'Fish the real hazard in South China Seas', *Asia Times*, 25 July 2013; and 'Fish: the overlooked destabiliser in the South China Sea', *Stratfor*, 12 February 2016.
‡ Christopher P. Cavas, 'China's "Little Blue Men" Take Navy's Place in Disputes', *DefenseNews*, 2 November 2015.

Scarborough. (That there are three different names for the same set of uninhabitable rocks tells you much of what you need to know about the region.) He described a 'cabbage strategy' which entails surrounding a contested area with so many boats – fishermen, fishing administration ships, marine surveillance ships, navy warships – that 'the island is thus wrapped layer by layer like a cabbage'.*

Recently China has become more willing to claim parts of the South and Near China Seas as its own, even though sovereignty of these areas is disputed by many governments. In a recent example, it seems at least 100 naval vessels from the People's Liberation Army Navy (PLAN) surrounded a gas rig that Vietnam claims is an illegal effort by China to claim their territory. Vietnamese and Chinese vessels faced off with water cannons and rammed each other. Ultimately China removed the drilling rig, but not before fully demonstrating how powerful the cabbage strategy is.

In a more concerning development, Chinese workers and Chinese-owned factories in Ho Chi Minh City in Vietnam have been attacked as a result of local anger about this dispute. Some 3,000 Chinese were evacuated from Vietnam after several Chinese citizens were killed in the violent confrontations there in May 2014.

The South and East China Sea are now at the heart of a great contest. Countries are fighting for valuable assets: control of shipping lanes and food and energy supplies. These assets are worth fighting for. They represent real cash flows. On the surface of things, the US and America's allies are aligned with China by many common interests. Below the surface, and in the air, however, the US and China are increasingly in conflict over these strategic assets.

* Jeff Himmelman, 'A Game of Shark and Minnow', *New York Times Magazine*, 27 October 2013.

Flipping the bird

The signals are compelling. On 29 October 2015, the US and China announced a Memorandum of Understanding in which the military pilots on both sides agreed to refrain from making obscene hand gestures at each other.* Now, imagine for a moment how close a spy plane and a fighter jet need to be for the pilots to be able to see the other guy is 'flipping the bird' at him.

Chinese fighter jets and US spy planes have been coming into increasingly close contact in recent years. On 18 August 2014 it seems a US P-8 Spy plane, America's most sophisticated reconnaissance aircraft, flew near Hainan Island. There were Chinese military exercises at the time, but Hainan is widely suspected to be a major submarine base and the home of China's new 'carrier-killer' submarines (the YJ-12) which can, in theory, attack a US carrier from beyond the limits of an American Aegis combat system. Its weapons are apparently faster than America's anti-missile systems. It was reported that a Chinese SU-27 fighter jet was sent up to push the US spy plane away. This led to news headlines along the lines: 'Did China Just Re-Enact the famous "Birdie" Scene from *Top Gun* With US Plane?'† Word is that the two planes not only came within twenty feet of each other but the Chinese pilot 'barrel-rolled' his fighter jet over the much larger and more lumbering spy plane, thus revealing that the weapons on the fighter jet's underbelly were fully loaded and armed.

Since then there have been more 'flipping' events. All these maritime craft and aircraft keep getting closer as both sides jockey for physical control of territory. Perhaps the most recent events give a flavour of the situation.

* Christopher Bodeen, 'China, US stress good manners in avoiding aerial incidents', *Military Times*, 26 October 2015.
† Elias Groll, 'Did China Just Re-Enact the famous "Birdie" Scene from *Top Gun* with US plane?' *Foreign Policy* magazine, 22 August 2014.

USS *Lassen* and USS *Curtis Wilbur*

On 30 January 2016 the USS *Curtis Wilbur* was sent in to patrol Triton Island, part of the disputed Paracel Island chain*. It wasn't the first incursion by an American destroyer navigating within China's perceived territorial limit. In October 2015 USS *Lassen* did the same thing in the Spratly Archipelago, deliberately testing the twelve-mile limit of Subi Reef in the vicinity of Fiery Cross. Here, on what was once a series of uninhabited rocks jutting out of the Pacific, China has constructed a large, seemingly military-grade runway. Chinese commercial airliners began making landings there in early January 2016, prompting many protests from the US and the countries that claim all or part of the Spratly Islands, including Vietnam and the Philippines.

The Chinese response was very clear: if the US passed beyond the 12-mile limit, the Chinese would open fire. President Obama ordered USS *Curtis Wilbur* to proceed anyway. Nothing happened, although the fear of a confrontation was so great that the Australians volunteered to use one of their naval vessels. Both the US and China told Australia to, putting it plainly, 'shut up.'

Confrontations between American and Chinese naval vessels date back to about 2006. On 26 October that year a Chinese Song-class submarine managed to surface inside the carrier battle group of the USS *Kittyhawk*, America's only forward deployed aircraft carrier in the region at that time. This meant the sub had arrived, completely undetected, well within missile distance, less than 9 kilometres off the carrier itself. It seems it was not spotted by any of the 5,500 personnel on board until an American pilot, who happened to be practising training runs, looked down from his plane and apparently realised the large object in the water below him was not a whale. Such 'pop-up' surprises are now standard.

---

* David Larter, 'South China Sea standoff: "Both sides need to step back"', *Navy Times*, 1 February 2016.

USS *Kittyhawk*

In 2008, China denied the *Kittyhawk* the right to berth in Hong Kong, thus depriving many personnel and their families of the opportunity to participate in the annual Thanksgiving weekend that had been a fixture of the Pacific Fleet's timetable for many years. Shortly after being turned away from Hong Kong without reason (China later said it was a 'misunderstanding'), *Kittyhawk* was confronted by a Chinese destroyer, the *Shenzen*, and Song-class submarines. USS *Kittyhawk* went to full battle stations. The stand-off lasted a day. The US responded by stating that China would not be permitted to control American access in the Straits of Taiwan.

USS *Cowpens* and the *Liaoning*

Tension between the two sides escalated on 5 December 2013, when one of the vessels forming an escort for China's sole aircraft carrier, the *Liaoning*, almost collided with the USS *Cowpens*, a Ticonderoga-class guided missile cruiser. According to news reports, the Chinese view was that *Cowpens* was tailing and harassing the *Liaoning* within Chinese-controlled waters. The American view was that *Cowpens* was in international waters when a People's Liberation Army Navy Amphibious Dock Ship veered directly into the path of the *Cowpens* and stopped, leaving less than 500 metres between the two ships. USS *Cowpens* was forced to take evasive action to avoid a collision. Whoever started it, it is clear that both sides were taunting one another. Both battle groups were well within the other's 'inner defence layer'.*

With so much at stake and with both sides provoking one another, these tensions and disagreements increasingly raise the spectre of conflicts that would take effort to defuse. In early 2014, Herbert

* David Alexander, 'US, Chinese warships narrowly avoid collision in South China Sea', NBCNews.com, 13 December 2013.

'Hawk' Carlisle, Executive Director of America's Pacific Air Combat Operations Staff, said,

> If you look at some of the things that have been going on in the East China Sea, both militaries [US and China] have been conducting themselves very professionally. But the potential for something, a mistake to occur or miscalculation or misunderstanding to occur, is out there. There is significantly more activity from both nations around the disputed territorial claims, and that to me is a risk.*

Territorial claims

The territorial disagreements centre on long-standing disputes over the many islands that lie within the 2.25 million square-kilometre radius of the South China Sea.†

The greatest and most obvious source of strain in Asia is the island of Taiwan, which is technically in the East China Sea and not part of the disputed island issue, except that China claims that Taiwan *is* China. The US President is somewhat obliged by law to defend Taiwan under the terms of the Taiwan Relations Act of 1979, so, while there is a lot of noise in the arguments over Taiwan's status, China has used economic policy to calm the issues. China permits Taiwan's business community to become enriched by China's economy. China wins more support in Taiwan by deepening economic ties and encouraging wealth creation among the Taiwanese than by threatening military confrontation.

While Taiwan is the primary reason for America's forward presence in the region, with the nuclear threat posed by North Korea providing further justification, much of the tension between China and the US is driven by disputes over the many chains of islands that riddle the South China Sea. For the most part these chains consist of craggy barren

* 'US general criticises Japan, Philippines' anti-China Views', *Sydney Morning Herald*, 10 February 2014.

† Beina Xu, 'South China Sea Tensions', *Council on Foreign Relations* news brief, 11 January 2013.

rocks that cannot be inhabited, yet their ownership is forcefully, and militarily, contested by China and most of its neighbours.

Follow the dotted lines

In 1948 a privately published map of the South China Sea showed eleven dashes forming a line to indicate which islands were owned by China and which were governed by Taiwan. Naturally, the two governments still argue about where those dashes ought to be drawn. The complicating factor is that other governments in the region also claim ownership of those islands. In 2009 China submitted a modified nine-dash-line map to the UN. The line skirted close to the shores of every other nation in the region. Protests were filed by Brunei; the Philippines; Vietnam and Malaysia, which filed jointly; and even Indonesia, though it had no specific territorial claims. China responded by telling two senior US officials, the then US National Security Council Director Jeffrey Bader and Deputy Secretary of State James Steinberg, that this part of the world was now a 'core interest' for China.* The phrase 'core interest' has been used by China to indicate when an issue is non-negotiable. Initially it was applied to Taiwan. In 2008 it was applied for the first time to Tibet and to Xinjiang.† By 2010 it was being applied to the East and South China Seas.‡ In other words, China has tried to declare the territorial disputes of the South and East China Seas 'off limits' to outside parties.

There is lively debate about President Xi Jinping's supposed use of the term 'core interest' with regard to the Senkaku Islands, which Japan claims as their own.§ General Martin Dempsey, then chairman of the

---

* Edward Wong, 'China Hedges Over Whether South China Sea Is a "Core Interest' Worth War', *New York Times*, 30 March 2011.

† 'China's Evolving Core Interests', *New York Times 'Sunday Review'*, 11 May 2013.

‡ Joseph Kahn, 'Turnaround by China: Centre Stage at Talks on North Korea', *New York Times*, 28 August 2003.

§ 'In Summit with Obama, Xi Declares Senkakus China's "Core Interest"', *Asahi Shimbun*, Asia & Japan Watch, 12 June 2013.

Joint Chiefs of Staff, was told in private meetings in Beijing in April 2013 that the term 'core interest' was now applied to the Senkaku. This was quickly followed by a statement by Hua Chunying, a Chinese Foreign Ministry spokesman, who said, 'The Diaoyudao Islands [China's name for the Senkaku] are about sovereignty and territorial integrity. Of course it's China's core interest.'*

ADIZ

At the Third Party Plenum in November 2013, China announced the creation of a National Security Council. Its aim: to consolidate existing foreign policy and the defence structures underlying it, and to counter 'hostile anti-China forces from abroad.'† On 23 November the nation's first action after establishing this new Security Council structure was to announce the creation of an 'East China Sea Air Defence Identification Zone' (ADIZ).‡

The map of this zone reveals that ADIZ covers some of Japan and extends all the way to Taiwan's airspace, as well as taking in some of South Korea's airspace. The Chunxiao/Shirakaba gas field falls right in the middle of the zone.§

The US launched an aggressive response to the creation of ADIZ, immediately sending two B52 bombers over the Senkaku/Daioyu islands, unannounced. According to a report in *The Economist*, China declared that 'all aircraft intending to enter the zone had to file flight plans with the Chinese authorities, maintain radio communications and follow the instructions of Chinese controllers – or face "defensive emergency measures". The B52s did not. Suddenly a stand-off loomed

---

* 'China officially labels Senkakus a "core interest"', *Japan Times*, 27 April 2013.

† Willy Lam, 'Xi's Power Grab Dwarfs Market Reforms', *Asia Times*, 21 November 2013.

‡ Justin McDonnell, 'Five Questions on China's Air Defence Identification Zone', *The Diplomat*, 29 November 2013.

§ 'China, Japan conflict on Chunxiao/ Shirakaba gas field', *Turkish Weekly*, 25 July 2013.

between the world's superpower and Asia's emerging great power.'*

The South Koreans and the Japanese also began flying into the new zone without first obtaining China's permission. South Korea announced the expansion of its own ADIZ in early December 2013 by 66,000 square kilometres. It now covers some of the territory that China claims.

In December 2013, the territorial disputes once again escalated when US Secretary of State John Kerry said:

> Today, I raised our deep concerns about China's announcement of an East China Sea Air Defence Identification Zone. I told the Foreign Secretary that the United States does not recognise that zone and does not accept it. The zone should not be implemented, and China should refrain from taking similar unilateral actions elsewhere in the region, and particularly over the South China Sea.†

Clearly the US believes that the extension of the ADIZ by China remains possible, if not likely.

Tomahawks from Ohio

From a Chinese perspective, it was the US who escalated first. At a meeting of the Association of Southeast Asian Nations (ASEAN) in Hanoi in 2010, Secretary of State Hillary Clinton directly challenged China in front of this regional security group, which China views as a congregation of adversaries. Clinton said, 'The United States, like every nation, has a national interest in freedom of navigation, open access to Asia's maritime commons, and respect for international law in the South China Sea.'‡

---

* 'Regional turbulence: China escalates a dispute, angering Japan and unnerving its neighbours'. *The Economist*, 28 November 2013.

† John Kerry, Secretary of State Department of Foreign Affairs, 'Remarks with Philippine Foreign Secretary Albert del Rosario', Manila, Philippines, 17 December 2013.

‡ Hillary Rodham Clinton, Secretary of State, National Convention Centre, Hanoi, Vietnam, 23 July 2010.

This was the diplomatic equivalent of firing a machine gun into the air.* If you missed it, the relevant words were 'has a national interest': a declaration that the US and China have directly opposing interests in the region.† Clinton significantly elevated the high seas issue by calling for 'a resolution of the sovereignty dispute over the Spratly Islands and maritime borders in the South China Sea'. She said this was a 'leading diplomatic priority' and 'pivotal to regional security'.‡

Words were accompanied by actions, as reported by *Time* magazine. At the time of the speech,§

> A new class of US super weapon suddenly surfaced nearby (China), an Ohio-class submarine, which for decades carried nuclear missiles targeted against the Soviet Union, and then later Russia. This one was different: for nearly three years, the US Navy has been dispatching modified 'boomers' [submarines] to who knows where (they do travel underwater, after all). Four of the 18 ballistic-missile subs no longer carry nuclear-tipped Trident missiles. Instead, they hold up to 154 Tomahawk cruise missiles each, capable of hitting anything within 1,000 miles with non-nuclear warheads.

The US also arranged for a number of aircraft carriers to arrive in the region that very same day. The USS *Michigan* appeared in South Korea and the USS *Florida* arrived in Diego Garcia, an island the Pentagon calls 'Camp Justice' and the 'Footprint of Freedom', which is central to America's capabilities across Eurasia. Diego Garcia has been the main base for staging bombing runs on Afghanistan and Iraq.

As *Time* put it: 'In all, the Chinese military awoke to find as many

---

* See 'Secretary Clinton delivers remarks at ASEAN Ministerial' on YouTube.

† Daniel Ten Kate and Nicole Gaouette, 'Clinton Signals US Role in China Territorial Disputes After Asean Talks', Bloomberg.com, 23 July 2010.

‡ Kathrin Hille, 'China blasts Clinton's Maritime Adventure', *Financial Times*, 30 July 2010.

§ Mark Thompson, 'US Missiles Deployed Near China Send a Message', *Time*, 8 July 2010.

as 462 new Tomahawks deployed by the US in its neighbourhood.' These are subsonic, long-range, low-altitude 'smart weapon' cruise missiles that are the most feared in modern warfare. No wonder it was rumoured that President Hu immediately summoned his security advisors. The spokesman at the Chinese Embassy in Washington DC said, 'We hope the relevant US military activities will serve for the regional peace, stability and security, and not the contrary.'

Space and cyberspace

How could China respond to these developments? China has started trying to match the US and its allies by building a 'blue water' navy with aircraft carriers and the like. But it would probably be smarter, cheaper and more effective to simply disable the other side's logistical capabilities, hence the intense focus between the US and China on space (satellites) and cyberspace.

The White House launched the new 'National Space Policy' in late June 2010. This reinforced the high-tech ban the US maintains on China that, among other things, precludes all US companies and American employees who work on satellites or space projects from entering China or having unreported contact with Chinese nationals. Overall, America's stance has been to maintain logistical dominance over China by denying it access to most high technology through control over space and satellites, which irks the Chinese terribly.

Is Google the CIA/NSA?

China has always been suspicious that America's dominance of the Internet has a nefarious side. *Wired* magazine's article, 'Exclusive: Google, CIA Invest in "Future" of Web Monitoring' only confirmed China's suspicion that Google *is* the CIA and the NSA (National Security Agency).* Ironically, these fears were confirmed for them,

---

* Noah Schachtman, 'Exclusive: Google, CIA Invest in "Future" of Web Monitoring', *Wired*, 28 July 2010.

and many Americans as well, the very week that President Obama and President Xi met in California in June 2013. A young NSA officer called Edward Snowden took a thumb drive loaded with critical classified information from the NSA, which revealed America's systematic efforts to spy on China and on US citizens alike. It is perhaps no coincidence that Snowden went straight to a protectorate of China, Hong Kong, to reveal America's spying efforts to the world. This event further confirmed for China that the central target of America's cyberspace efforts is indeed China. In Snowden's words, 'Thousands of technology, finance and manufacturing companies are working closely with US national security agencies, providing sensitive information and in return receiving benefits that include access to classified intelligence.'*

In 2017 Wikileaks claimed that US intelligence agencies have the capability to use smart devices to spy on anyone using then, thus fuelling China's concerns. It's clear that hacking, whacking and espionage activities in cyberspace are extensive.

Meanwhile, the US has upped the rhetoric about China's cyberspace capabilities. In 2010 the four-star general and military intelligence officer Michael Hayden, the twice-former head of the CIA and retired head of the NSA, said of the Chinese campaign to wrest industrial and defence secrets from major Western companies: 'As an intelligence professional, I stand back in absolute awe and wonder . . . It is magnificent in its depth, its breadth and its persistence.'†

Hackers and whackers

China's hackers (those who steal information) and whackers (those who damage systems) have repeatedly managed to get into the Pentagon at all levels, including the personal laptops of various

* Michael Riley, 'US Agencies Said to Swap Data With Thousands of Firms', Bloomberg.com, 14 June 2013.
† Joseph Menn, 'Ex-CIA chief downplays claims of China's "cyber war"', *Financial Times*, 30 July 2010.

secretaries of defense, into the Patriot missile systems, the F-35 Joint Strike Bomber, the silent P-C3 submarine technology and many other critical defence systems. It is assumed that these targets go far beyond the military and include US banks, the Congress, America's power grids, technology firms, defence contractors, energy companies, human rights groups, law firms, private equity firms and any other entities that can provide useful information in China's search for critical hard assets.

For their part the Chinese are offended by America's repeated efforts to spy on them and potentially inhibit their internal systems. Given the US government's systematic and comprehensive spying programme, it would be a reasonable bet that they have accomplished the same kind of penetration of targets in China. In 2006 the US started sending spy satellites over China, explaining that it wasn't its fault that it can't watch the nuclear threat from North Korea without catching a glimpse of China. China responded by 'blinding' America's satellites with land-based lasers as they passed over. The US then shifted to higher-orbit satellites, only to find Chinese anti-satellite tests proved that it was only a matter of time before they could hit a US military satellite even in high altitude. The US then engaged in its own ASAT tests, but instead of destroying the whole satellite, they knocked off just a corner of it, thus proving the US has something China lacks: precision. The two countries remain locked in this competition as to who can throw further and more precisely.

Reconnaissance aircraft are permanently deployed by both countries against each other. This is what led to the accident over the disputed Paracel Islands in April 2001, when an American EP-3 spy plane from the 'Worldwatchers' Squadron came within a few coats of paint of a Chinese J-8 spy plane. The Chinese pilot, Wang Wei, was killed and the US crew were forced to make an emergency landing on Hainan Island, the very location they had been spying on. It took a week of tense diplomatic negotiations to get the US crew back home. The plane was returned months later in July 2001, fully disassembled.* The Chinese had the hollowed-out carcass delivered to the US by Polet, the Russian Airline, no doubt to make a point.

Chinese and American spy planes continue to buzz each other, though they do so more carefully now. Who's to say who is right? What is clear is that there is a new kind of Cold War and it is focused on ownership of commodities. If the old Cold War was the CIA in Langley versus the KGB in Moscow, perhaps the new war in cyberspace is the NSA in Fort Meade versus People's Liberation Army Unit 61398 on the Datong Road in Shanghai. Russia too is involved. It is believed that the Russian intelligence services use internal and outsourced cyberwar experts. It has been argued that the majority of 'denial of service' cyber attacks actually come from Ukraine. If this is true, it provides yet another reason for Russia to care who has authority over the future of that nation.

Huggers and sluggers

The Chinese understand very well that there are two broad camps in the US when it comes to China. There are 'China Huggers' and 'China Sluggers'.† The Huggers want to embrace Chinese efforts to reform and to align the common interests between the two countries. China Sluggers focus on the competing and conflicting interests between the two. The Sluggers take every incident as justification for further enhancing America's military and technological dominance over a potentially hostile China. The end result has been something US officials call the 'Hedge Strategy'.

Ashton Carter and Jennifer Buckley explained America's dilemma with great clarity in Harvard's *Pacific Asia Review*:

* Erik Eckholm, 'China Agrees to Return Partly Dismantled Spy Plane as Cargo', *New York Times*, 29 May 2001.
† Sometimes called 'Panda huggers' and 'Panda sluggers'.

China's military future is not a secret it keeps from the world – it is a mystery even to those inside the country. Not even top leaders know whether China will become the United States' friend or foe in the decades ahead . . . Given this strategic uncertainty, the United States has no choice but to pursue a two-pronged policy toward China. One prong is to engage China and encourage it to become a 'responsible stakeholder' in the international community. The second is to engage in 'prudent hedging' against competitive or aggressive behaviour by China, pursuing continued engagement rather than treating the country as an enemy.*

Japan

Another aspect of cat and mouse is apparent from the continuing intrusions by China and Japan into each other's airspace, thus forcing both sides to scramble their fighter jets. China's first incursion into Japanese airspace since 1958 took place in late 2012. That year, Japan scrambled a record 306 times in response to Chinese jets breaching Japanese airspace. These numbers have increased each year. Japan has complained about Chinese submarines and ships using weapons-targeting and fire-control radar on Japanese vessels. Prime Minister Abe said, 'This was a dangerous action that could lead to unforeseen circumstances . . . At a time when there were signs that there could be talks between China and Japan, it is extremely regrettable that China should carry out such a one-sided provocation.'†

In addition, Chinese military vessels are now regularly seen moving around Japan in sea-lanes as far north as the Soya Strait north of Hokkaido and around the 'first island chain' that Japan considers its first 'Defence perimeter'. This runs from Okinawa to Taiwan. Japan's 'second island chain' runs from Japan's southern islands all the way to

* Dr Ashton B. Carter and Jennifer C. Bulkeley, 'America's Strategic Response to China's Military Modernisation', *Harvard Asia Pacific Review*, Winter 2007.
† John Brinsley and Isabel Reynolds, 'Abe Calls China Radar Targeting of Japan Vessel Provocative', Bloomberg News, 6 February 2013.

Guam. This is now the site for drills by Chinese military vessels. On 11 September 2012 the government of Japan purchased a number of small islands in the disputed Senkaku area from their 'private Japanese owner', much to China's chagrin. Chinese ships apparently sent military vessels into the Senkakus 'on 229 days and Japanese territorial waters around the islands on 54 days'.*

Russia, too, has been buzzing around Japan with visits by Russian Bear Bombers, Fulcrum Fighter jets and nuclear submarines. Japan and Russia have never formally ended the Second World War by signing a peace treaty. They remain in dispute over the Kuril Islands in north Japan. (The latter is a long-standing issue; the two countries have been arguing over these islands since the Edo period.)†

QE as defence policy

This increased strategic threat is in part what led Japanese Prime Minister Abe to announce the record quantitative easing in Japan. Japan doubled the monetary base in a single year. The Chinese know full well that this was not a purely economic decision. By stimulating the economy, Prime Minister Abe believes he can support his principal goal: the rearmament of Japan. Keynesian economic policy is expected to expand and support the economy, making it easier to spend more on defence, which itself further stimulates economic activity.

Expanding economic policy is intended to allow Japan to strengthen its defence capabilities at a time of increasing threat perception. The Prime Minister has called for a change to the Constitution to permit Japan to be removed from the constraints imposed in the aftermath of the Second World War. Until now, Japan has only been permitted to maintain a 'self-defence force', leaving Japan to rely entirely on the US for its defence. Now the Prime Minister wants to formally re-establish

---

* 'Insight: China puts Japan on notice that warship drills are now routine', *Asahi Shimbun*: Asia and Japan Watch, 30 July 2013.
† From 1603 until 1868.

a Japanese Navy, a Japanese Army and a Japanese Air Force. Japan is evoking bygone days when it was the major aggressor in the region by calling for the use of the old 'Rising Sun' flag and naming its new naval vessels after Imperial Navy warships. Their first helicopter carrier was called the *Izumo* – named after the flagship vessel that defeated China in 1937 during the battle of Shanghai.

In the ever-intensifying game of diplomatic chess between the US and China in the Pacific, Japan is viewed by China as an arm of the US in the region. The more the US and Japan collaborate on defence, the more this notion is reinforced. In February 2014 the Japanese Defence Minister, Fumio Kishida, hinted that US nuclear weapons would be permitted to be deployed inside Japanese territory if there were a 'clear and present danger'. Clearly this potentially significant break with past policy is aimed at China.

Horcruxes

Meanwhile, the signals from geopolitics are rattling the economic cage ever more loudly. Bloomberg posted a story entitled 'How to Prevent a War Between China and Japan',* thus acknowledging that the signals from both countries, Japan and China, are not positive. One such signal emanated from the pages of the British press at the end of 2013 when the Chinese Ambassador to the United Kingdom, Liu Xiaoming, wrote in the *Daily Telegraph*:

> In the Harry Potter story, the dark wizard Voldemort dies hard because the seven horcruxes, which contain parts of his soul, have been destroyed. If militarism is like the haunting Voldemort of Japan, the Yasukuni Shrine in Tokyo is a kind of horcrux, representing the darkest parts of that nation's soul.†

---

* Kishore Mahbubani, 'How to Prevent a War Between China and Japan', Bloomberg. com, 29 December 2013.

† Liu Xiaoming, 'Liu Xiaoming: China and Britain won the war together', *Daily Telegraph*, 1 January 2014.

Japan's Ambassador to the United Kingdom responded a few days later, also in the *Daily Telegraph*: 'There are two paths open to China. One is to seek dialogue, and abide by the rule of law. The other is to play the role of Voldemort in the region by letting loose the evil of an arms race and escalation of tensions.'*

ED problems

In February 2014, Daniel R. Russel, Assistant Secretary of the US State Department's Bureau of East Asian and Pacific Affairs, announced in Congressional testimony that the US does not recognise China's 'Nine-dash Line': 'Any use of the "Nine-dash Line" by China to claim maritime rights not based on claimed land features would be inconsistent with international law.'† In May that same year, China placed an oil rig in waters that Vietnam perceived to be within their territory and proceeded to protect the rig with more than one hundred naval vessels and five fighter jets. US Secretary of State Hagel said, 'China has undertaken destabilising, unilateral actions asserting its claims in the South China Sea'.‡ In response, Zhu Chenghu, a two-star general who is the dean of China's PLA National Defence University, said that America suffers from 'extended deployment' which, he went on, 'has become the male type of ED problem: erectile dysfunction'.§

On a less humorous note, President Xi Jinping said in July 2014: 'Sino-US cooperation will achieve things that are beneficial to both countries and the world, while confrontation will be disastrous.' Clearly it is worth paying attention to the signals emanating from this issue.

---

* Keiichi Hayashi, 'China risks becoming Asia's Voldemort', *Daily Telegraph*, 5 January 2014.

† Testimony Before the House Committee on Foreign Affairs Subcommittee on Asia and the Pacific by Daniel R. Russel, Assistant Secretary, Bureau of East Asian and Pacific Affairs, State Department. Washington, DC, 5 February 2014.

‡ 'Chuck Hagel: Beijing "destabilising" South China Sea', BBC.co.uk, 31 May 2014.

§ William Kazer, 'Chinese General Says US Foreign Policy Has "Erectile Dysfunction" Problems', *Wall Street Journal Asia*, 2 June 2014.

Managing expectations

One of the great social issues of our time, for the world and for China, will be breaking the news to one billion Chinese workers, let alone all the other emerging-market workers: 'We're terribly sorry, but you are no longer competitive in the world economy, so it's time to go back to the farm, reduce your expectations and we look forward to hearing from you when you invent a new business model now that cheap labour is not working for you any more.'

As the old song title goes, 'How Ya Gonna Keep 'em Down on the Farm (After They've Seen Paree)?' China's testosterone-rich and cash-poor workers will not go home quietly, and neither will all the emerging-market workers that compete with China. Huggers and Sluggers alike fear instability in China and across emerging markets as much as the leadership of these nations do.

In short, America hopes for the best and prepares for the worst when it comes to China. Similarly, China hopes for the best and prepares for the worst when it comes to the US. This is true whether Republicans or Democrats are in power, and whether hardliners or reformers are in charge in Beijing.

The US and China alike prepare for the worst by placing more and more military assets in the region. These include ships, aircraft carriers, basing stations, communications, cyber capability and deepened relationships with regional partners.

OBOR

There is, however, a new response from China which will profoundly alter the situation. In October 2013 President Xi Jinping announced a very clever idea to save China from the various pressures that I have described, declaring his intention to build 'One Belt, One Road'. 'One Belt' refers to the old land route we know as the Silk Road, which begins in Xian in China and reaches all the way to Venice, Piraeus Port in Athens, Madrid and to the ports of Duisberg in Germany, Antwerp in the Netherlands and to the railway hub in Liege Belgium.

'One Road' refers to the maritime version of the Silk Road, which runs from China's coastline, along the coasts of Thailand, Indonesia, Burma, Bangladesh, Pakistan, India and Sri Lanka and into the Middle East and on to Western Europe through the Suez Canal, then into the Mediterranean and on to the Atlantic.

This may sound fanciful, but in late February 2015 the first train completed the 26,000-kilometre round trip on the Yixin'ou line, which runs from Yiwu in China all the way to Madrid. It took the train and its eighty-two containers some two months to complete the journey and deliver the Christmas trinkets it carried from Yiwu, and the return cargo of olive oil from Madrid.* In January 2017 another train left Yiwu for London and completed the 12,000-kilometre journey in just sixteen days.†

The grand strategy serves many important purposes. In addition to helping China secure stronger access to critical supplies of food, energy and materials, it will generate demand for Chinese goods and services. China's excess capacity in concrete and steel can now be sold to the locations that will be building new ports, roads, bridges, airports and the like along these two routes. In other words, the initiative may allow China to replicate the effect Special Economic Zones had inside China. Now they aim to create Special Economic zones abroad.

AIIB

OBOR is financed by a new institution, the Asian Infrastructure Investment Bank. The AIIB opened in May 2016 with a balance sheet of some $250 billion, which made it bigger than the World Bank on its very first day of operation. Many countries quickly signed up as

---

* Alistair Dawber, 'China to Spain cargo train: successful first 16,156-mile round trip on world's longest railway brings promise of increased trade', *Independent*, 25 February 2015.

† Wade Shepard, 'The real impact that the new China–UK rail line will have', *Forbes*, 6 January 2017.

founder members and supporters. But the US opposes the AIIB and has scolded allies that have joined it. For example, when Britain decided to become the first founder member from the G7, the news was greeted with dismay by some in Washington. The *Financial Times* reported that this resulted in a 'rare breach' of the 'special relationship' when an anonymous person in the White House was reported to have said that the UK was engaging in the 'constant accommodation' of China.*

Some will argue that China has no money to finance such a grand scheme. China has been bleeding foreign exchange reserves, especially since the US began to pursue a higher interest rate policy. Once the Americans began to nominally tighten policy it caused most emerging-market currencies to commence extremely severe devaluations. China let its currency weaken a little, but it lost competitiveness against the many countries whose currencies plummeted in value. The Russian rouble, the Brazilian real, the South African rand, the Kazakhstani currency, along with many others, fell to record lows.

This has not stopped China from pursuing some very substantial projects that include plans to expand the Suez Canal. This makes sense now that China has emerged as the biggest buyer of Saudi oil in the world.

The perfect circle ends in OBOR

The AIIB marks a determined effort to change how and where capital flows in the world economy. In the past China and other emerging markets recycled their domestic savings into the sovereign debt of the US, Britain, Europe and Japan. This helped these nations live beyond their means because inbound emerging-market money financed the gap between what these nations spend and what they earn. Going forward, the capital markets will be profoundly changed as this money no longer goes into paper financial assets but into real economy activities like

* Geoff Dyer and George Parker, 'US Attacks UK's "constant accommodation" with China', *Financial Times*, 12 March 2015.

railways, ports and airports. The investments will be made into a wide array of countries and not just the major industrialised nations.

Reform or replace

OBOR aims to change the rules of the game. Remember that China and other emerging markets have campaigned for years to repair and reform the existing rules and institutions of international finance, such as the World Bank and the IMF. China wanted more representation in the World Bank and the IMF, especially if they were going to pay more money in. They wanted the renminbi recognised as a reserve currency that would be included in the IMF's basket of SDR (Special Drawing Rights) currencies. The US opposed them on these and other counts. The perception has grown that reform is not a viable option, given American resistance. Worse still, the perception has grown that the US is prepared to tilt the system towards its own interests.

A social contract concept underpinned the perfect circle. The idea was that membership in a US dollar-based world economy and its institutions, like the World Bank, the IMF and the International Trade Organization, would serve everyone's best interests. But emerging markets are beginning to question this now, given what they perceive as America's willingness to pursue policies that suit their own interests without regard for the international spillovers or consequences.

As a result, China and others now seek to replace the social contract that has ceased to serve them. Instead of redeploying savings into Western debt instruments like Treasuries, Gilts and Bunds, they want to build a new international social contract – one that is more in keeping with the domestic social contract.

They will ask the world to trade with them in their own currencies instead of being forced into a US dollar regime. They will create their own institutions and rules. They will try to pursue their own interests now – commercial, diplomatic and military interests – in their own way.

The String of Pearls

OBOR will inevitably help China expand its influence and perhaps strengthen its military security in the process. The military and strategic issues won't be ignored even though China will insist that these are not central objectives for them. To understand why, we need to get to grips with something the Americans refer to as the 'String of Pearls'. This nickname was coined in 2003 by a team of Booz Allen consultants, who said Chinese efforts to build a string of ports outside China, funded and effectively controlled by China, would help diminish the threat posed by the US presence along the critical shipping lanes.*

China's String of Pearls begins in Hainan Island, which is said to be the centre of its efforts to build a blue-water navy – i.e., a navy like America's, positioned far from home, in blue water. China has investments in and expansion plans for many ports, starting with two that belong to Myanmar: Sittwe and the Coco Islands. The latter are reputed to be home to a Chinese listening station that is principally aimed at India, a country China views as America's proxy in the region, certainly since the US–India Civil Nuclear Agreement of 2005. Under this framework the US shares all technology with India and establishes joint defence capabilities. Bear in mind that while the US is prepared to share nuclear technology with India, it maintains a severe country-specific ban on all tech transfer to China. President Obama also announced a ban on the purchase of Chinese-made computer technology, based on concerns about the possibility of a Chinese cyber attack.

As a result of Chinese mistrust of India, it is pursuing a policy of developing ports and infrastructure around India. These include the ports at Chittagong in Bangladesh and Hambantota in Sri Lanka. And on 18 February 2013, Pakistan gave China full operational control over the port in Gwador. Rumours abound that the Maldives has awarded

* Julie A. MacDonald, Amy Donahue and Bethany Danyluk, 'Energy Futures in Asia', Booz Allen, 17 January 2005.

the Chinese the contract to build its new airport in Malé. The Seychelles is allowing China to refuel its navy there, and there is talk of Chinese listening stations in Madagascar and the Maldives.

In the past the Middle East has been difficult for China, given that all Middle Eastern oil producers except Iran were aligned with the US, at least until recently. President Obama's efforts to normalise relations with Iran have forced China to diversify its interests but, conveniently for China, America has managed to alienate many of its other allies in the region. Both Saudi Arabia and Israel were alienated by America's support for the rebels in Libya and regime change generally during the Arab Spring. American efforts to increase fracking and reduce dependence on Saudi oil further damaged relations with the Saudis and most other ruling houses in the region. Talk of US energy independence has led to anxiety among the energy-producing countries of the Middle East, who realise the Americans may no longer need their assets. Indeed, the US may now become a competitor in the energy markets rather than a reliable consumer.

The tectonic shift in its relationship with the USA resulted in Saudi Arabia turning down a valuable seat on the UN Security Council in 2013, which meant the US lost a Security Council ally. Prince Bandar, the Saudi Ambassador to Washington from 1983–2005, said, 'This was a message for the US, not the UN.'* This breakdown of the Saudi-American relationship has opened the door for China to deepen diplomatic ties with Middle Eastern oil producers, especially now that the US presence in the region is diminishing, given the committed withdrawal of troops from Iraq and Afghanistan.

In the meantime, China has reached out to East Africa, where it is building or extending ports in Djibouti, at Port Sudan in Sudan, Lamu in Kenya and Bagamoyo in Tanzania. Chinese entities have invested in

---

* Ellen Knickmeyer, 'Spy Chief Distances Saudis From US: Prince Bandar's Move Raises Tensions Over Policies in Syria, Iran and Egypt', *Wall Street Journal*, 21 October 2013.

similar infrastructure in South Africa and West Africa – particularly in Nigeria.

Most recently, China has sought to take advantage of the 'fire sale' in Western Europe. Greece, being cash poor and deeply indebted, sold its largest port, Piraeus, to Chinese investors and granted them some shipping lane rights too. China is investing in Adriatic ports such as Rijeka in Croatia, Venice, Ravenna and Chioggia in Italy, enabling them to handle the new mega-ships, such as the Maersk Triple E class, which is four times the size of the largest existing container ships. These mega-ships will be required to move goods to and from China.

In addition, China appears to have leased the old Lajés Field NATO base on Terceira in the Azores.* The Azores, lying right in the middle of the Atlantic, are considered by some in the defence community to be as strategically important for China as Diego Garcia† is for the US. The Portuguese decided to lease it to the Chinese after the Americans decided to close large parts of the base there.‡

The New Great Game

It would be a mistake to think that China alone is an aggressive actor on the world stage, competing nose to nose with the US and its allies for control over various locations on the global landscape. The US has its own 'String of Pearls' which include their footholds in Japan, Korea, the Philippines, Vietnam, Australia, New Zealand, Diego Garcia, India, the UAE, some parts of East Africa, all that NATO controls and onward.

It is as if the US and China are playing a game of Monopoly. Each is aiming to control or influence parts of the global map. Lord Curzon,

* Felix Seidler 'Will China's Navy Soon Be Operating in the Atlantic?' Centre for International Maritime Security, 8 February 2013.

† Diego Garcia is little island in the middle of the Indian Ocean. Many of the bombing runs the US has conducted during the course of the conflicts in Afghanistan and Iraq have taken off from there.

‡ Julian E. Barnes, 'US, Portugal Wrangle Over Fate of US Base in Azores', *Wall Street Journal*, 16 June 2015.

the British Viceroy of India, said in 1898 that countries are 'pieces on a chessboard upon which is being played out a great game for the domination of the world'. He was making reference to a popular book by Peter Hopkirk, *The Great Game* (1842), which chronicled the exploits of the British, French, Germans, Russians, Chinese and many others to gain control over various territories and countries around the world. President Obama made a similar reference when he spoke about Syria in 2013:

> We are no longer in a Cold War. There's no Great Game to be won, nor does America have any interest in Syria beyond the wellbeing of its people, the stability of its neighbours, the elimination of chemical weapons, and ensuring it does not become a safe-haven for terrorists.

Instead, he said, 'I believe that America is exceptional' in its ability to 'stand up for the interests of all'.[*]

It may be that the US chooses to believe the Great Game era is over and that it stands for the interests of all, but others may disagree. China and many emerging markets certainly no longer agree. There is still a scramble for influence and assets.[†]

The end of the peace dividend

All nations must be able to supply food and energy to their populations at a reasonable price or risk anger and resentment, if not rejection and revolution. This is what compels emerging markets to join in the competition for control over valuable assets and supply chains. Most emerging markets are even more vulnerable than China because

---

[*] Christopher Dickey, 'Obama's American Exceptionalism', *The Daily Beast* (www. thedailybeast.com), 24 September 2013.

[†] For more on the new 'Great Game' see Dambisa Moyo, *Winner Take All: China's Race for Resources and What it Means for Us*, Penguin Books, 2013; and Elizabeth Economy and Michael Levi, *By All Means Necessary: How China's Resource Quest is Changing the World*, Oxford University Press, 2014.

they lack the size, the resources and the state power to pursue their goals. And yet they must. Failure to protect citizens from the world economy's vice of pain – the deflation and the inflation – can cause social unrest and the downfall of governments.

This is how economic forces have paved the way for geopolitics to move from the wings to centre stage across the world economy. It is not that anybody wants confrontation. Neither China nor the US, for example, have anything to gain by entering into conflict. But economic forces are driving both nations into a more confrontational stance.

Consider another angle. It is possible that defence spending and infrastructure investments are really just another way to pump money into the economy. Some say China is as indebted and broke as the West. China says the West is broke too. Should it come as any surprise then that there is an inclination to use strategic security issues as an excuse for spending? Might QE4 (quantitative easing mark four) arrive in the form of defence and infrastructure spending in future?

It would be folly to assume that emerging-market workers, whether in China or anywhere else, will accept a falling standard of living without a fight. I cannot imagine how we tell these workers that they must postpone their dreams of a better life, of more meals with meat, of becoming rich before they get old, until they become more productive. This is why we should be vigilant for signals that a loss of faith and hope in the future is provoking arguments and fights and competition for scarce assets.

The substantial jump in defence spending around the world is an important signal. Government are rearming and shares in defence firms have risen dramatically. The peace dividend is transforming into what we might call a conflict premium.

9

Enter Geopolitics:
Russia, the Middle East and Oil

—

Admiral Mark Ferguson is Commander of the Joint Allied Force Command, in charge of US Navy forces in Europe and Africa, so it means something when he says that the seas around Europe are now a 'contested space' with Russia. On 6 October 2015 he coined a new phrase – 'Arc of Steel' – that reveals the extent of the new stress between Russia and NATO and more specifically between Russia and the US:

> ... remilitarisation of Russian security policy is evident by the construction of an 'arc of steel' from the Arctic to the Mediterranean. Starting at their new Arctic bases, to Kaliningrad in the Baltic, and Crimea in the Black Sea, Russia has introduced advanced air defense, cruise missile systems, and new platforms. It is also building the capability to project power into the maritime domain. Their base in Syria now gives them the opportunity to do the same in the Eastern Mediterranean. This is a sea denial strategy focused on NATO maritime forces. Their intent is to have the ability to hold at risk maritime forces operating in these areas and thus deter NATO operations. They are also expanding the reach of assets to project power from this arc. Specifically, the proficiency and operational tempo of the Russian submarine force is increasing.[*]

[*] Daniel Schumacher, 'Remarks as delivered by Adm. Mark Ferguson at the Atlantic Council', 6 October 2015.

President Putin clearly has a similar view of the US and NATO. In early January 2016, Russia released a new strategy document, 'About the Strategy of National Security of Russian Federation', which listed the US and NATO as one of the primary national security threats Russia faces today. This was the first time since the end of the Cold War that Russia had explicitly named the US as a strategic security threat.

Things have deteriorated since then. On 12 February 2016 Russia's Prime Minister, Dmitry Medvedev, said that the West would be 'unleashing a new world war' if certain options, like ground troops, were pursued in Syria.* On 14 February, news headlines quoted Medvedev as saying 'We have slid into a time of a new Cold War.' The love affair is clearly over. Now we need to process the divorce between the hope that geopolitics will resolve itself and the reality that Russia and the West are engaged in nose-to-nose brinksmanship, with ongoing near misses involving spy planes, fighter jets and naval vessels. An era of Le Carré-type spy stories and Clancy-esque invasive military events on or across each other's borders has commenced. Only a few years ago it would have seemed laughable to suggest that this could happen. In 1997 that President Clinton managed to embrace Russia and charm the G8 into welcoming them into their meetings. By 2014, three days after 'Moscow annexed Crimea', Russia quit the G8 before the angry group could kick them out.†

Whether we like it nor not, Russia's view is that the US and NATO are re-arming and being increasingly aggressive. They would argue that America is using both economic and military tools to undermine and damage Russia's national interests. It can be no surprise if Russian behaviour reflects this view.

The return of geopolitics to the 'Russian front' is no more random than the situation with China. Economic forces are driving the drama

---

* Richard Spencer, Mathew Holehouse and Louisa Loveluck, 'Russia warns of "new world war" starting in Syria', 12 February 2016.

† Kenneth Rapoza, 'Russia Quits G8', *Forbes*, 5 June 2014.

that is playing out more visibly every day. The following events sound like something Hollywood made up – except, they actually occurred.

Spy stories

In late 2015 Steven Spielberg released *Bridge of Spies*, a film that tells the story of the famous swap of spies over a bridge in Berlin. The Americans handed back Russian spy Rudolph Abel in exchange for the American pilot Gary Powers, who had been spying on Russia from a U2 spy plane, and a young American student whom the Russians deemed to be a spy. It was fascinating that a similar series of events was unfolding between Russia and Estonia (a NATO member) just as the film hit cinemas in late 2015.

On 5 September 2014 the FSB, Russia's secret service, 'snatched' Eston Kohver – who worked for Estonia's counter-intelligence agency, the Kaitsepolitsei (aka KaPo) – and took him back to Moscow for interrogation. It remains unclear which side of the border Kohver was on when it happened. A couple of weeks later the Estonians arrested two Russians who were found 'fishing' on the river Narva, inside Estonia's borders; both men had formerly worked for the FSB.* In the end the Russian 'fishermen' were sentenced to two months in prison, while the Estonian government agreed to trade Kohver for Alexei Dressen, a former member of the Estonian secret service who had been arrested two years earlier and imprisoned on charges of spying for Russia. In a scene straight out of the movie, the swap took place over a remote bridge that crosses the Piusa River, connecting Russia and Estonia.†

The Wikileaks and the Edward Snowden cases ended up revealing that the US had commenced spying on its supposed ally, Germany. Angela Merkel grew up in East Germany, speaks Russian and fully understands the Russian mentality. She also fully understands how

---

* Michael Amundsen, 'Estonia arrests former KGB officers', *Guardian*, 3 October 2014.
† Shaun Walker, 'Russian "spy swaps": the cold-war cliché making a comeback', *Guardian*, 29 September 2015.

vulnerable Germany is to Russian energy, especially now that Germany has decided to end its nuclear energy programme, so it makes sense that there would be a dialogue between the two countries.

Of course it's long been the case that allies, even G7 members, spy on each other. My father has fascinating stories to tell about how the French were better at this than the Russians or even the Israelis. Given the revelations about ECHELON surveillance programme, which permits the US to work with Britain, Australia, Japan and Canada – the so-called Five Eyes – to monitor and intercept communications,* there can be few who don't believe the US is spying on just about everything that goes on in the world.

The publicity surrounding the leaks story meant Merkel needed to be seen to be doing something. Germany ended up deporting the CIA station chief, ostensibly on spying charges, and they arrested a double agent from Germany's own intelligence community who was allegedly working for the Americans. The Chancellor announced that the BND, Germany's intelligence service, would commence actively spying on the US and its closest intelligence partner, Britain.† In fact, the German leadership requires that senior officials prepare truly sensitive documents on typewriters instead of computers, while classical music is played in offices in order to make it harder to eavesdrop. According to reports in the *Süddeutsche Zeitung*, Edward Greig's Piano Concerto in A minor is a popular choice.

Given that the whole purpose of the US military presence in Germany and across Europe is to defend Germany and Europe from Russia, this is what might be termed a geopolitical problem for the world.

Other spy stories have since emerged. In January 2015, the US Attorney for Manhattan, Preet Bharara, said, 'More than two decades after the presumptive end of the Cold War, Russian spies continue

---

* To add some levity to the serious gravity of these developments, I find it quite funny that the NSA is now considered to be the only part of the US government that listens.
† Tony Paterson, 'Germany's Plan to take on NSA: Block Eavesdroppers with classical music, and use typewriters', 15 July 2015.

to seek to operate in our midst under cover of secrecy.' In late 2016, President Obama expelled thirty-five Russian diplomats on the allegation that Russia had interfered with the US presidential election process.* President Trump fired Bharara in early 2017, and investigations continue.

Death 11 and Death 12

Spying isn't the only Cold War activity to see a revival in recent years. Russia and the West have been engaged in military face offs too.

In June 2014, while President Obama was travelling in Air Force One en route to Japan, a Russian Su-27 Flanker fighter jet flew within 100 feet of an American spy plane (an RC-135U Combat Sent electronic intelligence plane), somewhere over the Sea of Okhotsk, near Japan.† The Pentagon did not disclose that the event had occurred until the story leaked. When asked why they had not mentioned it, the Pentagon spokesperson said 'I don't have a good answer for you yet.'‡

In 2015, Russian bombers flew some ten miles off the coast of California, forcing NORAD§ to scramble F-22 fighter jets to wave them off.¶ It turns out that this was not an isolated incident. Russian military jets had been breaching and violating the airspace of its neighbours since April 2002, when there were reports that Russian Bear Bombers had flown within 37 miles of Alaska. They were intercepted and waved off by two American F-15s.

In January 2004 a crew member of the USS *Kittyhawk*, the nuclear-

---

* 'Obama expels 35 Russian diplomats in retaliation for US election hacking', *Daily Telegraph*, 30 December 2016.

† David Lerman, 'Russian Military Jet Intercepted US Plane Near Japan', Bloomberg, 4 June 2014.

‡ Department of Defense Press briefing by Colonel Warren via Teleconference from Bagdad Iraq, Department of Defence Press Office, 24 November 2015.

§ North American Aerospace Defense Command is responsible for providing aerospace warnings for the defence of North America.

¶ Brian Todd and Jethro Mullen, 'July Fourth message not the first from Russian Bombers', CNN, updated 24 July 2015.

powered American aircraft carrier, filmed a Bear Bomber as it buzzed the *Kittyhawk* at 2,000 feet (well within hitting distance) while the carrier was on manoeuvres in the Sea of Japan. In 2005 a Russian fighter jet crashed near the city of Kaunas in Lithuania. Lithuania, Latvia, Estonia and several other former members of the former Soviet Union had only recently joined NATO, the West's primary military alliance, much to Russia's displeasure. The North Atlantic Treaty Organization traditionally served as the principal military opponent to the Soviet Union.

The first post-Cold War air incursion into Britain seems to have happened on 10 May 2007, when two Russian Tupolev Tu-95s headed into British airspace, forcing the Royal Air Force to scramble fighter jets from RAF Leuchars Fife, in Scotland. It later emerged that the Norwegian Air Force had scrambled their jets that same day because the Bears passed over Norway en route to Britain. The Russians said that the flight was a training mission.

Occasional training missions have now given way to something more sustained and more serious. Japan has scrambled their fighter jets on more occasions in recent years than at any point since the end of the Cold War. According to official government statistics they did so 810 times between April 2013 and April 2014 in response to incursions. Chinese incursions occurred 415 times. Russian incursions occurred 359 times in 2014 and 248 times in 2013. In April 2016, it was reported that Russian SU-24s made a 'simulated attack' on the USS *Donald Cook*, leaving only thirty feet between them.*

In the meantime, Western spy planes have also been conducting training missions and turning up in unexpected places, which indicate that the incursion and spying issues are broad based. In early June 2014, two US B-2 Stealth bombers (with the call signals Death 11 and Death 12) and three B-52 Stratofortress aircraft arrived at the Fairford Royal

---

* David Blair, 'Russia jets make "simulated attack" on US warship in "aggressive" Baltic incident', *Daily Telegraph*, 14 April 2016.

Air Force Base west of London.* Amateur plane spotters were excited because these aircraft are usually based in Missouri at Whiteman Air Force Base, and it is extremely rare for these strategic nuclear bombers to be seen outside the US. They would only be there if there were a need for them to be there.

Strangely, on 30 April 2014, the Federal Aviation Authority confirmed that the presence of an American spy plane over LAX Airport in Los Angeles had zapped computers and scrambled air traffic control systems, forcing the cancellation of 50 flights and the delay of another 455 flights.† Perhaps America now flies spy planes over California because they suspect that Russians are engaging in flights that are ever closer to the US?

Why?

Russian forces have been expanding their reach in the air, on the sea and on land in a multitude of ways for some years, though increasingly aggressively since the US began to pursue QE. Why are the Russians doing this?

The constant expansion of NATO eastward since the fall of the Berlin Wall is viewed by Russia as a clear provocation. A glance at a map of NATO, seen from a Russian perspective, looks much worse than the occasional air incursions undertaken by Russia in recent years.‡ The systematic effort by the US and Europe to expand NATO into formerly Soviet satellite countries like Poland, Estonia, Hungary, the Czech Republic and the like has deeply unnerved Russia's leadership. From a Russian perspective, it's as if the West 'took advantage' of the period when the Soviet Union ceased to exist and before Russia was able to re-establish itself in its rightful stance as a nuclear super-power.

* Dave Cenciotti, *Aviationist*, 8 June 2014.

† Laura Stampler, 'FAA Confirms Spy Plane caused LAX Chaos', *Time Magazine*, 6 May 2014.

‡ See 'The Expansion of NATO', a YouTube video posted on 9 February 2014 or the Map of EU/EEC, NATO, Warsaw Pact 1949–2015 posted 19 May 2015.

It's as if the US 'stole' Russia's sphere of influence during a period of the Great Game when Russia could not defend its own interests. And not for the first time. Russia loyalists are quick to say that Premier Nikita Khrushchev gave up Ukraine and Crimea in a moment when the Soviet Union was briefly on the back foot in the 1950s.

The restoration of Russia's pride and the physical reach of the former Soviet Union, or maybe even the former Russian Empire, has proved to be immensely popular in Russia, lifting Vladimir Putin's popularity to levels that are almost unimaginable for any Western or emerging-market leader.

I believe that the current Russian leadership do indeed view the world from a 'Great Game' perspective and are surprised that the US does not. One hears constant jokes from the Russians about how President Putin is playing chess while President Obama is playing golf. Given this mindset, we can begin to see how Russia came to view QE with suspicion. To them, QE looks like a hostile act committed by a US government intent on pursuing internal interests at the expense of everyone else's. Russians believe that the efforts by the US to save themselves from the debt problem necessarily involves sacrificing Russia's interests.

The impact of QE on Russia, as it proceeded and as it is unwound, is significant and quite negative in both directions. More than that, it changes the value of assets in the 'Great Game'. If America is exporting inflation, or conditions that give rise to inflation in the world economy, then Russians think they should be ready to take advantage of the changed value of assets. Seen this way, we might ask what is the value of Ukraine or the Baltic or the Mediterranean or Syria to Russia in a world where American monetary policy dominates and NATO expands?

Ukraine and Crimea

There are many competing narratives around Ukraine and Crimea. It's a 'he said, she said' kind of situation. What is clear is that by 2013 and 2014 it was obvious that Ukraine had an unpayable debt problem, with a debt-to-GDP ratio so large it was killing all prospects of growth. Food prices and energy prices in Ukraine had been rising for nearly three years in advance of the events in Crimea. It was long suspected that the then President of Ukraine, Viktor Yanukovych, a close ally of Russia, seems to have been artificially suppressing the inflation data, trying to mask the upward pressure in the cost of living. At the time it was estimated that Ukrainians were spending more than 50 per cent of their income on food alone. As a result of the squeeze, many Ukrainians began to ask that important social contract question: 'Why is the wealth in my society going to someone else and not to me?'

For some the answer lay in pushing the seemingly Russian-backed President, Yanukovych, out of power and moving towards a closer alignment with the European Union. The EU encouraged this. For others, such as the majority of citizens in Crimea, the solution lay in pushing for independence from Ukraine and closer alignment with Russia. The Russians encouraged that. Whatever longstanding allegiances had been in place, the economic pressures caused, or forced, people to choose sides. By February 2014, the citizens of Ukraine, Crimea and Russia had calculated their geopolitical interests and concluded it was worth making changes. Some Ukrainians pushed for EU membership. The Russian-speaking citizens in Crimea began a separatist movement that they hoped would end in independence. Russia naturally began to support the breakaway pro-Russian separatists – after all, Ukraine owed a good deal of its debt to Russia, so a default would be painful for Russia. More than that was at stake though.

It is always difficult to pinpoint the start of a geopolitical event, but when the EU invited Ukraine to join its membership, Russia's leadership felt confronted by a singularly important geopolitical issue – security. Russia did not want the EU or NATO to gain control over a country that was not only on their border but which contained so many genuinely valuable assets.

The Russian Ambassador to the UK, Alexander Yakovenko, once asked me, 'Have you Americans completely forgotten about the Cuban

Missile Crisis?' In other words, do you not see how provocative this is? My answer was, 'Yes. We have completely forgotten about the Cuban Missile Crisis.'* We have forgotten that America was threatened by Russia's attempt to place nuclear weapons in Cuba in 1962 and we, in the West, sometimes fail to appreciate (or even desire) that a Ukraine inside the EU would also likely be a Ukraine inside NATO. We therefore cannot grasp that potentially facing NATO nuclear weapons on its border would be as unacceptable for Russia as it was for America during the Cuban Missile Crisis.

There is more though. Beyond preserving a buffer against NATO, I suspect that Russia's leaders also appreciated that the most valuable assets in Crimea are food and energy. Ukraine is the breadbasket of the former Soviet Union and one of the largest producers of food in the world. It has the highest concentration of black topsoil of any nation in the world, which amounts to some 30 per cent of the world's supply. It is one of the world's largest fertiliser producers as well. All this has real value if you suspect that inflation is coming your way. The Russians have been proved right in their fear. At the time of writing, Russian inflation is dramatically increasing. That's on the back of an official increase of 13 per cent in 2015, which probably seriously understates the true situation. It matters if Russians face much higher food prices.

In addition, Ukraine is the centre point of Russia's natural gas pipeline network, which supplies Western Europe. Russia artificially subsidised gas prices while Viktor Yanukovych was in power, but threatened to raise prices if he were to be thrown out. This merely heightened awareness of the dependency on Russia. At one point, as part of the protest, the Maidan People's Union – an alliance of Ukrainians opposed to Yanukovych and Russia – announced it was cancelling 85 per cent of all the natural gas contracts with Russia. Of course, there was no alternative source of supply, so the threat was hollow. But the

---

* I said this with some confidence because my father was one of John F. Kennedy's defence advisors at that time and worked on the Cuban Missile Crisis.

action heightened Russia's awareness of its vulnerability. Whoever controls the land the pipelines pass through has real power. It is real power if you can avoid being defaulted upon. And so we see another example of price pressures around commodities becoming a source of conflict in the world.

Other strategic interests and assets were at stake too. Sevastopol in Ukraine had been Russia's only or principal warm-water port since the late eighteenth century, when it became the home of Russia's Black Sea Fleet. In 2009 Ukraine had announced the lease with Russia would come to an end by 13 December that year. This happened to coincide with the deterioration of stability in Syria. Why was that relevant? Well, Russia's only other warm-water ports were located there, in Latakia and Tartus.* By June 2013, Russia had evacuated its personnel from these ports in Syria, leaving it with no other warm-water port options.† Sevastopol must have taken on new significance in light of the loss of the ports in Syria.

When Viktor Yanukovych's government dismissed the effort to have Ukraine join the EU on 21 November 2013, the Maidan alliance began to protest and then revolt, slowly at first but with ever increasing force. By 22 February 2014 Yanukovych had fled the country. By 27 February 2014 gunmen had begun to take control of Crimea. Then, in the first week of March, unmarked troops (some claimed they were from Russia's 76th Shock Troops unit, others claim they were local paramilitaries), took physical control over the ports, the airports and the regional parliament in Crimea, the Verkhovna Rada. On 6 March 2014 Crimea declared itself a new state.

According to press reports that emerged in early May 2014, Russia had engaged in a surprise simulated 'massive retaliatory nuclear strike'

---

* Fred Weir, 'Why Russia evacuated its naval base in Syria', *Christian Science Monitor*, 27 June 2013.

† Miriam Elder and Ian Black, 'Russia withdraws its remaining personnel from Syria', *Guardian*, 26 June 2013.

in mid April, just as things were heating up in Crimea.* They apparently launched weaponless ICBMs (which usually carry nuclear weapons) from two nuclear submarines within the Northern and Pacific Fleets and one RS-24 Yars from the Plesetsk Cosmodrome near Archangel, which hit its target in Kamchatka.

What prompted these actions? I come back to a central tenet of this book. The debt problem, combined with inflation pressure, created social pressures. Debt resulted in a loss of faith in the future of Ukraine that was felt on all sides. The local ethnic Russian population wanted the separatist movement to succeed due to their loss of faith in their state after Ukraine fell into overwhelming debt and lost the capacity to manage its internal affairs. The non-Russian population preferred an alignment with the EU, but this was unacceptable to Russia and, ultimately, unaffordable to the EU itself. With all the debt trouble within the EU and especially within the Eurozone, no one had any cash to bail out Ukraine. The Russians refused to allow Ukraine or any part of that nation to default on its debt.

The value of the assets involved was rising. The various social contracts involved were clearly breaking, including the international social contract. Instead of pursuing a policy of protecting the interests of all participants in the international financial system, Russia felt America had begun to pursue its own interest at everyone else's expense. This was especially true after the US (via Britain) suggested that sanctions should include excluding Russia from global financial and banking networks. These narrow, specific and painful financial sanctions caused Russia to feel less allegiance to an international financial system that was no longer serving their interests at a time when QE was changing the value of assets. This encouraged Russia to claim physical territory and to expand influence.

---

* 'Putin oversees Russian nuclear force exercise', Associated Press, 8 May 2014.

SWIFT and Mastercard

In October of 2014, in response to Russia's alleged involvement in Ukraine, the US proposed a number of financial sanctions. The UK suggested that Russia could be kicked out of SWIFT, the Society for Worldwide Interbank Financial Telecommunications, which is the core infrastructure of the global bank payments system. Without access, Russian money could not be transferred in or out of the country.* The US also encouraged Visa and Mastercard to stop processing Russian transactions as part of the sanctions.† The Russian response was to say the US and the UK cannot have it both ways. It cannot expect the US dollar to be the glue that holds the international financial system together and then use it as a gun to defend their own narrow national interests.

De-dollarising

Both Russia and China want to 'de-dollarise' the world economy and increase the amount of trade that occurs in renminbi and roubles as a result of America's seemingly poor or unfair stewardship. They too have economic policy initiatives to undermine America's power in this arena. As examples, in May of 2014, Russia and China's leaders signed a deal, the Agreement of Cooperation, which encouraged both countries to bypass the US dollar and transact increasingly in their own currencies. In June 2014 they signed the China–Russia Agreement, the biggest gas deal ever done in the world. Part of its purpose was to encourage the use of only roubles and renminbi to pay for gas, and for Russia and China to create their own natural gas benchmarks and pricing in their own currencies.

* Kenneth Rapoza, 'Russia to retaliate if banks given SWIFT kick', *Forbes*, 27 January 2015.

† Carol Matlack and Elizabeth Dexheimer, 'Russia gets ready for life without Visa and Mastercard', Bloomberg, 24 March 2014.

'Universal Diktat'

On 24 October 2014 President Putin gave a speech at the Valdai Discussion Club in Sochi in which he warned the world he was going to challenge what he called America's 'Universal Diktat', by which he meant the US dollar-led world order:

> First of all, changes in the world order – and what we are seeing today are events on this scale – have usually been accompanied by if not global war and conflict, then by chains of intensive local-level conflicts. Second, global politics is above all about economic leadership.

'We did not start this,' he went on, but if the US continued on this path states 'would be subjected to extreme hardship, or perhaps even total destruction'.

By invoking a reference to nuclear weapons, Putin drew attention to Russia's increased testing of nuclear and hypersonic missiles in the recent past. Within a few days of the speech, NATO was promptly compelled to respond to some twenty-six reported air incursions by Russian jets and bombers, which occurred over a forty-eight-hour period. That too is meant to serve as a signal.

The Russian Prime Minister, Dmitry Medvedev, also made an important statement on the SWIFT issue. He said, 'We'll watch developments and if such decisions are made, I want to note that our economic reaction and generally any other reaction will be without limits.'*

When I read this statement, which was reported by ITAR-TASS, Russia's official news agency, I assumed he meant that Russia could respond to the SWIFT issue by threatening nuclear weapons. I asked my friends at the Pentagon what they thought. They said 'What is

---

* Howard Amos, 'What would exclusion from payment system SWIFT mean for Russia?' *Moscow Times*, 28 January 2015.

SWIFT?' In the main, the US military were unaware of this market issue. When I asked traders in the financial markets what they thought Mr Medvedev meant, they assumed he meant that Russia would undermine the US dollar as a reserve currency. This explains Russia's efforts to align with China and push for a world where trade would be priced in renminbi or roubles or any currency other than US dollars.

Russia's intensified efforts to accumulate gold reflect this as well. They have pursued gold reserves on the assumption that US dollars would be worth less in future and that the rouble might be worth less too.* Once the rouble collapsed to its lowest value ever in early 2016, these gold purchases began to make more sense.

The notion that nuclear weapons could be back on the negotiating table was scoffed at and cast aside as a ridiculous notion. And yet, that seems to be exactly what has happened. Russia has increasingly sought to threaten the use of nuclear weapons.

Of course, their view is that the US and NATO provoked this. The US had been systematically decommissioning and drawing down nuclear capabilities by about 90 per cent in Europe from the end of the Cold War until 2012. In that year, President Obama began to reverse that process by announcing an upgrade of the B61 tactical nuclear weapons that remained to make them more 'usable'.† Since then the US has intensified and upgraded its nuclear presence in Europe.

Bornholm

So, considering all this, it would be strange if other valuable assets, and Russia's interest in them, stopped with Ukraine and Crimea. The commonly held view in the US and across the West had been that the whole Russia story was about Ukraine. But, for Russia, Ukraine is merely one part of the new 'Great Game'.

* Mark O'Byrne, 'Russia Gold "Buying Spree" Continues – Buy 22 Tons in November', *Goldcore*, 22 December 2015.
† Michaela Dodge, 'US nuclear weapons in Europe: critical for transatlantic security', American Enterprise Institute, 18 February 2014.

An interesting incident seems to have occurred in the Baltic in the summer of 2014. The Russians held the largest naval exercises in the Baltic since the Cold War. At the time, the Americans and NATO members I spoke to joked about whether Russia's ships would sink on the way out or on the way back. But at about that time, there were sightings of an unidentified 'foreign' submarine practically in the middle of Stockholm. It was widely assumed, rightly or wrongly, to be a Russian vessel. Later, Sweden denied that it was a submarine at all.

Then the DDIS, the Danish Intelligence service, released a statement saying that they had intercepted encrypted communications from Russian vessels in the Baltic indicating that Russia had 'simulated' a physical attack on Bornholm, a large island that sits smack in the middle of the Baltic Sea.* It happened that the alleged attack occurred during the very week that Danish politicians were gathered there for an annual conference.

This raised many issues for the US, Europe and NATO. How quickly could Russia take physical control of the Baltic if it really wanted to? It might not take long since no one in the Baltic had spent any money on defence since the end of the Cold War. The peace dividend shifted all that expenditure to other activities.

Would NATO defend Denmark? The initial reply was 'of course, yes'. NATO is obligated under Article 5 to defend any member against attack. However, everyone knows the US (and/or its president) is exhausted and not in a position to pursue another major confrontation given the draining situation in the Middle East. Would Americans really want to spend more resources defending a nation they could not place on a map?†

In any case, why target Bornholm? For an answer, one might need look no further than the island's location, the Baltic, with its vast supply

---

* Danish Intelligence Service report.
† This may not matter since it seems many Americans cannot pinpoint Afghanistan on a map of the world and some, in fact, seem to think Afghanistan is where Denmark actually resides.

of fish and protein. With Russian inflation rising, access to these critical commodities is essential. To put it in perspective, by January 2016 the value of 4.5kg or 10oz of Norwegian salmon (equivalent to a single fish) was worth more than one barrel of oil.* The island also sits in the middle of critical shipping lanes for Western Europe. It might be relevant that in 2014 Russia announced it was abandoning the agreement that permitted Lithuania to inspect Kaliningrad for weapons, including nuclear weapons. Kaliningrad is the enclave nestled between Poland and Lithuania on the Baltic Sea, which sits not very far from Bornholm and Denmark.

Or perhaps the Danish island was targeted because the head of NATO at that time was a Dane, which made it a higher-value target. It also happened that Denmark was considering using its fleet to enhance NATO's radar for their missile defence system. Russia responded to that possibility by threatening to aim nuclear weapons at Danish ships.†

By early 2017, Russian politicians were beginning to speculate that Russia might try to test NATO by attempting to provoke an Article 5 event, potentially in multiple locations. Kaliningrad is a possible flashpoint.‡ §

The Arc of Steel

So, like China's 'String of Pearls', Russia's 'Arc of Steel' is a line-up of strategic locations that one can see on a map. Let's have a look at the locations where competing national interests are increasingly apparent.

---

* Mikael Holter, 'One salmon costs more than barrel of oil as slump deepens', Bloomberg Business, 26 January 2016.
† 'Russia threatens to aim nuclear missiles at Denmark ships if it joins NATO shield', Reuters, 22 March 2015.
‡ Lizzie Dearden, 'Full list of incidents involving Russian military and NATO since March 2014', Independent, 10 November 2014.
§ Max Fisher, 'The risk of unintended war with Russia in Europe explained in one map', Vox, 9 February 2016.

The Arctic

It is estimated the Arctic holds as much as 13 per cent of the world's undiscovered oil and more than 30 per cent of the available natural gas, which would explain why Prime Minister Medvedev is reported to have called it the 'Mecca of resources'. This was echoed when Deputy Prime Minister Dmitry Rogozon briefly landed in Norway, near Svalbard, on 20 April 2015, without having alerted the Norwegians to his presence. He tweeted: 'The Arctic is Russian Mecca'. The Norwegians promptly summoned the Russian Ambassador for a dressing down.

There is a long history to Russia's interest in the Arctic. In August 2007 Russia sent a Mir submarine to go underneath the polar ice cap in the Arctic. From that vessel, Russia planted a titanium Russian flag a perilous 14,000 feet below the surface on the seabed of the Lomonosov Ridge, which divides the Arctic Ocean, to symbolise their claim that much of the Arctic belongs to Russia. Subsequently, President Putin gave a speech on the bow of a nuclear-powered icebreaker. He said that he expected some 20–25 per cent of Russian GDP to come from the incredibly rich Arctic resources, including oil, gas, minerals, gold, nickel and even diamonds. Russia subsequently established a new division of the Federal Security Service to deploy Special Forces commandos specifically trained for Arctic fighting.

Fears have been accelerating for some time in Norway that Russia would simply take physical control of parts of the country which are both undefended and perhaps indefensible, given the remote and cold nature of the terrain. It is telling – a signal, perhaps – that Norway too announced the creation of an Arctic corps of commando paratroopers, trained to protect and defend its Arctic interests. It has also moved its military command headquarters from Stavanger to Bodø, a location inside the Arctic Circle, which was originally built in the Cold War and designed to withstand a Russian nuclear attack.

Norway actively opposes China's efforts to become an observer on the Arctic Council and supports Russia's efforts to create an 'Arctic

Group of Forces'. Since 2006, Norway has held a military exercise called Cold Response in what it calls 'the High North', since four of the five countries that claim Arctic territory are NATO members: the US, Canada, Norway and Denmark. Finland and Sweden join in as well. But, somehow, despite the extraordinary training and skill required to be an Arctic commando, it does not seem likely that Norway will be able keep a strong enough foothold on the Arctic to prevent Russia and China from exploiting the territory first. This is why the Norwegians launched a $250-million Arctic spy boat, the *Marjata*, in 2014. According to the Head of Norwegian Intelligence, Lieutenant General Kjell Grandhagen, 'There is a demand from our political leadership to describe what is going on in this region,' and 'military aspects in terms of being able to defend that.'*

In another telling signal, October 2015 saw the screening of *Occupied*, a Norwegian television series based on an idea by thriller writer Jo Nesbø. The most expensive Norwegian TV programme ever made, it tells the story of a stealthy takeover of Norway's oil and energy assets by Russia (with the tacit approval of the EU and as a result of America's withdrawal from NATO). The Russians were deeply offended. The Russian Ambassador to Norway said:

> It's definitely very regrettable that in the . . . 70th anniversary of the victory of World War II, the authors of the series – as if they had forgotten about the heroic contribution of the Soviet army in the liberation of northern Norway from Nazi occupants – decided in the worst Cold War traditions to frighten the Norwegian audience with a non-existing threat from the east.

Clearly the Arctic has the potential to be a flashpoint on the Arc of Steel.

---

* Karl Ritter, 'Cold War spy games return to the Arctic', Associated Press, 12 June 2014.

The Mediterranean

Russia's desire for a presence in the Mediterranean has intensified for the same reason China's interest in the disputed islands of the South China Sea has grown: the discovery of energy reserves. There is a real possibility that the natural gas and oil reserves in the Eastern Mediterranean are extremely large and accessible given new drilling technology.* Of course, ownership of the gas fields is bound to be contested by many countries in the region, given that the value of the gas, once developed, could make whoever owns it the wealthiest in the world, per capita, even at a low oil price.

Based on the energy discoveries, Israeli firms have acquired most of the drilling rights and Israel's government seems to believe that this will lead to its energy independence from the rest of the increasingly turbulent and hostile region. The licences were granted by the owner, Cyprus, which is quite broke, incapable of defending the territory and partly controlled by the Turkish Republic of Northern Cyprus, which will also want to find a way to financially benefit from the gas fields. Eventually, Greece may challenge their ancient rival Cyprus over ownership, as will Turkey, Gaza, Syria and Lebanon, all of whom have coastlines that border these gas fields. Their entry into the conversation will not be a surprise. Meanwhile, Russia has much at stake. If the gas fields are as extensive as the geological surveys imply, Russia could lose the grip on Western Europe that it currently enjoys as the main nearby external supplier of gas.

One wonders whether Israel's neighbours really want to see that nation enjoying energy independence from the region. Moreover, it is widely suspected that Israel has upgraded its nuclear capabilities and can now potentially deliver such weapons via the Dolphin-class

---

* 10 trillion cubic square feet (TCF) at the Tamar gas field and 19 trillion cubic feet (TCF) at Leviathan gas field, both off the Mediterranean coast of Israel. Eran Azran, 'Is the Leviathan gas field a sure thing or a whale of a problem?' *Haaretz*, 26 January 2014.

submarines in its fleet.* This has special significance given that Russia has been deeply aligned with Iran for some time and provides most of the missile and anti-missile systems to that nation. Iran is viewed by Israel as a potentially mortal threat. For years financial markets and other observers have speculated whether Israel had the military capacity to 'take out' Iran's nuclear programme. The discussion mainly focused on the simple fact that Israel lacked the mid-air refuelling capacity to use planes for this purpose. It also lacked access to flight paths. The new submarine fleet may, in theory, allow them to overcome these constraints. Naturally, this is not in Russia's interests.

Russia announced its intention to maintain a permanent presence in the Mediterranean in June 2013.† The US announced its intention to 'ramp up' its presence in the Mediterranean in October 2015.‡ If there really are 122 trillion cubic feet of natural gas in the Eastern Mediterranean, then we have to expect that this part of the world will become geopolitically 'noisy' as key players in the region vie for control over the energy and its cash flows.

Greece

Russia offered Greece cash and credit if they would agree to leave the European Union. In exchange for money Russia expressed an interest in acquiring 'particular hard assets', as one anonymous Russian official was said to have put it. Greece did not go down that road but both EU and NATO officials have begun to accuse Russia of deliberately provoking the rush of refugees into Western Europe,

* Victor Gilinsky, 'Israel's sea-based nuke pose risks', *Bulletin of Atomic Scientists*, 8 February 2016.
† Alexei Anishchuk, 'Russia Announces Permanent Mediterranean Naval Presence', Reuters, 6 June 2013.
‡ David Larter, 'Navy 6th Fleet ramps up to face Russia, ISIS', *Navy Times*, 19 October 2015.

mainly through the Greek border. General Breedlove, the Supreme Allied Commander Europe of NATO, said, 'Together, Russia and the Assad regime are deliberately weaponising migration in an attempt to overwhelm European structures and break European resolve.'*

Kuril Islands

Not all flashpoints are to Russia's West. Some are to the East. Russia and Japan continue to argue over the disputed Kuril Islands, which both nations claim. Hardly surprising when the islands are reputed to have large natural gas deposits as well as the world's largest deposit of rhenium (which is essential for industrial engines), along with other minerals and resources. But perhaps most important for Russia is the fact that these islands are key to their ability to access the Arctic, as well as being a significant supplier of fish protein to Russia.

Russia and the Great Game

Russia's efforts to build and retain valuable assets are not restricted to its borders. Like China, Russia's reach is expanding. It plays its own hand at the 'Great Game'. On 26 February 2014, Russia's Defence Minister, Sergei Shoigu, said that Russia was preparing to build military bases in Vietnam, Venezuela, Nicaragua, the Seychelles, Singapore and Djibouti, among other far-flung locales.

Syria

If the top end of the Arc of Steel is the Arctic, then the bottom end is Syria. As I've said, Russia is keen to maintain ownership of warm-water ports there, at Latakia and Tartus, which they now use as the main bases for the military actions against DAESH/ISIS. We could go into the

---

* Matthew Holehouse, 'NATO Chief: Vladimir Putin "weaponising" refugee crisis to "break" Europe', *Daily Telegraph*, 2 March 2016.

history of Russia's recent involvement in Syria, but what might matter more is the simple fact that Syria represents a place where regional powers and global superpowers are now in close confrontation – with important consequences for the world economy.

Rather than viewing Syria as a local, isolated, standalone issue, it might be be helpful to put it into the context of a larger set of economic and geopolitical forces. It may be that Syria started out as a local and localised civil unrest problem, a civil war. But it is also the location of a conflict between Saudi and Iran, the two most important regional powers, as well as the flashpoint in which the nuclear superpowers, the US and NATO, come into conflict with Russia.

When I speak to policymakers from the region, I hear that they blame the US in large part for the unfolding events. Rightly or wrongly they claim that President Obama effectively abandoned America's principal allies in the region when the Arab Spring began – namely Saudi and Israel. The Saudis took grave offence that America chose to support the rebels throughout the region who were attempting to turf out their long-standing and autocratic leaders.

Every policymaker in that part of the world seems to think it is perfectly obvious that the rising price of wheat, bread and core food staples played a huge part in unleashing the anger that led to the Arab Spring. In the run-up, droughts in Russia and Australia had driven up the price of wheat and therefore bread. Caught between the pain of the global slowdown and the rising price of bread, anger turned into protest. Hosni Mubarak, who ruled Egypt for thirty years, used to say he did it by ensuring 'bread and circuses'. He meant this literally, at least in the case of bread. Egypt's political construct had long rested on one simple foundation: the provision of highly subsidised, practically free bread for the poor.

The central problem of higher wheat and bread and food prices across the region was the same for everybody. It raised awareness that the social contract was no longer serving the interests of the population. People began to ask why the bulk of the wealth was ending up in the hands of the few while the majority ended up with practically nothing.

There are those who object to this notion, of course. Some believe that, without much warning and after decades of dictatorship, the citizens of Tunisia and other countries in the region simply woke up one morning and proclaimed, 'Today is the day I have to have democracy!' This does not ring true. The populations of this region have long harboured grievances and endured unmet aspirations; what made them suddenly rise up at that particular time?

Perhaps it is not a coincidence that the man who triggered the Arab Spring was a fruit-and-vegetable seller. Tarek al-Tayeb Mohamed Bouazizi decided on 17 December 2010, at the age of twenty-six, to douse himself in petrol and set fire to himself in broad daylight in protest against the dictatorial leadership of Zine El Abidine Ben Ali, who had ruled Tunisia for twenty-three years. It wasn't just the fact that food prices were rising beyond the reach of his customers that pushed Bouazizi over the edge, though he would have noticed that, no doubt; his main complaint was that members of the state, including the police, were harassing him for ever-larger informal and even illegal payments. These 'taxes' for doing business are a staple in emerging markets. But the rise in his informal tax rate, combined with the marked rise in the price of fruit and vegetables, was more than he could bear. He chose to protest by 'exiting'. Bouazizi's death inspired the citizens at large to take to the streets and overthrow the dictatorship. His demise marks the start of the Arab Spring.

Once underway, the social protests spread across the entire region. Citizens everywhere were feeling the pain of global slowdown in conjunction with the higher cost of living. In retrospect, many concluded that quantitative easing had led to qualitative squeezing. But, whatever the cause of their pain, it was sufficiently serious for the public to push for a renegotiation of the social contract. People wanted a new social contract that would parcel out the wealth and economic opportunity more fairly and more sensibly.

The implications for Saudi Arabia have been enormous. The kingdom arguably has greater pressures than other countries in the region because of the nature of its social contract. It can be argued that the ruling family, the House of Saud, is given the latitude to remain in power, despite the fact that much of the population feel that the royal family might not be sharing the wealth fairly or even being the best guardians of Mecca. One take on the Saudi social contract is that it is based on a trade-off. The royal family agreed to permit the ultra-orthodox Wahhabi religious leaders a good deal of freedom (and perhaps financial support for their activities abroad) in exchange for being allowed to control the nation's substantial wealth.*

Saudi

So, what caused the oil price to fall so very dramatically? At the time of writing it is down some 70 per cent since June 2014. One view is that supply and demand got out of whack. It was simple economics:† Excess supply drove the price down. Another view is that the Saudis very deliberately pushed the price down. This was evidenced by their many statements, which confirmed their willingness to let the oversupply persist. In the oil world, the Saudis no longer control the pricing of the oil market but they remain the world's lowest-cost producer. So when they intimate that they will permit the price to keep falling (by not withholding supply) the markets take this to mean that they want the price lower.

Why would they do that? Well, there are conspiracy theories galore. But I think it's worth considering the geopolitical elements of the story, because the low oil price may be a signal that the Middle East is already 'at war'.

* Karen Armstrong, 'Wahhabism to ISIS: how Saudi Arabia exported the main source of global terrorism', *New Statesman*, 7 November 2014.
† Clifford Krauss, 'Oil prices: What's behind the drop? Simple Economics', *New York Times*, 9 February 2016.

First, who does a lower oil price hurt? Iran, Russia and the American fracking industry. All these were rivals to Saudi, threatening its influence on the oil price.

Most Saudis I have spoken to concur with the theory that is expressed in much of the mainstream media. The Saudis were shocked and outraged by the fact that President Obama chose to support the rebels, especially in Libya, during the Arab Spring. They were offended when the President began to speak of lessening dependence on the Middle East by building the US fracking industry. That meant cash flows to Saudi and other producers would be damaged over time. They blame the US for leaving the region in a messy nightmare, both with its intervention and its withdrawal from Afghanistan and Iraq. As a result of the latter, the old Sykes–Picot borders in the region, which were established in 1913, are now disintegrating. The vacuum the Americans are leaving behind is rapidly being filled by groups that are problematic for the Saudis, like DAESH/ISIS, Iran and Russia.

But perhaps the biggest problem, from a Saudi perspective, is that the US failed to assist them in the most pressing existential threat they face – the Iranian nuclear issue. In fact, the President did something the Saudis did not anticipate and are finding it hard to process: he decided to normalise relations with Iran and to make that the cornerstone achievement of his Presidency.

Of course, the Americans have their complaints about the Saudis too. Obviously there are long-standing and still unresolved issues regarding the export of Wahhabism by the Saudi leadership, not to mention the obvious problem of 9/11. What is clear, though, is that the relationship between Saudi Arabia and the US is perhaps irretrievably broken down as a result of all this.

Iran and Russia

The Arab Spring, in conjunction with all these other developments, has caused nations like Iraq and Syria and Yemen to fall into tribal and regional conflicts as the locals began to vie for power in the absence of a unifying force. By the Saudis' reckoning, this created an opportunity for Iran to 'have a go' at a weakened Saudi Arabia. These two countries are ancient rivals who have long sparred for the position of being leader of the Islamic world.

The Saudis believe that Iran's attempt to take control of Mecca on 20 November 1979 was intended to displace the House of Saud. The Iranian-backed Juhaymin al-Uteybi led a group of many hundreds of supporters who took physical control of Mecca for seven days. They declared a new spiritual leader of Islam, a 'Mahdi', who would be a better guardian of Mecca and Islam. The Saudis had to bring in French paratroopers to restore control over the holiest site in the Islamic world.

The Saudis, rightly or wrongly, believe that Iran is assisting Saudi opponents in Syria, in Yemen and in other parts of the region. Most analyses focus on the local political and social issues driving the Houthi rebellion in Yemen or the Byzantine politics of the Syrian situation; this ground-up approach has its merits, but there is a top-down aspect too. Saudi Arabia now views itself as being in a regional superpower war with Iran in local proxy locations like Yemen and Syria. They see these as places where the superpowers, namely the US and Russia, are engaging in proxy wars as well.

The alignment between Iran and Russia and China makes sense on one level: Iran was the only major oil supplier in the region that was not aligned with the US. Russia sells sophisticated weapons systems to Iran, such as the Almaz-Antey S-300 and S-400 long-range high-altitude surface-to-air missiles that can target and find planes and missiles well beyond Iran's borders. Their presence on the Iranian side has led to much speculation about how American weapons systems would fare against them.* China too provides Iran with

---

* Dave Mujamdar, 'American F-22s and B-2 Bombers vs Russia's S-300 in Syria: Who Wins?' *National Interest*, 22 September 2015.

sophisticated weapons systems from J-10 fighter jets to advanced cruise missiles.

One school of thought is that the Saudis believed, by pushing the oil price down, they could deprive Iran and Russia of the budget they needed to pursue this regional proxy fight. Certainly, a lower oil price would hurt the Saudis too; but they could hold their breath longer than Iran and Russia, who needed oil to fetch well above $120 a barrel for their budgets to break even and would be devastated by the loss of income. Of course both Iran and Russia deny that they are in trouble.

What no one seems to have anticipated is that the Saudis would be unable to bear the pain. Though, even before the oil price collapsed, there had been signals that the Saudi government was reining in its budget: in 2013 the kingdom abandoned its thirty-year effort to grow wheat in the desert, saying it had become too expensive.* By 2016 the new Deputy Crown Prince, Mohammed bin Nayef (known as MbN), son of the former Head of Intelligence and the nephew of King Salman, had begun to make announcements that confirm the Saudi economy is in trouble. Moreover they signal that the social contract in Saudi is unravelling.

After years of providing subsidised petrol, food and housing, on 28 January 2016 the Saudi government announced that subsidies would be substantially reduced, with electricity, diesel and kerosene all affected, and the subsidy on petrol falling by 50 per cent. On top of this VAT would be implemented, raising the cost of goods by something like 20 per cent. And for the first time in the kingdom's history, sovereign debt would be issued. In addition, the Kingdom began to float the idea that Saudi Aramco, which controls the bulk of Saudi oil production, would potentially be sold to investors in an IPO. All this confirmed that the social contract in Saudi was under historic financial pressure.

---

* Diana Al-Jassem, 'Kingdom to halt wheat production by 2016', *Arab News*, 14 April 2013.

I say the social contract because it is clear that the citizens in Saudi, as elsewhere in the region, are no longer content to see so much wealth end up in the hands of so few. Increasingly the public across the Middle East are requiring the royal families to share their wealth more broadly at the very moment that their capacity to generate revenue may be weakened by the fall in the oil price.

This all comes at a time when the dissolution of regional borders and the intensification of regional wars is giving rise to a refugee problem of epic proportions. Saudi has been extremely reluctant to take any refugees or to finance them. This is in part because the budget is already overwhelmed, a fact which makes them appear vulnerable to their opponents in the region, like Iran, which seems emboldened to challenge them as a result. They can no longer 'buy' the peace by simply writing cheques to the public.

Time, inflation, war

So, taken together, what we see are many signals both driving and emanating from the geopolitical landscape. China, Russia and regional powers in the Middle East are all critically aware that food prices and domestic stability are inseparably linked. Oil itself has emerged as a signal of military tension and geopolitical confrontation. The social contracts in all these places need to be met one way or another. One possibility is for governments to find new forms of spending. Could it be that QE4, which the markets are so anxious to have, may come in the form of military spending? Finding an opponent abroad can help divert the local population's anger about the fact that their social contract is unravelling. The Americans are quick to say that this is what is happening in both Russia and China. But those two are equally quick to point out that America, too, needs an excuse to pump money into the economy given that it's hit the 'zero bound'* of interest rate policy. Most of the emerging markets can't help but

---

* 'Zero bound' is when interest rates have fallen to zero or nearly zero.

view America's efforts to generate more inflation as hostile to their interests.

The fact that the US tells them to take responsibility for their own economies merely increases the chances that they will do just that. They will reach harder for what they need to survive. In this way, we may find that protein is the new oil. The Arc of Steel and the One Belt One Road are simply answers to the problem posed by a world in which the indebted countries try to deal with their debt by fomenting inflation. It is a worrying signal that the Western allies seem to be squabbling amongst themselves while some play Greig's Piano Concerto in A minor.

As Carl von Clausewitz memorably said, 'War is the continuation of Politik by other means'. By 'politik' he meant all 'policy' and 'politics'. Perhaps this same idea is in play today and military conflict is merely a continuation of monetary policy by other means.

The stakes here are very high

The historian Margaret Macmillan has warned of dangerous parallels between the situation today and the run-up to the Great War of 1914. In *Rhyme and Reason: Why 2014 doesn't have to be 1914*, she writes: 'The 100th anniversary of 1914 should make us reflect anew on our vulnerabilities to human error, sudden catastrophe, and sheer accident.' The difficulty of managing such vulnerabilities may be even worse today because 'the speed of communications puts greater than ever pressure on government to react to crises . . . before they have time to formulate a measured response.'[*]

All this begs us to recall the open letter Ernest Hemingway wrote in September 1935 in which he warned of the risk of another war in Europe: 'The first panacea for a mismanaged nation is inflation of the

---

[*] Margaret Macmillan, *The Rhyme of History: Lessons of the Great War*, Brooking Institution, 14 December 2013.

currency; the second is war. Both bring a temporary prosperity; both bring a permanent ruin.'*

War is obviously nobody's first or even last choice. No one wants war, but in a world where there is excess capacity and/or too much money, economic forces can conspire to destroy excess capacity and excess capital. Nothing is more efficient at this destruction than conflict. Today the stage is increasingly set for war. States are competing with each other over physical spaces for access to commodities, for the loyalty of their disillusioned and pained citizens. Accidents can happen. Mistakes can be made.

We must be careful or at least cognisant of our choices.

It might be worth revisiting the notion that there are only a limited number of paths out of a burdensome debt problem:

1. Take the pain and accept the deflation. Be like Japan or Continental Europe and sacrifice many years of growth and a generation or two to the process of managing the debt without default;
2. Introduce inflation;
3. Conflict and war;
4. Or, grow your way out through innovation.

Luckily, innovation is underway, as we shall see . . .

* 'Notes on the Next War: A Serious Topical Letter', first published in *Esquire* magazine, September 1935.

10

Innovation

This all sounds pretty tough. The terrain is rocky. Faith and confidence seems to have hit an especially rough patch. In spite of all the QE and cash that has gone into the world economy, confidence and growth are faltering. All the good things we wanted in exchange for QE have not yet arrived, and many of the ill-effects have gained momentum. Unemployment and rents are both too high. Growth and lending are too low. Financial markets worldwide opened with stunning losses in 2016.

Yes, the pressures are grim, but they promote the one thing that is required for the economy to sustainably grow: innovation. If I stick to my belief that GDP is created in the human soul, then tough circumstances are exactly what lead to the soul-searching that in turn leads to calculated risk-taking and innovation which forms the foundation of tomorrow's economy.

Unbelievers will say it cannot be done. They'll assert that there is no new Silicon Valley, no new equivalent of the financial services sector, no new product that can replace those parts of the economy that have crashed and burned. But the fact is, there is no way to anticipate what people may create. The only real question is whether or not we choose to 'be the change'. The only other option is to surrender to the change the global economy will force on us, whether we like it or not. Mahatma Gandhi's advice was to be the former: 'If we could change ourselves, the tendencies in the world would also change. As a man changes his own nature, so does the attitude of the world change towards him . . . We need not wait to see what others do.'*

Some will say that's all very well, but nothing positive can happen because capital will be scarce for those who need it most. The central banks may have expanded their balance sheets by many multiples, but it is much harder now to get a business loan, an overdraft or a mortgage. However, limited resources can actually stimulate people to pursue the ideas that really pay off. Jeff Bezos, founder and CEO of Amazon, believes that lack of access to capital is a great discipline. He says the most successful business decisions at Amazon have usually been made by the teams that were the most capital constrained and therefore forced to use imagination and ingenuity to solve problems.

It may be useful to remember the words of Admiral Jacky Fisher, who served as the First British Sea Lord in 1904. He scrapped a large chunk of the British fleet because the ships were 'too weak to fight and too slow to run away', and replaced them with HMS *Dreadnought*, the biggest gunship ever constructed at the time – in spite of a general cash crunch. He is attributed with making the observation that Winston Churchill loved to use: 'Gentlemen, now that the money has run out we must start to think!' Circumstances demand a new way of thinking.

Happily, I see many signals that fear, pain and loss have indeed stimulated innovation. People are already busy building the economy of tomorrow.

Nuts to soup

Damon Baehrel must be nuts. He was a very successful motocross champion (which is already a little nuts) until an accident put him out of action. He then decided to become a chef and restaurateur without

---

* Often paraphrased to 'Be the change you wish to see in the world'. The original quote is in the *Collected Works of Mahatma Gandhi*, Vol. 13, Chapter 153 ('General Knowledge About Health').

having one iota of background or training in the subject. Well, actually, he decided to turn the whole business model of restaurants and cooking on its head. He told Bloomberg, 'I learned bits and pieces along the way, but I never did the research, never looked in a cookbook. In my family, we just learned to do it ourselves, and the inspiration came from nature.'*

Baehrel opened a little restaurant in Earlton New York. He is the sole employee and staff member, except for his wife who does the books. His restaurant has twelve tables, no business manager, no advertising and a five-year waiting list. Based on that, he takes home about $700,000 free and clear each year. He started the venture in 2006, just before the financial crisis, and has thrived in spite of it. He says, 'I'm the chef, the waiter, the grower, the forager, the gardener, the cheese-maker, the cured-meat maker . . . everything comes from this 12-acre property.'†

His restaurant is referred to with reverence. It is considered a worthy rival to The French Laundry, which was America's top restaurant for many years. Stephen Spielberg apparently complains that it's hard for him to get a reservation there.

The moral of this story is obvious: Innovation rarely comes from doing things the way they have always been done, or from people who are playing it safe. It comes from people who have no choice but to take a risk – like Saeed Pourkay. He opened a one-man soup stand in the corner of a New York City restaurant where he makes and serves a complex Iranian soup called *Asheh Reshteh*. His career in the soup business is a story of our times:

> I ate my investments, I ate all my savings. I ended up leaving my wife, and when I separated, I have no place, no money. I got depressed a little bit, and it was difficult for me to find out what my

* Sean Patrick Cooper, 'Damon Baehrel, Chef of Most Exclusive Restaurant in the US, opens up', *Bloomberg*, 12 December 2013.
† www.damonbaehrel.com.

passion is at the age of 55. What else can I do that I don't make a mistake again?'*

Yet somehow he ended up getting a corner of a bigger restaurant and launched his soup business. Queues formed. Reviewers raved. Customers spread the word. He succeeded.

Some will say such examples of innovation are not useful because they are small, one-off cases. Others will rightly point out restaurants are notoriously difficult businesses to run. They have one of the fastest turnover rates for all businesses, meaning they open and then close at mach speed. I know that from hard personal experience. I was involved in a savoury pie business that failed. For every restaurant that opens, there are some three others, or more, that go under. But even if just one person can figure out how to make a living from selling food, that creates wealth, growth and GDP. All those who fail also contribute to GDP along the way. And they learn many priceless lessons from failing. I know I did.

What all these people are doing, the successes and the failures alike, requires hubris but on a scale they can manage with the skills they happen to have. In a world overcome by the pressures I have described, such efforts are to be celebrated. The fact that these particular people did it without being trained or educated to do it is an incredibly encouraging sign. Their success should be a signal to others who might have equally crazy or strange ideas: you can be the change.

Being the change is risky

Luckily, there are those who will not or cannot wait for economists to compile enough data. They do not want or need any declaration or proof that recovery from the financial crisis is comfortably underway. They will not or cannot wait for historians to explain what went wrong or what the right solutions should be. Instead, the sharp demands of

* Alex Gallafent, 'This chef serves Persian comfort food from the corner of a pizza joint in New York City', www.pri.org, 11 December 2013.

reality draw forth strength of character and cause them to explore and exploit change without certainty.

There is no nobility in this idea. Risk-taking and innovation are not luxury items. Some of us are not trying to reinvent the definition of a restaurant. No, we are merely trying to keep our own fridge full. That's spur enough. The great thing about the economy is that it has a place for those with great noble visions and those who are just trying to make ends meet.

Whatever the cause, acts of risk-taking are signals, beacons that lead the way out of the storm and into the economy of tomorrow. It takes hubris to engage in such great leaps of imagination and edgework. It takes a willingness to break with conventional expectations about how we should behave, what we should believe, and what is expected from us.

Signals about tomorrow's economy arise from this kind of individual action. The MBA finds she cannot become an employee because no one is hiring, so she reinvents herself as an entrepreneur. The retiree realises that she cannot survive on a fixed income because interest rates are at record low levels, so she starts to find ways to work part-time. Companies drop the business lines that no longer generate positive cash flow and enter the business lines that do. Citizens ask questions about the social contract that's in place and seek to modify it or reinvent it. The process of innovation is the positive outcome of pain.

So, while no one can prove that any of the stories that follow are going to be enduring successes, I can make the case that people everywhere are trying to build tomorrow's economy. Perhaps their calculated risk-taking, whether they succeed or they fail, will serve to encourage the rest of us to pursue our own vision. The purpose of this chapter is to try to tilt things towards hubris, so that more people will begin to make their own contribution to tomorrow's economy. Yes, hubris got us into this mess. Ironically, it's hubris, albeit balanced by a sensible calculation of the risk, that will get us out of it.

Innovation is the one truly effective and desirable way out of the formidable pressures that are bearing down on the world economy and on social contracts today. Innovation stands in stark contrast to the one truly ineffective and undesirable way out: the continued bickering about how to redistribute a stagnant or declining pool of GDP which goes on while governments find ever more clever ways to take or expropriate more of their citizens' money. Arguing about the redistribution of wealth is a mug's game that causes the character of the economy and public debate to degenerate into nasty arguments in which all sides adopt intractable, ideological positions. Innovation, on the other hand, creates wealth, enhances productivity and facilitates the transition from past limitations to future opportunities.

But, to be clear, we are still faced with a contest, a race, between the power of the state to tax versus the power of the individual to generate a profit. Both the state and the individuals in it are innovating in their efforts to 'win' this race.

Not tech

Too often it is assumed that innovation means a new gadget or implies technology in some way. Yet innovation can mean the act of *personal* reinvention, when we change career or come up with a new vision for our individual, corporate, communal, national or international future.

It is sometimes said that life begins at the end of our comfort zone, which is where a lot of people, balance sheets and nations have found themselves in recent years. We know the social contract needs rejigging. We know that no one is happy about the perceived injustice of a world in which a few benefit at the expense of everyone else. We know that we have been favouring the interests of the speculators over those of the savers and that the injustice of that is not sustainable. We know that we do not want to stumble into a Third World War. We know that the numbers don't add up.

There is both a reluctance to abandon old models, ventures, policies and definitions and a pressing need to explore new ones. Today individuals, families, communities, companies and countries are all changing the definition of who they are and what purpose they serve, and they're figuring out how to make ends meet in new ways. All these are entrepreneurial endeavours.

It does not matter whether we consider ourselves entrepreneurs or intrapreneurs (expressing entrepreneurship in the context of a large organisation); whether we are government officials or ordinary citizens. What matters is that now we are all being forced by extraordinary economic pressures to ask the question that Peter Drucker said we should ask ourselves every three years: 'If we were not already doing this, would we be doing it now?' It is a shame it takes a crisis to compel us to consider this question, but it's when we find ourselves unhappy with the status quo that we start thinking about alternatives.*

Some have already begun to build the economy we will have tomorrow, even as the debris from yesterday's economy continues to be sifted through, sorted, explained, defended and perhaps eventually vilified. The British social philosopher Charles Handy called this the 'Sigmoid Curve'† Like a radio wave, the economy has ups and downs but the next upturn starts well before the last downturn is over, just as the next downturn will begin before the last upturn is over. Our job is to find the signals that allow us to manage both. Here are some signals that innovation is both possible and underway.

One Million Cups

Consider the story of 1MC, which is a grass-roots effort by the Kauffman Foundation, based in Kansas City. It's an organisation that brings together investors and other interested parties (such as possible employees), with people who have new ideas for starting businesses.‡

---

* Peter Ferdinand Drucker, *Classic Drucker: Wisdom from Peter Drucker from the Pages of Harvard Business Review*.

† Charles Handy, *The Age of Paradox*, Harvard Business School Press, 1994.

‡ I am grateful to Barbara Mowry, the Chairman of the Kansas City Federal Reserve Bank, for bringing this organisation to my attention.

Each business gets ten minutes to talk about its idea and a sponsor pays for the coffee, which, as the organisation grows, will amount to a million cups or probably more. These events are full in every location they are held in across the United States. Hundreds of people come along to hear about ideas and to see if there is an opportunity for them to invest or find a job or work with these new ventures in some way. They are looking for signals about the future and hoping to be a signal to others.

Crowd funding

The financial system is surely innovating. One positive outcome of the financial crisis is that the world economy will never be so dependent on banks for lending again. The Internet has enabled people who want to invest to connect with people who need investment. 'Crowd-sourced' financing allows a maker of goods or a provider of services to sell the wares in advance of production. When someone wants to float an idea for a product, they can turn to IndieGoGo, Kickstarter, Funding Circle or a wide array of Internet platforms and raise money quickly. These platforms allow the purveyor to see if there is a market for their idea, product or service. In short, you can get your customers to pre-buy your product and thereby pre-fund your production. In addition, such crowd-funding efforts, even if they don't raise much money, provide pretty cheap advertising and marketing opportunities.

It is true that some crowd-funding initiatives fail. Investors lose money now and again. In the last few years I myself started a business manufacturing drones with my business partner. That's one of my bolder efforts to 'be the change' in the world economy. We witnessed a spectacular crowd-funding failure in the drone space. In 2014 Zano raised a massive £2,335,119 from more than 11,000 backers to finance the creation of a new drone, making it the largest-ever European Kickstarter crowd-funding campaign. Unfortunately, it seems the firm behind the drone, Torquing, never figured out how to make the drone actually fly (which is exceedingly common in this space), and ended up declaring bankruptcy.* So, yes: crowdfunding can fail. Then again, banks have made some pretty bad loans over the course of history too. Traditional lending has a failure rate. Bad bank loans were a major contributor to the debt mess we have today.

It is also true that crowd-sourced funding has only touched a tiny fraction of the world economy. The typical corner shop or small business still needs an overdraft, a line of credit and a bank manager who can cut them some slack when the funds have not yet arrived from an invoice. So it is important that even big businesses are beginning to find ways – in addition to crowd funding – that allow them to bypass the traditional lending system and sort out their own cash flows without the help of a bank.

Invoice factoring

Invoice factoring is thus one of the most exciting developments on the financial services horizon. Essentially, a company is now able to sell their invoices to investors who take a bet that the invoice will be paid in full and on time. The investor provides the business with cash in hand today and takes the risk that the invoice might not be paid within the specified period, which is usually something like three months. The business employs a lot of people and it is profitable, but waiting three months for an invoice to be paid ties up a lot of cash flow.

An investor charges something for taking the risk the invoice might not be paid on time or at all. But to the business, it is a small price to pay for cash in hand today. Invoice factoring permits firms to negotiate harder with banks and forces banks to lower the interest rates on their loans.

Company loans

One of the strangest and most deplorable side-effects of quantitative easing has been that very big companies can raise money on the capital

---

* Samantha Hurst, 'Largest UK Kickstarter Campaign Ever Zano Goes Bust. Begins Creditors' Voluntary Liquidation', www.crowdfundinsider.com, 18 November 2015.

markets at the drop of a hat. Really big firms can 'issue paper' (in essence, sell a piece of paper that says 'I owe you' in return for cash) very easily and at very low interest rates. But, their suppliers, who are a lot smaller usually, have not been able to secure any bank lending and they are too small to go to the capital markets. Assuming a bank is prepared to extend them a loan in the aftermath of the financial crisis, it will impose a hefty interest rate. This, of course, is one way that the central bank can recapitalise the banks. It permits a bank to borrow at a super-low interest rate but does not permit the business community to do so. As a result, businesses get charged for the losses the bank had made in the past.

However, many big firms found that their suppliers were disrupted by their inability to manage their cash flows. The price a bank charged for a loan was too high. So, in addition to invoice factoring, big firms said, let's be a banker to this supplier. After all, who knows the business and the collateral better than the biggest customer? Big firms are better placed than the very best banker to understand which suppliers would be fine and which would not. So, the very old-fashioned lending model of the 1950s and 1960s came back to life.

All of these new channels for capital prove one thing: there are profits in lending. One of the most extraordinary and positive developments in the world economy in recent years is that the real economy has provided better returns than the financial markets. I have seen lenders make well over 15 per cent each year making plain vanilla loans (everyday simple loans) to real businesses on a highly collateralised basis (offering ownership of equipment or buildings, for example, if the loan was not repaid). This has drawn banks back into the lending game.

Who started the lending? Wealthy individuals, businesses and even hedge funds began to realise that the rates of return in lending are very high if banks are refusing to lend. So, new lenders began to displace the banks. In recent years the rates of return for investors have been very high.

The average return from a hedge fund in 2015 was 'dismal'. It was mainly negative during 2014 and 2015 and averaged out at a few per cent for each year. This helps explain why hedge funds became the principal investors in crowd-funding platforms. Lending has been outperforming trading.

These returns helped to induce banks to re-enter the lending market, and they put pressure on banks and fund managers in other ways too. After all, if plain vanilla lending on a highly collateralised basis makes over 15 per cent per year, why is it that fund managers everywhere say we must get used to very low rates of return? Why bother with a sophisticated fund management product like a hedge fund if plain old lending gets you such a big return? Such returns are a powerful signal for the asset management industry. This just goes to show that innovation in the real economy is starting to displace old business models and old notions of how things should be done.

A banker and sewage

I know one fellow who lost his job on Wall Street. He had been an equity salesman for a major investment bank. He was cagey and reluctant to tell me about his new life when I talked to him. He sheepishly conceded that he had been forced by difficult circumstances to join a friend who was running a small sewage company in New Jersey, to which I replied, 'How fabulous. Now that's something with a genuine demand and a genuine cash flow!' Sewage treatment is an essential service that protects the population from untold horrors. Encouraged by my enthusiasm, he began to explain how they intended to improve cash flows, buy out competitors and eventually take the company to an IPO.

Job losses in financial services are bound to continue. Society will no longer permit banks and the financial services sector to gamble away a nation's financial future. Slowly, as we realise that the reckless losses in financial services actually jeopardised the social contract, citizens will demand that financial services be constrained. As financial services shrink, the weaker players will be pushed out. They will return to the real economy, because it's the only place they can go – and, frankly, the real economy can benefit from their skills.

For example, the algorithm experts of Wall Street will slowly end up as algorithm experts in manufacturing operations in the Midwest and the Midlands. Think of it another way: where is the most interesting place to pursue algorithms today? It is no longer the trading floor of a major bank. It is in a manufacturing operation or in the world of 'big data'.* Of course, not everybody has the required skills, especially mathematics skills, to succeed in these areas. But education is changing to accommodate this problem.

Lifelong education

Higher education and universities have got themselves into a financial mess in the same way as nations and other balance sheets. They built an infrastructure that is expensive to maintain and now lack the revenue to cover those costs. Students cannot afford to pay or are having to borrow enormous sums only to find that when they graduate there is no possibility of the kind of job that would permit them to pay off the loan. The value of a degree seems to have diminished now that there are so many graduates, and many firms are prepared to train their own staff. Many graduates don't have the mathematics and writing skills that the modern workplace demands. We now worry that the Indians and Chinese get better scores in mathematics, which means graduates cannot keep up with the higher standards being established abroad. In addition, many universities lost their endowments and fundraising collapsed in the aftermath of the crisis. As a result there is a good deal of soul-searching going on in the realm of education.

People are trying to build new business models. Luckily, many have

---

* For an excellent and comprehensive study of big data and its applications to politics see Nate Silver, *The Signals and the Noise: The Art and Science of Prediction*, Penguin Books, 2012.

concluded that education is a lifetime undertaking and there is more and more content for learning available for those who wish to upgrade their skills. Consider the story of MOOCs.

MOOCs

It is now relatively easy to access to free online education from some of the best universities and teachers in the world through Massive Open Online Courses (or MOOCs). A global audience can access education through a laptop. With less cash for shoes, clothes, technology and other 'stuff', people are instead spending more on opportunities to learn new skills. In the immediate aftermath of the financial crisis, there was a leap in demand for online education. Common sense tells us we must reinvent ourselves if we are going to find a job or sustain our earning power in a world where growth is low and unemployment is high. Indeed, if we live longer we may have to reinvent ourselves several times in a lifetime.

The aptly named Phoenix University is a good example of the new increased demand for skills. In Ancient Greek mythology, the phoenix was a magical bird* that lived for a thousand years, at the end of which it built its own funeral pyre, threw itself into the flames, burned and then rose from the ashes to live for another thousand years.

The founders of Phoenix were early pioneers in a phenomenon that is now becoming extremely popular: online education. They launched in 1986, in the midst of the Savings & Loan crisis, with one class of eight students. Today Phoenix has campuses in forty states in America as well as in Europe, China and Mexico. At its peak it had 200 campuses, although it closed the majority of them after the financial crisis. Today it is suffering because competitors including Harvard, Stanford and MIT are copying their success with MOOCs. Newer, virtually unknown competitors are emerging, further revolutionising the delivery of

---

* The phoenix myth is found in many stories of transformation, most recently J. K. Rowling's *Harry Potter and the Order of the Phoenix* (2003).

online education. For example, Southern New Hampshire University (SNHU), which few have ever heard of, was named by *Business Week* as one of the fifty most innovative companies in America in 2013.[*]

The President of SNHU, Paul LeBlanc, has lifted the enrolment from 2,000 students to 22,000 and launched College for America – an online, competency-based degree programme that costs $2,500 per course and $38,000 for the degree. Instead of requiring credits or a certain number of hours in the classroom, the course allows students to proceed based on competency. This means smart and dedicated students can finish the programme in as little as six months instead of the usual two years. SNHU expected to have 500 students but some 5,000 signed up. As *Business Week* reported, LeBlanc says his goal is 'to reach out to students whose next best educational option is nothing at all':

> The total price of Southern New Hampshire's online bachelor's degree, $38,000 isn't cheap, but it's far less than the $112,000 – not including housing or meals – the university charges undergrads for four years at the brick-and-mortar college. For the current academic year, the university is projecting a $29 million profit from the online college, which amounts to a 22 per cent margin.

In another example, the economist and Harvard University President Larry Summers chose innovation in education as his next venture after losing the nomination for President Obama's first choice to replace Ben Bernanke as the Chairman of the Federal Reserve. Summers and a small team of highly experienced academics have joined the American entrepreneur Ben Nelson, who founded the online digital photo-printing service Snapfish, to create a new university called Minerva. It aims to offer first-class teaching from real-world practitioners, without the overheads of a traditional campus, to capture the gap in the

[*] John Hechinger, 'Southern New Hampshire, a Little College That's a Giant Online', *Business Week*, 9 May 2013.

education market at the high end.* Students are chosen from those that can gain admission to, but cannot afford, the world's best universities. The recruitment and teaching will take place worldwide. Faculty will be brought in according to skills rather than the traditional academic tenure system.

Meanwhile, the pressures on budgets have pushed students out of some universities and into others. I am on the advisory board at Indiana University's School of Public and Environmental Policy for one reason. I felt that the recovery in the US was more likely to happen in the Midwest than anywhere else. So, I wanted a connection, a reason to be there. As it turns out, *US News and World Report* ranks SPEA as the second best school of public policy after Harvard's Kennedy School. But it costs a fraction of the price. So while Harvard's enrolment has been falling, SPEA's is increasing so fast that the university can hardly hire and build fast enough. These are all good examples of the kind of change that push the economy forward.

Spending on experiences

In a world where we are caught in a vice between debt deflation and rising cost of living, spending has to be curtailed. It seems that this makes us less inclined to spend money on things that will start getting old or becoming outmoded from the moment they are acquired. A cash-constrained person would rather spend their money on an experience that makes them feel good, special, privileged, that they can go on talking about long after the experience has ended. Spending on experiences is a powerful emerging trend.

Realising this, shopping malls and department stores have started to offer 'experience' content to their customers. Westfield, one of the world's leading shopping mall firms, have offered experiences in their Australian malls for a long time, being an Australian firm, but now they extending the policy globally. Their malls have all the usual sorts of

* See minervaproject.com.

shops but they also offer massages and manicures, simulated race car driving, ice skating rinks, and places where kids bungee jump or romp in jungle gyms. Their malls have valet parking and offer a dry cleaning service while you shop. Westfield is truly redefining the 'shopping' experience.

Secret cinema

Entertainment is another experience cash-constrained consumers will spend money on. And there have been some fantastic innovations in the delivery of entertainment.

Consider Secret Cinema. In 2012, 80,000 British film lovers spent £40 (about $70) on a ticket to a film-based entertainment event without having any idea what the event was. This was because Fabien Riggall, the founder of Secret Cinema, realised that films and concerts needed to be reinvented. Film lovers were becoming bored by much of what Hollywood was churning out and uninterested in paying a high price to visit a cinema where popcorn cost as much as the film ticket. The Hollywood studio system and the movie theatres alike are collapsing under the weight of their own hubris and being eroded by online film access from Netflix and iTunes, as well as the illegal bootlegging that technology makes easier every day. Riggall came up with a new way of entertaining people with film.

Imagine receiving a text message that tells you the date, but not the location, of an unnamed film, and says that you must bring long johns* to secure admission. Then another text arrives telling you the event is being held at an abandoned prison. You buy a ticket in advance and later find yourself being checked into prison like a convict. Everyone agrees to give up their personal belongings, including their mobile phones. Initially no one realises that the prison insurrection, which soon breaks out, is led by actors, who are posing both as prisoners and prison guards. The film shown is *The Shawshank Redemption*, but this is preceded by

---

* Long johns are underpants with ankle-length, close-fitting legs.

time in the prison laundry and the prison workshop, where guests learn to make little metal chairs from beer cans. After the show, some guests elect to stay the night in the 'hotel'. The sound of prison doors locking down echoes through the old building as they lie in their cells. The lights go out. Everyone wonders, 'Did I really pay to be locked up overnight without my mobile phone?' Suddenly, a spotlight goes on and a stunning woman in an elegant burlesque costume and high heels begins to walk through the dark prison, singing. It's many a prisoner's dream! The event is a mini concert as well as a film screening.

Secret Cinema has created a cult-like following, and its fans adhere to the company motto, which is an admonishment to 'tell no one'. You can't get Secret Cinema guests to tell you when or where or what. It's a secret club that anyone can join. That alone may be worth the ticket price.

Riggall launched his concert business, Secret Music, by holding a show with the folk musician Laura Marling at an abandoned Victorian Gothic building. Dubbed 'The Grand Eagle Hotel' for the night, the interior was designed to reflect her dream state, with 1960s furniture and fittings, vinyl records scattered alongside photographs of the era and windswept autumn leaves on the floor as Marling drifted from room to room giving small private concerts to whoever happened to be there at the time.*

What Riggall is doing is reinventing the business model, the film experience, and the traditional film and music business models. He is redefining modern entertainment and is now in great demand to produce and franchise film and concert events around the world.

I once met Harvey Goldsmith, one of the world's greatest concert promoters. He has staged tours for everyone from the Rolling Stones, Elton John and Madonna to Muse. As I listened to him, I realised that music fans are less inclined to spend money on huge music tours

---

* The concerts are recorded and available online from LauraMarling.com or SecretMusic.com.

where they hear the same old songs in large venues and where the same show is played over and over again for high ticket prices. There is still a market for these events, but increasingly audiences want to attend events that are cheaper and more exclusive. They prefer smaller venues where they are closer to the artist in a space that permits the artist to innovate.

Smart singers and musicians are seeking out these one-off opportunities, which is why Riggall is besieged with phone calls from famous musicians. This also explains the immense success of music festivals around the world, from Burning Man in Nevada to Glastonbury in England. These used to be 'cult' events for a small crowd of edgy people. Now they are more mainstream and generating revenues that were unimaginable even five years ago.

Pop-ups

Pop-up restaurants, clubs and shops similarly reflect the desire for a unique experience. Now we see the concept come into the workplace as well. Companies increasingly offer a lounge area instead of a staid reception area. Often there is a private business providing the coffees and doing the catering. In fact, the workplace is changing even more profoundly. More and more businesses are forming that permit people to work together in places where they can share overhead costs. As a manufacturer of drones, I have looked carefully at new options where the team can rent a space that includes access to 3D printers, metal lathes and welding equipment.

The phenomenon was made possible because property owners had to become creative in managing the declining cash flows associated with properties. In the immediate aftermath of the financial crisis, property values fell as people stopped going out and stopped shopping. Many businesses not only downsized, they moved to cheaper parts of town.

Suddenly it made sense to cadge income where you could. Forget the annual fixed rent contracts. Getting a little cash in for a few months was better than nothing. This was ideal for small businesses, which could not afford to commit to an annual rent in a fixed location while still testing out a new idea.

Restaurants go in and out of business notoriously quickly. In recent years the two sides have started to come together, solving each other's business model problems. When old businesses went bust and defaulted on their rental contracts, landlords needed to compensate by accommodating short-term renters who might then share part of their profits rather than paying a predetermined rent. The Internet facilitated the launch of these short-term 'pop-up' restaurants, shops and clubs. They could be advertised worldwide, attracting enough clients to fill the place. The brevity of the experience compelled even more innovation because it had to be fresh and different each time. Derelict and underperforming spaces suddenly became a perfect venue for an edgy innovative experience.

I spoke at the 'Makegood Festival' in 2014 in London. It was held in the Old Selfridges Hotel, which is a stripped-out, disused building. The floors are concrete. The walls are uncovered and reveal exposed electrical wiring and pipes. The Makegood Festival used the space for three days to showcase small manufacturers from all over Britain. The purveyors came from every sector: people were making textiles, handbags, shoes, whiskies, champagne, chocolates, jams and many other things. The 'pop-up' experience was a great success, according to the companies that came. Selfridges got some revenue from an otherwise unusable space. The companies got a place to display their wares to the public. Everybody benefitted.

Invention

Some acts of innovation are really acts of invention. Mikkel Vestergaard's father ran a clothing company in Denmark that supplied Scandinavians with hospital uniforms. Mikkel decided to go off to Africa instead. Once there, he realised there was a profound need for malaria netting and thought his family firm could start making medical textiles.

He created a fabric that is impervious to malaria-carrying mosquitos. The number of people who sleep under Vestergaard malaria nets is apparently larger than the number of people who use Facebook.

Mikkel did not stop there. He realised that countries like India lose as much as half their crop each year to pestilence and disease. So he invented a grain sack made from a textile that cannot be penetrated by disease or rodents. In 2012, India announced it was prepared to allow foreign direct investment into grain storage for the first time. I remember looking at a project that involved upgrading India's grain silos and improving storage. No one could comprehend that today's new silos only need ten people to operate them; that would mean displacing the 2,000 people who place grain in sacks with every single new silo. Mikkel's idea addressed the problem without displacing the people.

Dark farms

Ferran Adria ran El Bulli in Spain for many years. It was consistently ranked the best restaurant in the world. He is world famous for his ability to extract flavour from food. His cooking was more like an alchemical process than cooking. He has now closed El Bulli and is spending some of his time developing 3D printed food and opening a cooking lab called the *El Bulli Foundation*. It sounds disgusting, but modern technology permits the fusion of first-class flavour and texture with formerly unpalatable proteins. Plain vegetables like cassava can be converted into something flavourful. More challenging is the idea that powdered and crushed insects can be a palatable source of protein too. But, the innovations in the 3D printing of food are likely to astonish us. They are also capable of reducing the supply shortages that currently plague the world economy, with 3D printed food technology permitting increased nutrition even for the poor and the sick. Hospitals can anticipate 3D printers that allow doctors to adjust the nutritional content to fit an individual patient's needs. So people recovering from surgery could soon have identical meals with differing nutrition or, even better, whatever meal they want with exactly the nutrition the doctor 'ordered'.*

There is no doubt that many innovations are being brought to bear on farming and food production. Satellite-based laser resurfacing can make land far more productive. The new mega tractors can tell the driver the exact value and weight of different grades of grain being harvested while the driver has no need to even touch the steering wheel.

Caleb Harper runs City Farm at the MIT Media Lab. He aims to grow food inside urban areas, in and on urban buildings. His approach needs no soil, little water, no chemicals, very little fertiliser and a manageable amount of energy, especially when compared to how much energy is used to bring in food from rural areas. His approach propagates plants three to four times faster than traditional methods. Urban food for urban consumption will diminish food vulnerabilities.

The innovations in the food sector are astonishing. The only question is how fast they actually happen. Can they happen fast enough to avoid more Arab Springs and more social unrest in the near coming years? Probably no. Can they be counted on to change the future we will face over time? Probably yes.

Starbucks and genetics

Stefan Roever is an entrepreneur who has backed several Silicon Valley ventures and is deeply interested in innovation. He has a strong personal interest in genetics and so noticed when the guy in front of him at the Starbucks in Silicon Valley had a book on genetics. He struck up a conversation. It turned out this new acquaintance had dropped out of Berkeley University, where he had been studying the subject, in order to devote his time to building a machine that could identify

* I am grateful to Egbert-Jan Sol who is the Director of Innovation for High Tech Systems and Materials at TNO in the Netherlands for this insight.

genetic markers without requiring samples to be sent off to a lab. He was building this machine in his garage, with no funding, no partners and no certainty it would ever work. Stefan had a look at his project, concluded he was on to something, agreed to back it and became the CFO of what is now known as Genia. The company's goal is to reduce the cost of genetic testing to $100 from its current price of thousands of dollars and to provide an on-the-spot answer to almost any genetic question, rather than oblige the patient and doctor to wait for test results from a lab. Genia is on the path to revolutionising genetic medicine, and has now been acquired.

Bio-warfare

This kind of invention has spurred another sort of innovation which militaries and defence departments are now alert to: the possibility of bio warfare based on genetics. In November 2012 *The Atlantic* published an article called 'Hacking the President's DNA'* in which they suggested that governments everywhere are keeping the DNA of their own leaders safe (which seemingly involves asking the Secret Service to vacuum everything the President touches) and trying to get hold of the DNA other leaders leave lying around. This is because, in theory, diseases can now be created that will attack the one person it has been designed to attack. This constitutes a sobering innovation in how modern warfare and even diplomacy may be conducted.

Today we can build things as complex as genetic testing systems and new kinds of drones in our garages because we have access to computing power and materials that used to be available only in a classified defence lab. I mention drones because I decided to demonstrate my own commitment to innovation by co-founding a robotics firm that makes helpful drones. They can be used to help a paralysed

---

* Andrew Hessel, Marc Goodman and Steven Kotle, 'Hacking the President's DNA', *The Atlantic*, 24 October 2012.

person experience real-time 'flying' and enable them to go 'chat' with a neighbour. They can be used to survey buildings, agricultural farmland and pipelines. They can help athletes see themselves real time as they perform sports as diverse as skiing, rowing and running. And, they can help first responders find and have a conversation with accident victims faster. The manufacturing of the drones has taken place in my office in London. There are soldering irons, glue guns and bits of electrical wire everywhere. Once the orders start coming in and production really gets under way, we intend to move to larger premises. But in the meantime the noise my office produces is a signal that gives me great comfort that the economy of tomorrow is being built today.

Angels and Hailo

Many new businesses are launched from around a kitchen table. No mathematical skills or degrees are required for this kind of innovation. Consider the story of Hailo. Three London taxi drivers found themselves unable to generate sufficient income after the financial crisis. The rich bankers and fund managers in London weren't taking taxis as often. The taxi drivers schemed with some friends who were tech experts about how to better connect with possible customers and came up with a novel idea. What if the customer could 'hail' a taxi by using a mobile phone? Surely GPS technology would make it easy for the driver to decide whether it was worth a short drive to collect a passenger and whether it was worth it to the passenger to wait a few minutes for a taxi that would come to the door. The idea took off. Nearly half of all London taxis signed up for Hailo, it has become hugely popular and has expanded into cities across Europe, North America and Asia. Smart investors like Accel and the founders of Spotify and Skype backed it. It worked beautifully until they raised their minimum fare to £10 on a weekday and £15 on a weekend. At that point another taxi App came into fashion: Get Taxi. That company has now expanded into the US, Russia and Israel.

The American equivalent is Uber, which connects drivers who have downtime and passengers who need a lift. The limos that hover around airports often have downtime between jobs, so they log on to Uber, as do the customers who know they can get a nice limo fast for a ride that doesn't cost much more than a taxi.

By the summer of 2014, taxi strikes were called in London and other cities as traditional taxi drivers began to comprehend the meaning of Uber. But, they still don't 'get' what Uber really means. In August 2013 Google invested US$258 million in Uber – 86 per cent of the fund that Google had set aside for interesting acquisitions. Google simultaneously announced the acquisition of the first fleet of driverless cars, which will, no doubt, be used by Uber. Soon after the acquisition, Mercedes announced that its first driverless cars will be available to the general public in 2015. So, driverless limos are not far away.

Apparently such driverless cars now have a collective 700,000 miles on the road and few accidents. No human being could match that. Speaking of cars, the co-founder of Paypal, Elon Musk, has revolutionised car design with his new company, Tesla Motors, and has created a hugely successful luxury car from scratch (the Tesla Model X and Model S). Yes, it has had problems. The lithium battery has a tendency to catch fire when it smashes into something. Then again, I have seen car engines in flames on the roadside and they have a lot less innovation and glamour behind them. Musk's design is immensely innovative. The engine is underneath the passenger seats, leaving the front of the car for storage and a highly effective crumple zone to protect passengers from any frontal impact. Overall, it has the look and feel of an overgrown iPad and even plugs into normal electricity mains.

In the meantime, 3D printing has enabled customers to 'print' highly customised professional racing bikes, such as the titanium Empire Cycles MX-6 full suspension bike and the titanium Flying Machine. Even motorcycles can be 3D-printed these days. The Italian Energica Ego bike is one example. Victory Motorcycles, the classic Indian motorcycle brand, has been brought back to life through 3D printers that copy the original designs.* Happily, 3D printing has also been used to reconstruct the face of a Welshman who came off his motorcycle. Surgeons simply 3D-printed the missing parts of his skull, including the eye socket. Printed body parts and organs are becoming closer to everyday reality. Innovation is everywhere.

Couture

All sorts of businesses can spring to life from small ventures. It would be a mistake to think that the skills of a geneticist or a car manufacturer are necessary. It is also a mistake to believe that only 'hard industry' which involves the manufacturing of metal and machinery matters. Clothing, textiles and fashion move the economy too.

Consider the story of Ralph & Russo. This couture clothing company creates fabulous fashion, from stage costumes for Beyoncé to wardrobes for official state visits by various royal families. A dress from Ralph & Russo can easily cost tens of thousands of dollars running into the hundreds of thousands. Everything is made by hand for its clients from an atelier in Sloane Street in the epicentre of one of the most expensive megacities in the world, London. Tamara Ralph and Michael Russo, both Australians, met walking down the street in London, became friends, eventually married and founded their couture label. For Tamara, sewing was a family craft, passed down from several generations. Michael was a young entrepreneur who had launched several ventures. They started the business in 2007, just before the financial crisis, with only one sewing machine and no contacts among high-fashion customers. Their biggest problem has been a shortage of workers with sufficient haute couture sewing skills.

Tamara told me, 'Everyone wants to be a "designer", but nobody wants to sew.' The fashion world is full of people who can draw or style,

* Scott J. Grunewald, 'Classic American Motorcycle Brand Indian Motorcycle Ressurected With 3D Printing', *3D Printing Industry*, 14 March 2014.

but is exceptionally short of craftsmen who actually know how to sew, how to work with beading or leather, how to perform the detailed and highly skilled techniques associated with making haute couture gowns. For me, this signals something everybody knows about the modern educational system. It is preparing people for a white-collar world that no longer exists and has failed to provide people with the real-life skills that give rise to innovation in the real economy. Thankfully, education has begun to innovate to reflect these changes. There are many signals of the kind of edgework and reinvention that leads to economic recovery, growth, the creation of wealth and GDP. Rather than waiting for economists to confirm that change in the economy is occurring, or for historians to explain it, edgeworkers are assessing the landscape, looking for signals, balancing the drive of their hubris against their fear of nemesis and choosing to 'be the change' in the world economy.

Knitting and quilting

This brings me to a curious story. In 2012, I happened to sit next to a quiet lady at the open-air lunch. Everyone at the table was craning their heads to hear what the influential policymaker sitting there had to say. I started to chat to her instead (because I already knew what he was going to say). After some gentle prodding, she revealed that she had started a knitting shop that sold specialist wool and provided classes to people who are serious about the knitting craft. This shop launched during the financial crisis but made a profit pretty much immediately. After all, there are always people who love knitting and who are always hunting for innovative yarns and designs. I said I believed that the weakened economy would cause more people to take up knitting. Why buy a sweater when you can knit one for far less money but with more originality? Knitting is a good example of spending less money on things and more money on experiences. Meanwhile, as Bangladeshi and Chinese factory workers clamour for higher wages, the cost of a manufactured sweater is rising.

The presence of such an entrepreneur in the midst of policy-makers struck me as a signal itself. How strange to be sitting next to a real, live example of the market finding its own solution, while surrounded by people who don't believe that this person exists. Worse, policymakers have chosen to define 'the market' as Wall Street or the City rather than a place where one can find millions of people like this who are pursuing business ventures. But people like this do exist. They quietly build interesting businesses all the time. Consider the 'Queen of Quilting', Jenny Doan. According to the *Wall Street Journal*, more than a million people (a number that most music bands would envy) have watched her YouTube videos in which she shows you how to make quilts easily and quickly.* Her shop, the Missouri Star Quilt Company in Hamilton, employs around eighty people, and as many as fifty to a hundred customers arrive every day who buy everything needed to make an imaginative quilt. Apparently the local diner and hardware store are doing extremely well too as the spouses of the quilters entertain themselves.

Why are these stories important?

The Federal Reserve and other central banks believe that the failure of every large bank and many businesses in the economy at one moment in time could never be fixed or offset by even a million Jenny Doans, Tamara Russos and Elon Musks. No doubt this is true in the moment of a financial-market-and-economy-wide emergency. Central banks should stand as the lender of last resort under such conditions, but when does the helping hand of central bank support in an emergency become the hand of government that crushes the entrepreneurial spirit? No econometric model can tell us where that line is drawn. It will be in a different place in every society depending on the prevailing social contract. It will take creative thinking to figure out where it is and where it could be, wherever you happen to live.

* Jim Carlton Short, 'Entrepreneur Stitches Together a Quilting Business', *Wall Street Journal*, 31 January 2014.

The whole point of the central banks' response to the crisis – the low interest rates, the unlimited liquidity, the asset purchases – is to hold up the market, because if it were allowed to fall the economy would descend into oblivion. These policymakers believe that Jenny Doan, Tamara Ralph, Stefan Roever and the owners of knitting shops and drone ventures alike cannot be trusted to discern the signals for themselves, to see when rents fall to an all-time record low, to realise that the financial strains on families will result in people wanting to make their own quilts or sweaters.

Animal spirits and hubris

Central bankers fear that the entrepreneur or 'mompreneur' and even the consumer cannot overcome their fear. They need encouragement to begin risk-taking and spending again. Their 'animal spirits'* have to be enticed into action (and then restrained later when all is going well). It will take shockingly low interest rates to compel them and other risk-takers to take their cash out of their bank account and put it to work in the market.

It is possible that the failure of a major bank was enough to paralyse risk-taking in the economy. After all, the failure of Lehman Brothers was a lightning flash that exposed the fact that almost every financial institution was potentially illiquid, if not insolvent. 'Panics,' as John Stuart Mill observed long ago, 'do not destroy capital; they merely reveal the extent to which it has been destroyed by its betrayal into hopelessly unproductive works.'† The Lehman Brothers event, and the panic and crisis that ensued, revealed that almost every industrialised

---

* This term was first used by J. M. Keynes in his book, *The General Theory of Employment, Interest and Money* (1936) and more recently revived by the Nobel laureates George Akerlof and Robert Schiller in their book, *Animal Spirits* (2009), in which they write: 'The proper role of the government, like the proper role of the advice-book parent, is to set the stage. The stage should give full rein to the creativity of capitalism. But it should also countervail the excesses that occur because of our animal spirits.'
† John Stuart Mill, *On Credit Cycles and the Origin of Commercial Panics* (1867).

economy had a debt problem that could not be financed if the banking system failed.

Freshwater and saltwater thinkers alike were compelled to grab the steering wheel from a market that was punch-drunk on its own hubris. Having taken control of that steering wheel and seemingly guided the economy back to a safer place, it is understandable that policymakers are reluctant to relinquish control of the unpredictable market to a sea of unknown anonymous individuals engaging in seemingly small ventures from their kitchen tables and garages. That same sea is filled with the killer sharks from the financial markets who will take the free money and still savage their prey. This is an important signal of hubris itself. Perhaps when policymakers moved the losses from the banking system and placed them on the government's balance sheet (i.e., on the shoulders of the taxpayers), they also unwittingly allowed hubris to move from the financial market into the heart of government. Policymakers now trust their own capabilities more than those of the markets. They believe they have control over the outcomes.

The Great Depression

It is hard to know whether QE and other government efforts are prolonging the slowdown or quickening the recovery. The debate harks back to the Great Depression years. Saltwater types tend to love President Roosevelt. They believe his efforts to put the nation back to work with the building of the Hoover Dam, the Tennessee Valley Authority and the many 'ditch-digging' programmes saved the nation from an even worse outcome. However, there are others who believe that Roosevelt's ditch-digging efforts actually prolonged the Great Depression. I find myself in agreement with the author Amity Shlaes,* who believes that Roosevelt's efforts to control the price of milk and

* Amity Shlaes, *The Forgotten Man: A New History of the Great Depression*, Harper Collins, 2007.

steel and other core goods actually destroyed the market mechanism and doomed the economy to an unnecessarily prolonged recession. The economy would have revived but government intervention inhibited the recovery by interfering in prices. Today many governments from Latin America to the Middle East to Asia are once again seeking to control the price of food by restricting exports, taxing imports and setting prices instead of allowing markets to do this. But the most important development in the world economy today is that many governments are artificially suppressing the single most important price in any economy: the price of money.

While these two camps debate counter-factuals, the facts for today's financial crisis seem clear. In response to a historic loss that jeopardised many nations' citizens, governments gave the financial services sector a blank cheque. Far from being held to account for the losses, the financial services sector was given access to so much cash that it no longer had to sell its broken assets. Meanwhile, the real economy has learned to manage without them. With seemingly unlimited support, banks can just wait for the economy to improve and sell when prices return to normal levels.

Some policymakers explained to me that their purpose in bailing out the banks was to buy time, to hold open the window of opportunity to sell. They fully expected banks to sell their broken assets so that the market could invest again and the banks could strengthen their balance sheets. This plan backfired. The free money from government allowed the banks to not only retain these assets but to double up on them.

Profits vs revenues

What matters now is whether the policy stance of government is stopping or slowing innovation and the building of the economy of tomorrow. In his book, *Competition as a Dynamic Process* (1961), the American economist John Maurice Clark wrote that competition that keeps prices down is fair, but there are 'enabling' and 'underlying' conditions' for innovation. These include 'the character of the people', which we've discussed, and whether the 'problem-solving' population 'should operate under a secular government and religious attitudes that are hospitable to its exercise'.

That's our question now. Are policymakers and governments 'hospitable' to risk-takers and innovation? As it stands, most governments want to tighten control. This issue stands at the heart of modern political economy. Yes, there is innovation as we have seen here, but can the innovations of the small business, the anonymous risk-taker, outrun the innovations of the state? As I mentioned in chapter one, the world economy can be reduced to two fundamental forces: the power of the state to tax and the power of the individual to generate wealth. Both must balance hubris and nemesis within themselves to coexist with each other. This is why we now need to understand that the state is innovating too.

Marijuana

In 2012, the state of Colorado announced it would be legalising marijuana.* By 2017 many more states had done the same. Hawaii has considered decriminalising just about every sort of drug. Washington DC is decriminalising marijuana. Current and former presidents of Mexico have said that Mexico is on the same path and will certainly legalise if California does.

Why? Did public morals in Colorado and all these other places suddenly change? No. The simple fact is that if you make something legal you can tax it. It is no coincidence that Colorado announced the opening tax rate of 30 per cent on sales of cannabis. On 1 January 2014, the first day of legal trading, the state-regulated pot industry set a price

---

* New York's Governor Cuomo has announced plans to loosen the terms under which seriously ill patients can be permitted to use it, but not to fully legalise it. New York will be the twenty-first state to pursue this idea. (Susanne Craig and Jesse McKinley, 'New York State is Set to Loosen Marijuana Laws', *New York Times*, 4 January 2014.

of $250 per ounce and generated sales of over $1 million.* Colorado expects some $600 million in sales and nearly $70 million in revenue in 2014 alone. It turns out 'Maui Wowie' can generate an awful lot of revenue for state and local governments.

If this continues to unfold, not only will it add to tax revenues, but it will dramatically diminish the resources needed to enforce against its use. The Mexican Drug War has generated immense negative publicity. Some 100,000 people have died or gone missing and the continuous headlines about headless corpses frighten investors and tourists alike. So, any effort to change the focus of policy will probably work to the benefit of both sides of the border. The costs of drug enforcement for California, Columbia and Mexico would probably fall. There will always be those who argue that legalising one drug will simply fuel the trade in illegal ones. That may be, but what matters is that these local and national governments are trying to innovate their way out of a problem without killing the entrepreneurial efforts of the citizens.

The dog and the Frisbee

Generating fines is a favourite way for governments to raise revenues. Naturally many policymakers and the general public are keen to constrain the financial services sector, considering the havoc it has wreaked. So we see a lot more regulation and fines being put in place in this arena. The financial services sector has been subject to an endless stream of fines related to tougher enforcement of existing rules and the introduction of new ones. J. P. Morgan has emerged as one of the most fined financial institutions. By the end of 2013, it had been subjected to a record $13 billion in fines in a single settlement with the US government over allegations that it had misled investors over mortgages in the run-up to the financial crisis.† It paid another $1 billion

---

* Alec Torres, '$1 Million in Pot Sold in Colorado on First Day of Legal Sales', *National Review*, 3 January 2014.

† 'JP Morgan in record $13bn settlement with US authorities', Business News, bbc. co.uk, 20 November 2013.

in fines over trading losses associated with its Treasury function, the 'Chief Investment Office'.* The cumulative fines are hard to estimate because there have been so many in the aftermath of the crisis, ranging from claims of market abuse to misleading investors.† One thing is certain, however: every bank feels it is under far more rigid scrutiny than ever before and regulators want them to feel this pressure. The fact that such pressures generate revenue is an added bonus.

But is this going to achieve the right outcome? Is it going to make the finance sector behave better? Is it going to shut down finance or restore it as a means of lubricating the normal functioning of the economy?

Andy Haldane, an Executive Director of Financial Stability at the Bank of England and a member of its Financial Policy Committee, suggests a simple analogy: you can't teach a dog to chase a Frisbee; they just do it.‡ Knowledge of physics and flight dynamics will not help a dog to catch a Frisbee any better. Similarly, excessive efforts by governments to direct the hounds of the financial markets towards the right outcomes are likely to fail.

Some will object to the financial market participants being referred to as dogs, but I was one of them for many years and here is what I know about them: they are very good at finding the juicy red meat that we call profit. Assuming we do not support Communism or Socialism as an economic model, profit is the lifeblood of the economic system. (If we do support these other systems, then we still need to figure out how to generate more income than the government is paying out or else face certain bankruptcy as a nation.) If the economy fails to generate profit, it will kill any business and any nation as well. The puzzle is therefore how best to do this while avoiding the disasters that can occur

---

* This was the so-called 'Whale' scandal.

† 'JP Morgan Chase's Long List of Expensive Legal Settlements Grows Even Longer', TheDailyBeast.com, 20 September 2013.

‡ Andrew G. Haldane and Vasileios Madouros, 'The Dog and the Frisbee', Federal Reserve Bank of Kansas City's 36th economic policy symposium, 'The Changing Policy Landscape', Jackson Hole, 31 August 2012 (www.bankofengland.co.uk).

when the hounds of the financial market are left unleashed and savage the innocent public. Record fines are one innovation governments are imposing to achieve this goal, but they may not address the central driver of behaviour.

Sheep dogs and pit bulls

I recall the words of John Whitehead, whom I met when I served in the White House. As the Managing Partner at Goldman Sachs, he developed the Fourteen Principles that should guide the firm in its actions:

> Our assets are our people, capital and reputation. If any of these is ever diminished, the last is the most difficult to restore . . . We are dedicated to complying fully with the letter and spirit of the laws, rules and ethical principles that govern us. Our continued success depends upon unswerving adherence to this standard.*

He wrote this in the 1970s, a time when Wall Street and the financial markets were dominated by partnerships in which each partner was liable for any losses the firm might incur. After Wall Street and the City shifted to a limited liability model in which the company could go bust without impacting on the personal liability of the senior management, the incentives changed.† John Whitehead was, in a sense, a sheepdog. He could perfectly well go after the profits but would always do so without savaging the innocent sheep in the pen (pensioners, savers and the man on the street). As banks began to have shareholders instead of partners, as unlimited liability gave way to limited liability, it started to make sense to test the 'letter and spirit' of the law. After all, the greatest profits are often found at the edge of the law and regulation.

---

* Goldman Sachs' 14 Business Principles can be read on the website, www. goldmansachs.com, under 'Business Principles' in the 'Who We Are' section.
† I am grateful to Dr Ngaire Woods, Dean of the Blavatnik School of Government at Oxford University, for her work on the subject of incentives arising from the public listing of banks.

The presence of shareholders and the incentive of a rising share price seem to encourage greater risk-taking than the old partnership structures. When unlimited liability gave way to limited liability, the signals changed in ways that encouraged the transformation of sheep dogs into pit bulls. I have yet to see a government innovation that encourages better behaviours.

Instead, the policy response has been similar to the punishment the Ancient Greek gods inflicted on Tantalus. The word 'tantalise' comes from the legend of a man who angered the gods by not only stealing their ambrosia and nectar and revealing their secrets, but also sacrificing his own child and serving him up at the gods' banquet. As punishment, Tantalus was condemned to stand up to his neck in water, within easy reach of the low-hanging fruit on a tree, but whenever he reached for the fruit, the branches extended away from his grasp, and whenever he bent to take a drink, the water receded away from him. The markets are now subject to a similar torture. Yes, there may be endless liquidity, but most of the time market participants are punished for actually using it.

The Gods of Regulation want banks to make plain vanilla loans to real businesses and real people. This is trickier than it sounds, because the banks fired all the lending officers years ago and replaced them with algorithms that have been proven to not work. For most other activities, banks are faced with a range of regulatory obstacles, from investigations* to caps on pay-outs, that effectively prevent them from using the free money in the system. The problem with the 'Tantalus punishment', which lasts for eternity, is that it renders the banking system incapable of getting on with the work society wants and needs it to do. Profits need to be captured. Disasters need to be avoided.

We have to think about something John Coates writes about: the 'hour between the dog and the wolf' which is when a testosterone surge or a biochemical change causes traders to focus on their prey (a

---

* Such as the Libor and Foreign Exchange abuse investigations.

profit).* We want a dog that hunts. We don't want a massacre. The question is how to balance the hubris and the nemesis in this context. The subject of incentives lies at the heart of our social contracts: how can bad, overly risk-taking behaviours be disincentivised and good ones incentivised? Of course, it is quite awkward asking this question, given that the central government policy in most industrialised countries has been to reward epic losses by making a semi-permanent commitment to handing the financial services sector a blank cheque in the form of low interest rates and virtually unlimited free money.

Exhibition Road

Friedrich Hayek was as influential and renowned as J.M. Keynes but not quite as famous. His views counterbalanced those of Keynes, who believed government could and should intervene in the economy whenever trouble appeared. He described how both the political left and right begin to offer state planning and redistribution as a means of relieving the citizen of the burden of figuring out how to manage the economy after a crisis. The moderates in the middle warm to the idea that a 'little' state protection is warranted, given the damage that the 'free market' has inflicted on the citizens. This is how we find ourselves stepping back on to what Hayek called 'The Road to Serfdom': the road to less freedom, less choice, less productivity and less GDP.†

Perhaps another road could be considered.

Exhibition Road is in the South Kensington neighbourhood of London. The striking quality of this road is that there are no street signs. There are no markings to distinguish the kerb from the road itself. There are no parking lines on the ground, or any 'street furniture' such as road signs, speed limit signs, traffic signals or anything else to indicate where to walk, park, drive or stop. I recall the first time

---

* John Coates, *The Hour Between the Dog and the Wolf: Risk-taking, Gut Feelings and the Biology of Boom and Bust*, Fourth Estate, May 2012.
† Friedrich Hayek, *The Road to Serfdom*, Routledge, 1944.

I stepped into Exhibition Road. I felt a distinct wave of unease come over me. I was disoriented. A car drove by very close to where I was walking. I realised I wasn't at all sure whether I was on the pavement, where pedestrians are supposed to be. There were cars parked at odd angles and seemingly in the middle of the street. I literally stopped in my tracks and focused on my surroundings. This is the intention. The absence of signals and signage compels everyone to slow down and concentrate. Drivers and pedestrians alike realise that they must take responsibility for their own safety and their own actions. It turns out that when signals and signage are removed, the accident rate collapses.

Yacht racing

During my time working in the financial markets I realised you could see things as something like a yacht race. Players in the financial market always have the best and most expensive boats and equipment, which enhances their ability to push hard against the boundaries of the rules and regulations. They are fast and focused. Meanwhile, the regulators are usually in the equivalent of a dinghy, unable to keep up with or even see the race as it takes place. They tend to find out what happened well after the events have already occurred. So, more rules, more regulations and more law does not usually fix problems. It often exacerbates them and sometimes gives rise to unintended consequences.

Consider the birth of the Eurobond market. Some $4 trillion a year is raised through Eurobonds. Companies issue debt in foreign currencies or issue debt in their own currency abroad. This permits firms to raise money from investors worldwide in the currency of their choice.

Eurobonds began in 1962 when John F. Kennedy, then President of the United States, came to believe that the debt problem was so large it had to be addressed at once. Little did he know how large it could become. He announced the imposition of a financial services tax* that would be applied to the sale of all US government bonds. In

---

* The Interest Equalisation Tax, 1962.

response, a young man named Stanislas 'Stanley' Yassukovitch, who headed Merrill Lynch in London, realised that US government bonds could easily be sold from London, where they would be exempt from that tax. Yassukovitch is said by some to be the godfather of the now massive Eurobond market because he pursued this innovative idea that, ever since, has permitted companies to raise some $4 trillion every year from investors outside the United States.*

Foreign firms can also raise funds in foreign currencies on the Eurobond market, hence Dim Sum Bonds (which are denominated in Chinese renminbi), Samurai Bonds (denominated in Japanese yen), Kangaroo Bonds (denominated in Australian dollars) and even Pho Bonds (denominated in Vietnamese currency).

Inflation as a tax

There are many examples of government innovation and its intended and unintended consequences, but I'd like to come back to the idea that inflation is an innovative method of taxation. It is an innovation today in the sense that it has revived an old idea that most have forgotten. Milton Friedman wrote:

> Since time immemorial, the major source of inflation has been the sovereign's attempt to acquire resources to wage war, to construct monuments, or for other purposes. Inflation has been irresistibly attractive to sovereigns because it is a hidden tax that at first appears painless or even pleasant, and, above all, because it is a tax that can be imposed without specific legislation. It is truly taxation without representation.†

In theory, the bond market should serve as the brakes on government

* This story was related to me by Michael von Clemm, another 'father of the Eurobond market' before his death in 1997.
† Milton Friedman, 'Monetary Correction: A Proposal for Escalator Clauses to Reduce the Costs of Ending Inflation', Institute of Economic Affairs, London, 1974: Occasional Paper, no. 41.

efforts to inflate. If money is debased too much, if interest rates are kept too low for too long, if too much money is printed, then the bond market ought to sell it off. This places a constraint on the ability of the government to persist with inflationary policies, but there are innovations that governments can make to prevent the bond market from responding or slowing the inflation pressure. For example, we can already recognise and anticipate the introduction of regulations that compel pension funds and banks to own 'safe' assets. The definition of 'safe' is the one thing that an investor wants to sell when governments are inflating or debasing paper money but which the government wants them to own: government debt.

This is a silent and effective way of forcing the losses away from the government's balance sheet and into the citizens' pocket. Of course there are other ways. Government can just take the money out of your bank account. This is what happened inside the Eurozone in Cyprus on 16 March 2013. On that day the World Bank, the International Monetary Fund and the European Union together demanded that the Cypriot government take a 'one-off "stability levy" of 6.75 per cent on all bank deposits of €100,000 or less and 9.9 per cent for deposits over that amount, with the aim to raise €5.8 billion'.* Cyprus was also required to tighten the national budget by about 4.5 per cent of GDP and the central bank of Cyprus was asked to sell almost all of its 13.9 tonnes of gold for cash.

This expropriation was a condition the EU had set for Cyprus to qualify for a €23 billion bailout, which had become essential once it became clear that the Greek default had exposed the fact that the Cypriot banks and government were no longer just illiquid, they were insolvent and in need of life support.

In exchange for their cash, the depositors at the Bank of Cyprus were issued with the stock of their bank. This was presumed to be nearly

---

* See Eurogroup Statement on Cyprus, 16 March 2013 at www.consilium.europa.eu/press/press-releases/2013/03/pdf/Eurogroup-Statement-on-Cyprus/

worthless. Depositors at Laiki Bank got nothing. Obviously, such an event would normally prompt depositors to transfer their money abroad, so capital controls were introduced simultaneously with the expropriation announcement. Daily withdrawals from cash machines were capped at €260 for individuals and €500 per day for companies. Ultimately, according to some analyses, the expropriation came to roughly 47.5 per cent of the cash in every bank account in the Bank of Cyprus and Laiki Bank that contained more than €100,000.*

Innovation versus Intervention

Individuals and companies are perfectly capable of innovating their way out of the debt mess as long as governments don't try to kill the goose that wants to lay golden eggs. Martin Wolf, editor of the *Financial Times*, points out:

In 1816, the net public debt of the UK reached 240 per cent of gross domestic product. This was the fiscal legacy of 125 years of war against France. What economic disaster followed this crushing burden of debt? The Industrial Revolution.†

Wolf is arguing that innovation can create GDP, which is true. He is hoping that some anonymous person(s) or process will suddenly become wildly successful so that we find ourselves with a revolutionary new economic engine. I believe this can happen, given my confidence in the ability of the common person to innovate and navigate the complexities of the world economy. There are many examples that such innovation is already underway, as we shall see. The greater the economic pressures, the greater the capacity for innovation and reinvention. But just because a new Industrial Revolution is possible does not mean it will happen. And even if it did, it does not absolve

* 213 Menelaos Hadjicostis, 'Bank of Cyprus depositors lose 47.5 per cent of savings', *USA Today*, 29 July 2013.

† Martin Wolf, 'Austerity loses an article of faith: The UK industrial revolution shows the Reinhart-Rogoff thesis on debt is not always right', *Financial Times*, 23 April 2013.

governments of the need to sort out their financial messes in the meantime, especially because the debt, sadly, is not static. It is alive.

So, we come back to the social contract. If we want to deal with the debt and progress the economy simultaneously, we are going to have to think very hard about how to balance the interests of the citizens and their power to innovate versus the power of the state to help or hinder that process.

11

Cutting Through the Gordian Knot

—

The world economy finds itself twisted into a Gordian Knot. This is a problem that becomes more intractable as you push and pull at the individual strings and threads that constitute the many conflicting facts and commonly held views about what should be done. It comes from an old tale about a very old man named Gordias who had a simple oxcart. He became king through sheer dumb luck. Apparently the local oracle had seen a sign: an eagle landed on Gordias's oxcart. Based on that, the oracle declared that anyone entering the city on that particular oxcart would become king. Naturally, Gordias tried to tie up his cart as securely as possible for fear of losing his new-found power. He tied it to a tree using an especially complex knot that could not be undone or unravelled and which actually became tighter the more one attempted to undo it – the fabled Gordian Knot.

There are so many different threads and skeins to the story we hardly know where to begin, just like a Gordian Knot. We know central banks have collectively cut interest rates some 637 times since March 2008. They have purchased some $12.3 trillion dollars' worth of debt. And yet, it is entirely unclear whether these efforts are not working at all, not working yet, or working entirely too well already. Much depends on your perspective and whom you talk to – emerging-market officials or industrialised country officials, hawks or doves.

As Christine Lagarde, Head of the IMF, noted: 'If inflation is the genie, then deflation is the ogre that must be fought decisively.'* Deep divisions exist over whether it is really possible to conjure forth the genie of exactly the right amount of inflation and put it back in the bottle before it hurts anybody. Killing deflation seems to require giving life to at least a little inflation, which certainly benefits some at the expense of others.

Deals with the devil

If a deal is going to be made with a genie and an ogre, shouldn't we at least get a wish or two (or three) in exchange? As Larry Lindsey, a former Governor of the Federal Reserve and Economic Advisor to the President wisely observes, even in deals with the devil you usually get something in exchange for selling your soul. So far, none of the obvious three wishes has been granted. Unemployment everywhere remains too high, lending remains too low and the debt problem continues to grow. In the US alone the debt expanded to a record $19 trillion in 2015 and looks set to hit $30 trillion by 2020 according to the Congressional Budget Office. The average American now owes some $154,161 but only earns less than $55,000 according to the Census Bureau. The picture is similar across the industrialised world. Due to compounding, the value of the debt is rising far faster than wages are.

Meanwhile, the signs of life in the world economy, though welcome, further fuel the demands for a fairer distribution of wealth. Wages as a percentage of GDP remain at an all-time low while profits remain at an all-time high. We no longer have 'haves' and 'have nots'. We have 'haves' and 'have a lots' and 'have nothings'. Capitalism is the only way forward, since everything else has failed far worse, but we must redouble our efforts to define that correctly. We need to balance the interests of the savers and the speculators better.

---

* Sandrine Rastello, 'Lagarde Warns Officials to Fight Deflation "Ogre" Decisively', Bloomberg.com, 15 January 2014.

We need to ensure that individual sections of the population do not automatically or unfairly profit at an unbearable cost to others.*

I am reminded of the German economist and statesman Ludwig Erhard, the man who restored Germany's market economy after the Second World War. After years of inflation, most prices in Germany were fully controlled and administered by the state. Germany had inadvertently become a state-controlled economy. Erhard's job as Finance Minister in the 1950s was to return Germany to being a free market economy. It may well be that this is exactly the path we need to follow today. When reflecting on his experience, Erhard wrote:

> To achieve increased prosperity, any policy which prefers apparent success to real progress must be abandoned. Whoever is serious in this must be prepared to energetically oppose all attacks on the stability of our currency. The social market economy is unthinkable without a parallel stability of the currency. Only a policy of this kind guarantees that individual sections of the population do not profit at the cost of others.†

Abba's costumes

The problem lies at the heart of the Gordian knot. I've talked about the balance of power between the ability of the citizen to generate a profit and the ability of the state to tax it. The question is what is the right balance in the society you live in?

There is no doubt that governments can compel citizens to do things they would not otherwise do. I am always both amused and horrified by the story of Abba's costumes. For those who may be too young to remember, Abba was an uber-popular Swedish music band whose outlandish costumes were as distinctive and renowned as their music. It turns out that the tax code at the time in Sweden permitted deductions of costume costs, but only if you could prove the costume

---

* Friedrich Hayek, *The Road to Serfdom*, 1944.
† Ludwig Erhard, *Prosperity Through Competition*, 1957.

could never be worn anywhere but on stage. Obviously the spangles, exposed tummies and massively flared pants trimmed with feathers rendered these clothes entirely ridiculous if worn on the street. In this way Abba qualified for the tax deduction.

So, we need to be thoughtful about what government is asking its citizens to do. That means government and policymakers must be truly honest about their own convictions.

One hopes that the beliefs of our policymakers are real and grounded in reality. Think about Richard Feynman's wise observation. This world-class theoretical physicist was called upon to investigate the Space Shuttle *Challenger* disaster of 1986, when the shuttle blew up soon after take-off, killing not only all seven astronauts but effectively killing the space programme as well. In his report, Feynman wrote, 'Reality must take precedence over public relations, for nature cannot be fooled.'*

This is where policymakers need to ask themselves whether they are suffering from the kind of blind overconfidence in their own views and abilities that renders them ever more vulnerable to preferring 'apparent success to real progress'.

Time is of the essence because, as Hayek noted in 1944, 'The one thing modern democracy will not bear without cracking is the necessity of a substantial lowering of the standards of living in peace time or even prolonged stationariness of its economic conditions.'†

People want answers. But everything is binary and at an impasse: freshwater and saltwater, left and right, deflationists and inflationists, policymakers from the industrialised world and those from emerging markets are all at each other's throats. No one can agree. Is QE the problem or the solution? Is the debt the problem or the solution?

It should not surprise us that there are already clear indications

* From Appendix F of the Report of the Presidential Commission on the Space Shuttle *Challenger* Accident, 'Personal observations on the reliability of the Shuttle', RP Feynman, 6 June 1986.
† Friedrich Hayek, *The Road to Serfdom* (1944), p. 216.

that many, especially the young, want to see if there is a 'third way', a socialist solution to all this. Perhaps Bernie Sanders, the American Democratic presidential candidate, personifies this approach with his campaign message. It could be summed up as 'Vote for me and I will give you what you want for free.' It sounds great. But in the end, it's your money.

Being bribed with your own money

Do we suffer from self-delusion? The American author Upton Sinclair (1878–1968) wisely noted that, 'It's difficult to get a man to understand something when his salary depends on him not understanding it.' How many of us depend on the continued postponement of the day of reckoning?

We would prefer to believe that everything is OK. Or, better still, we like confusing luck with skill. Here is another complicating thread of the Gordian Knot. Sheila Bair, the outspoken former regulator and former head of the Federal Deposit Insurance Corporation, has admonished all CEOs to ask themselves, 'Is it me or is it the Fed?*　How much of my company's share price reflects our work versus government stimulus policy [QE]?' Indeed, each one of us needs to ask ourselves this question. 'How much of my life is a result of my own hard work and how much is the result of government stimulus that, in the end, is my own money?'

Consider the nineteenth-century political thinker, Alexis de Tocqueville, who came to America in 1831 at the age of twenty-five, and went on to write the seminal work, *Democracy in America*. He is often attributed with the observation that, 'The American Republic will endure until the day Congress discovers that it can bribe the public with the public's money.' Whether he said it or not, it is a sobering thought.

---

* Jordan Carney, 'Bair: Economic Reform Requires Taking the Long View', *National Journal*, 22 November 2013.

Governments today are finding ways to bribe the public with their own money and many do not want to understand why. QE is an inducement, an encouragement, a bribery. Keeping interest rates low and offering 'free money' to the banking system, money that was yours to begin with as the taxpayer, is a way of provoking your 'animal spirits' and encouraging you back into taking risks that a rational person might not otherwise undertake.

Years ago, the *Washington Post* invited its readers to take any word from the dictionary and alter it by adding, subtracting, or changing one single letter, and then supply a new definition.* Two spring to mind today: 'intaxication' and 'cashtration'. 'Intaxication' is 'The feeling of euphoria at getting a refund or stimulus from the government, which lasts until one realises it was one's own money to start with.' The original *Washington Post* definition of 'cashtration' was, 'The act of buying a house, which renders the subject financially impotent for an indefinite period.' Today, I'd say cashtration is what happens when government policy seems designed to give you more cash in theory but, in fact, involves stealing your income from your back pocket through higher taxation and a higher cost of living. Or, more specifically, it explains the regulatory approach to the banking system: give the banks free money but excoriate and fine them for both using it too aggressively and for failing to deploy it in the form of lending that the government would like to see.

We no longer live in a world where markets decide who gets what. We live in a world where policymakers decide who gets what. In their efforts to protect Main Street they seem to have bestowed incredible largesse on Wall Street. This is the fundamental issue we need to consider today. Which is the social contract we want? One in which markets determine the distribution of goods and wealth, or one in which policymakers decide who gets what? How tragic if we think we already chose the former but somehow drifted into the latter.

* 'The Style Invitational' at www.washingtonpost.com.

Dissent

One of the surest signs of a problem is an increased unwillingness to tolerate dissent. We should celebrate and not stifle dissent. This book and its arguments forms a dissent to current popular opinion. But many others with even stronger credentials and vantage points than mine are dissenting today.

We must appreciate that there is a fight raging in the policy world and it matters who wins it. We should be wary when the views of dissenters are ignored, suppressed or maligned and when it becomes common wisdom that the views of the establishment will inevitably be proved right, good and true. I, for one, was very struck by the apology issued by Andrew Huszar, a former Federal Reserve staffer who went to Wall Street and was then asked back to the Fed to administer the first round of quantitative easing. In November 2013 he made the following statement:

> I can only say: I'm sorry, America. As a former Federal Reserve official, I was responsible for executing the centrepiece programme of the Fed's first plunge into the bond-buying experiment known as quantitative easing. The central bank continues to spin QE as a tool for helping Main Street. But I've come to recognise the programme for what it really is: the greatest backdoor Wall Street bailout of all time.*

What was especially striking was the revelation that the government forged ahead even though it was not at all sure of the efficacy or possible consequences of its choices.†

Nobody is exactly sure of what they are doing, which would make anyone less open to dissent and debate at the very moment that there is

---

* Andrew Huszar, 'Andrew Huszar: Confessions of a Quantitative Easer', *Wall Street Journal*, 11 November 2013.
† Bruno J. Navarro interview with Andrew Huszar, 'Ex-Fed Official: "I'm Sorry for QE"', cnbc.com, 12 November 2013.

more need for dissent and debate. At the 2014 meeting of the American Economic Association, Bill Dudley, the President of the New York Fed, apparently said, 'We don't understand fully how large-scale asset purchase programmes work to ease financial market conditions.'* In other words, QE is so innovative no one actually knows how it works or whether it works at all. It's end result is not yet known. Not enough time has passed. The facts are not in. Those who claim it has worked without causing inflation seem too content to trust their models and ignore the reality of daily life, preferring to follow an algorithm that may or may not present a realistic view. Those who claim QE will unleash inflation may have some evidence, but we will have to wait and see whether it becomes a generalised phenomenon.

Until then, central bankers have already told us that they intend to make interest rates go negative if they possibly can. Yet, in keeping with the analogy of a knotty problem central bankers often refer to the problem of zero interest rates as being akin to 'pushing on a string'.† Once interest rates fall to zero, and we hit their so-called 'zero bound', there isn't much more a central bank can do than to start buying assets. However, government intervention in asset prices such as stocks and bonds destroys the most powerful signals the economy generates and instead creates artificial mis-signals, thus distorting incentives. Once governments start buying and controlling prices in the stock market and the bond market, it becomes hard for them to stop.

* William Dudley, President and CEO Federal Reserve Bank of New York, 'Economics at the Federal Reserve Banks', American Economic Association 2014 Annual Meeting, Philadelphia, Pennsylvania, 4 January 2014.

† The origins of this phrase are often attributed to J. M. Keynes and also to Congressman T. Alan Goldsborough during the Congressional hearings on the Banking Act of 1935. When the Federal Reserve Chairman Marriner Eccles stated, 'Under present circumstances, there is very little, if any, that can be done,' Goldsborough replied, 'You mean you cannot push on a string.' Eccles responded: 'That is a very good way to put it, one cannot push on a string. We are in the depths of a depression and . . . beyond creating an easy money situation through reduction of discount rates, there is very little, if anything, that the reserve organisation can do to bring about recovery.'

Central bank independence

One fierce debate rages today over an important question: Have central banks already forfeited their independence? Most of the time, I find that this question is met by stony silence among central bankers who are outraged by the mere suggestion that this might be true. Yet, when the central bank becomes the largest buyer of a nation's government debt, can it reasonably be seen as truly independent any more? Are central banks simply funding governments in their efforts to buy votes and to deal with the debt by giving oxygen to inflation? But, central bankers reply, we had no choice!

The fact that this may have happened inadvertently does nothing to change the problem itself. We can't afford to pretend it did not happen or to ignore the problem.

One aspect of central bank independence is that it allows and even encourages lively debate. If a central bank begins to stifle dissent and shun alternative views it is an important signal. When the institutions of justice in a society, like the courts, become biased, everyone understands that justice will not be as fairly and impartially served. The central bank is also an institution of justice, given that it has the ability to change the balance of power between the lenders and the creditors, between the savers and speculators, between the state and the citizens. The decision to inflate is not just a technical economic decision, it is a political and social justice decision.

Governments may even be willing to forgo the long history of central bank independence. Politicians are inevitably drawn to the idea that they control the money supply and therefore can produce more money any time they want simply by printing it. However, this debasement of the currency makes prices unstable. Prices start to move (up, usually) in response to the fact that there is more cash chasing the same goods and services. This is why central banks came into being – they are, in theory, the guardians of 'price stability' or 'stable prices', meaning prices that don't swing around too erratically. Price stability is the Holy Grail of most of the economics profession. It is the most desired outcome and the most difficult to achieve.

It's been fought for before. The situation today is perhaps not so different from the financial landscape in 1951. During the Second World War, the Fed stepped in to buy US bonds to help finance the war effort and also to hold down interest rates, which they continued to do long after the war. By 1951 one of the Federal Reserve Board governors, Marriner Eccles, was agitated about this loss of independence and the rising risk of inflation. Eccles, who later emerged as the Fed Chairman and after whom the Federal Reserve Building in Washington DC is now named, articulated the problem clearly. The Fed had become 'an engine of inflation':

> As long as the Federal Reserve (or the Bank of England or any other central bank) is required to buy government securities at the will of the market for the purpose of defending a fixed pattern of interest rates established by the Treasury, it must stand ready to create new bank reserves in unlimited amount. This policy makes the entire banking system, through the action of the Federal Reserve System, an engine of inflation.*

Today, the US government, meaning the Treasury and the White House, is not specifically defining the acceptable level of interest rates. However, the Treasury and the White House are certainly pushing for a long-term commitment to ensure interest rates are kept low and under control. This suits the White House, which would be under far greater pressure – regarding the budget and fiscal policy, let alone the recovery – if interest rates actually started to rise. This is why the White House will want to load the Board of Governors with like-minded folks. This is why the Federal Reserve finds it necessary to repeat the view that tapering and withdrawal from asset purchases has nothing

---

* Robert L. Hetzel and Robert F. Leach, cited in 'The Treasury-Fed Accord, A New Narrative Account', US Congress 1951.

to do with interest-rate policy. It's a slightly awkward stance, since the purpose of the asset purchases was to hold down interest rates. This is why rate hikes will not be acknowledged or described as 'tightening' but as 'normalisation'.

The important point is that it is not enough for the markets to be ready for tapering, let alone ready for interest rate hikes. The White House and Congress have to be ready too. Consider this exchange between Eccles and the Texan Congressman, Wright Patman, in 1951:

> PATMAN: Don't you think there is some obligation of the Federal Reserve System to protect the public against excessive interest rates?
>
> ECCLES: I think there is a greater obligation to the American public to protect them against the deterioration of the dollar.
>
> PATMAN: Who is master, the Federal Reserve or the Treasury? You know, the Treasury came here first.
>
> ECCLES: How do you reconcile the Treasury's position of saying they want the interest rate low, with the Federal Reserve standing ready to peg the market, and at the same time expect to stop inflation?
>
> PATMAN: Will the Federal Reserve System support the Secretary of the Treasury in that effort [to retain the 2.5 per cent rate] or will it refuse? . . . You are sabotaging the Treasury. I think it ought to be stopped.
>
> ECCLES: Either the Federal Reserve should be recognised as having some independent status, or it should be considered as simply an agency or a bureau of the Treasury.*

Today, the Chinese and Russians would say it is certainly not pursuing the interests of the world economy any more. It is pursuing America's interests alone.

---

* 'The Treasury-Fed Accord, A New Narrative Account'.

The common wealth

Some careful thought has to be put into managing the 'common wealth' of the world economy in ways that meet everybody's needs. Price stability is perhaps an even more valuable 'common wealth' commodity than we ever thought. We should not have to learn the hard way that, for some, it may be worth fighting for militarily as well.

In the post Second World War era, the US led the creation of the 'Bretton Woods' system, which has underpinned the world economy ever since (even if parts of it have been eroded over time). In short, it stood for a world economy in which the markets determined who would get what (not states or governments) and almost every important asset, especially food and energy, would be priced in US dollars and the supply lines of food and energy would be policed by the US and its regional allies. No doubt that Bretton Woods system is very different today than it was when most nations signed up to it. The US and others have dramatically changed the system at times, such as when Richard Nixon abandoned the gold standard in 1971. But at its heart, there is one thing everybody has remained committed to. It is the most valuable commodity of all: price stability. Today, many question whether the US remains a steadfast guardian of that commodity.

Price stability is the holy grail of all central banking theory. If the post-war economic order is based above all else on a commitment to price stability, then it cannot be surprising that nations begin to object if they feel the US is abandoning price stability, or taking excessive risks with it, for their own benefit at the expense of the others. Ultimately each nation must be responsible for their own price stability, but this becomes much harder when the largest economies in the world are believed to be taking gambles with it.

The Federal Reserve may be right; perhaps they are not creating inflation, nor are they undermining price stability in any way. But the pain elsewhere is high enough that it has become worthwhile to pin the blame on someone or something else. Then again, the emerging markets may be right: record low interest rates and record injections of capital into the world economy are creating spillover effects, imbalances, inflation and causing the kind of pain that governments have no choice but to respond to.

I think today's leaders in Russia, China and elsewhere increasingly find it easy to think this way: You want to steal money from my pocket? Then this (land, asset, gas field, island, nation, shipping lane, etc) belongs to me. Many countries are beginning to fight for commodities and valuable assets in an effort to ward off the inevitable consequences of pain. The vice of economic pressure is tightening its grip on every person, every company, every community and every country.

Caught between loss of growth and loss of faith in the future on one side, and the rising cost of living, which means a falling standard of living, on the other, people are in pain. Whatever the degree of loss and pain, governments know that the public will remove from power a government that cannot deliver relief.

Sustained upward pressure on hard-asset prices brings geopolitical consequences because failure to deliver these items at the right time and the right price can propel people towards the ballot box or into the streets. The risk of higher hard-asset prices (whether correctly attributed to inflationary policies in the West, or as the result of policy in the emerging markets themselves) is leading to new-found competition among governments for access to necessary resources around the world. Now that the perfect circle is broken, politics and geopolitics have staged a comeback. The vice of pain is compelling people to ask that simple question: 'Why is the wealth in my society being distributed to someone else and not to me?' Suddenly, governments have to start thinking about how to ensure the delivery of whatever is needed and expected. Competition for commodities and for GDP now forms the basis for potential conflict in the world economy.

The return-free rate of risk

It is easy to dismiss the idea of outright price controls in the industrialised world. Nobody imagines these governments want to control the price of beef or chocolate, though they may concede such governments have an interest in the price of housing and wages. No, instead, the governments of industrial economies are intervening in the single most important price in any economy: the price of money. In the words of Friedrich Hayek:

> Any attempt to control prices or quantities of particular commodities deprives competition of its power of bringing about an effective co-ordination of individual efforts, because price changes then cease to register all the relevant changes in circumstances and no longer provide a reliable guide for the individual's actions.*

Keynes, too, felt controlling the price of money was especially noxious because 'the importance of money essentially flows from its being a link between the present and the future'.†

Interest rates are about as low as they have ever been since the Roman Empire.‡ What does the artificially low and subsidised price of money tell us about the future? It seeks to lure the public into borrowing and making investments, which they would not otherwise do. It seeks to make the public take a bet on asset prices and on the future.

No price can be more important than the price of money itself. Government intervention to suppress interest rates perverts the bond market, which has serious consequences. Government bonds are supposed to constitute the risk-free rate of return against which all other investments are measured and judged.

If your venture or investment cannot outperform the return on a

* Friedrich Hayek, *The Road to Serfdom*, 1944.

† J. M. Keynes, *The General Theory of Employment, Interest and Money*, 1936 (Chapter 21: 'The Theory of Prices').

‡ Sydney Homer and Richard Sylla, *A History of Interest Rates*, 2005.

government bond, then you are taking too much risk for insufficient reward. When governments buy their own bonds and thereby keep interest rates down, they support their own cause. Now government itself can borrow more cheaply and avoid the risk that higher interest payments would bankrupt them. This erodes, if not removes, the incentive to fix their debt problems.

This artificial control over the price of money means that, far from being a risk-free rate of return, the government bond market can be perverted into a return-free rate of risk.* It is return-free because interest rates are so low that holding bonds offers virtually no income to the owner. Should the government's effort fail at some point, should interest rates rise, the government would be the first to find it lacks the resources to repay its debt, other than relying on its ability to print its own money.

I mentioned an important signal in passing earlier. Japan moved into negative official interest rates in early January 2016. The very next official bond market auction in Japan failed, raising concerns about how we will fund sovereign debt if the return is negative.† This is the kind of signal we should be paying attention to.

Alexander the Great

So, what can be done? Well, there is only one thing you can do with a Gordian Knot, as Alexander the Great (356–323 BC) demonstrated. Alexander exhibited hubris on an epic scale; his combination of ego and arrogance has few equals in history. A brilliant military commander, he led his armies though Europe, India, Central Asia and the Middle East, capturing kingdoms and forcing them into submission, until he had formed a vast empire – and all this well before the age of thirty-three, when he died from food poisoning.

* Robert Jenkins (formerly on the Financial Policy Committee at the Bank of England), 'The Safety Catch, *Financial World*, July 2014.
† Japan cancelled the auction on 2 February 2016 to avoid it being revealed that there would not be enough buyers.

When he arrived in the small city of Telmissus, he discovered poor old Gordias and his knotted-up oxcart. Alexander assumed that it would be child's play to wrest control of the oxcart from a little old man, even if it was 'magical'. He tried to untie the knot, but, the more he tried, the tighter it became. So he pulled out his sword and sliced through the knot. Alexander entered Telmissus on that oxcart and as the oracle had predicted he was proclaimed king. Then he promptly moved on to his next conquest.

It takes enormous personal courage, indeed hubris, to slice through a Gordian knot. Preoccupation with the past and fear of the future sometimes preclude a clear vision of similar acts of hubris in the present. The sharp demands of reality draw forth strength of character and cause some to proceed with nothing more than conviction and a clarity of vision that others don't yet share or may never share. These efforts are signals – even beacons – in an economic fog, and lead the way into the economy of tomorrow.

I heard Steve Furber, the ICL Professor of Computer Engineering at the University of Manchester, say something interesting when he accepted his prize at *The Economist*'s Innovation Awards ceremony in 2013.* He and his colleague Sophie Wilson invented ARM chips, which now 'dominate the processor chips inside smart phones, digital cameras and other mobile devices'. Some 40 billion units have been sold, which lie 'at the heart of more than 35 per cent of all consumer devices worldwide'. Furber said, 'The young have a distinct advantage when it comes to innovation. They do not yet know what is impossible.'

Yes, we have an impossible task. That may be exactly the thing that forces us to use our imagination to solve this.

The following saying is attributed to the ancient Chinese philosopher Lao Tze (and sometimes to Henry David Thoreau): 'Watch your thoughts; they become words. Watch your words; they

---

* *The Economist*'s Innovation Awards 2013 at www.economist.com. The ceremony was held at the British Academy of Film and Television Arts (BAFTA).

become actions. Watch your actions; they become habits. Watch your habits; they become character. Watch your character; it becomes your destiny.'

Wait or create?

While writing this book, I was often asked, 'How does your book end? What is the solution?' The answer, dear reader, depends on you. You, too, are a signal in the world economy. What do you see? What do you think it means? Will you wait or create? When confronted by someone who has the hubris to engage in a great leap of imagination, what will you say? What would you have said to Miles Davis and Charlie Parker as they abandoned perfectly successful styles of music in order to create something new? 'Whatever for? Why change, you're a huge success as it is!' Or, 'Wow! How exciting! You have a vision for something unheard of.' What kind of signal will you be when someone you know decides to take a risk? Will you, as a friend or a colleague, welcome and encourage the act of reinvention, the pursuit of new ideas? Perhaps you will feel better advising them to wait until the economic recovery path is confirmed by the data and blessed by economists who won't sound the all-clear until the recovery is well under way? How will you calibrate the decision with the specific skills and character of the person undertaking the risk?

Demographics and sex

I wonder if my reader might indulge me in a humorous act of imagination? One way to solve the economic problems and to create a better social contract might be to think more about the role of sex in the economy.

There are those who will say that demographics is the key to economic success. No matter what innovations the government comes up with, demographics will define the outcome. There is a lot of truth to this. As mentioned earlier, the only debt burden that the US did not need inflation to solve was the debt burden accumulated from the

Second World War. Why? The baby boom more than compensated for debt and helped pay it down through wealth creation. I, for one, strongly support sex as an alternative to QE (on the assumption that more sex leads to more children, one way or another). You may laugh, but more people equals more opportunity for economic growth.*

Governments can innovate on this policy front too. Today Japan is buying more nappies for adults than for babies, as Gillian Tett of the *Financial Times* points out. Had Japan created incentives for families to grow, this might not be the case.† Meanwhile, in 2014, Kimberly Clark announced that it is decreasing the number of diapers in its packages (adult and baby versions alike) by 7 per cent, while selling them at the same price.‡ Is this a signal that inflation is causing the input costs for diapers to rise to the point that Kimberly Clark has to pass on the costs by engaging in 'shrinkflation'? Yes. And who will pay more? The elderly in Japan and the young elsewhere. I suspect Japan's demographics would look very different today if sales of baby diapers outranked sales of adult diapers instead of the opposite.

Let me put it more bluntly. Japan could solve its debt and growth problems if it would encourage women to enter the workforce. Productivity and performance would rise substantially. The question for Japan and everywhere else is: can you have more women in the workforce *and* more babies? This is a social contract question. Singapore addresses it differently than South Korea and Sweden. Singapore restricts the number of small one-bedroom flats to discourage people from remaining single for too long. South Korea signals its desire to increase the birth rate by holding 'Family Day' on the third Wednesday

---

* If anyone wants to support the idea that sex is a politically attractive alternative to QE, they should come out of the closet.

† Gillian Tett, 'Falling fertility rates pose threat to government revenues', *Financial Times*, 5 August 2013.

‡ Paul Ziobroa, 'P&G to cut package Sizes for Diapers', *Wall Street Journal*, 8 September 2013.

of every month, when the lights in offices must be turned off by 7 p.m. (in the hopes that workers will go home to engage in friendlier relations). Sweden, in contrast, makes it incredibly easy for parents of both sexes to take paid leave from work to commence the process of raising young children.

A baby boom could arguably do at least as much to stimulate growth as quantitative easing. However, the appetite for abandoning quantitative easing and substituting quantitative pleasing seems strangely small. Though this is exactly what stands behind China's recent decision to abandon the 'One Child' policy.

What leads us into error?

It makes no sense to ignore signals, or remain wilfully ignorant of them, simply because they don't fit a mathematical preconception of reality. This is dangerous. Hence J. M. Keynes' recommendation that economists pay attention to the things that don't 'fit' the model:

> The object of our analysis is, not to provide a machine, or a method of blind manipulation, which will furnish an infallible answer, but to provide ourselves with an organised and orderly method of thinking out particular problems; and, after we have reached a provisional conclusion by isolating the complicating factors one by one, we then have to go back on ourselves and allow, as well as we can, for the probable interactions of the factors amongst themselves. This is the nature of economic thinking. Any other way of applying formal principles of thought (without which, however, we shall be lost in the wood) will lead us into error. Too large a proportion of recent 'mathematical' economics are merely concoctions, as imprecise as the initial assumptions they rest on, which allow the author to lose sight of the complexities and interdependencies of the real world in a maze of pretentious and unhelpful symbols.*

---

* J. M. Keynes, *The General Theory*, Cambridge University Press, 1936.

I would like to think that there might be some consideration of the signals that fall outside the mathematical models. These signals might be considered and debated among the class of econometricians and statisticians on whose models the public depend. But the public can join in now. Only by asking such common sense-based questions about the signals we see can we create an economy where we won't be compelled to say, 'The algorithm made me do it.' This will require character. As Peter Drucker pointed out: 'Far too many people – especially people with great expertise in one area – are contemptuous of knowledge in other areas or believe that being bright is a substitute for knowledge.' The remedy: 'discover where your intellectual arrogance is causing disabling ignorance and overcome it.'*

My friend James Galbraith suggested that the picture I have painted in this book is one of 'Impressionist/ Pointillist' economics. Perhaps there is a place for this alongside the standard mathematical blueprint approach. Perhaps this approach would permit many more to see what's going on across the landscape.

I hope that my own observation of signals, and those made by others, can be met with a robust opponent who can help us discover where our own 'intellectual arrogance' has resulted in 'disabling ignorance'. This is as applicable to policymakers as to business people as to someone managing the household's finances.

By raising an awareness of the signals that we see every day, we can be empowered to make our own judgements and thereby better decisions about how to manage our economic life. No one has a monopoly on the truth, nor is there a crystal ball that empowers any one person or school of thought to predict the future with certainty. Instead, the world economy moves forward, or backward, based on a multitude of decisions, whether made by famous policymakers or by anonymous individuals. This requires, as the Queen of Hearts noted in *Alice in Wonderland*, imagination.

* Peter Drucker, 'Managing Oneself', *Harvard Business Review*, 1999.

Steve Jobs and eccentricity

Steve Jobs explained this with great clarity when he gave the Stanford University Commencement Address in 2005:

> You can't connect the dots looking forward; you can only connect them looking backwards. So you have to trust that the dots will somehow connect in your future. You have to trust in something – your gut, destiny, life, karma, whatever. Because believing that the dots will connect down the road will give you the confidence to follow your heart even when it leads you off the well-worn path; and that will make all the difference.*

The more lively and robust the debate about signals, the better, because each one of us will strike out on our own path and we will be more likely to succeed if we are better armed with knowledge of the forces and risks that may await us. No one should shy away from asking questions or making observations about the world economy; this could be what it takes to lead them 'off the well-worn path'. As John Stuart Mill observed: 'The amount of eccentricity in a society has generally been proportional to the amount of genius, mental vigour, and moral courage which it contained. That so few now dare to be eccentric, marks the chief danger of the time.'†

Some of those who have great expertise in economics will mock the average person who notices the world economy with naïve and fresh eyes and energetically enters the debate. They will probably knock down my simple suggestion that anyone is capable of identifying signals in the world economy and deciding for themselves what they mean. But such backward-looking, data-dependent naysayers would do well to remember Emerson's comment that 'an ounce of action is worth a tonne of theory'.

---

* Steve Jobs, 'You've Got to Find What You Love', 14 June 2005.
† John Stuart Mill, *On Liberty*, 1869.

There are many who are prepared to devote years of time and effort to figuring out whether what works in practice can be made to work in theory. Happily, there are more who are prepared to engage in the decisions and actions that will have great consequences for the character of our future economy. They do not need a tried-and-tested theory to engage in their edgework.

Signals can come from many unexpected places. A magazine cover from November 2009 still burns in my mind. It was a potent signal of how many are preoccupied with the question of blame. It showed a beautiful wealthy woman on the cover of *W* magazine, drenched in diamond jewellery and holding up the sort of cardboard sign favoured by tramps and beggars. It read: 'It must be somebody's fault'.* Witch

---

* Linda Evangelista, photographed by Pierpaolo Ferrari for the cover of *W* magazine, November 2009, www.fashiongonerogue.com

hunts are one way out of a Gordian Knot. But, going down this path will only leave us stuck in what Larry Lindsey calls 'The Recrimination Phase of the Economic Cycle'.* You find someone to blame and hang them from a high post (i.e., you put them on the front page and then in jail). This does not stimulate innovation or GDP. It does, however, win votes.

When I flip through women's magazines and see that the fashion industry cannot decide which hemline or silhouette to offer, it encourages me that there are profits and revenues to be made by someone who will boldly declare what 'the new look' ought to be. If you think this cannot happen, look at what Christian Dior did in Paris on 12 February 1947, when he unveiled his 'New Look' to the world, with its chiselled waistline and 'wasteful' round skirt that required reams of fabric simply for the purpose of serving beauty. He changed the way women dressed forever. And in the process he created GDP.

Some might still be scoffing at the idea that magazines can provide signals that are in their way as valid as mathematical models. But when I open any journal on the newsagent's shelf, from *Wired* to *Wooden Boat*, all I see is innovation. I see artists taking cast-offs from the Large Hadron Collider at CERN† and from Formula One cars and turning them into art, furniture and useful machines. On television, I see one of the world's most widely watched sports, cricket, innovating with the introduction of Twenty 20 Cricket.‡ Frankly, it's hard not to see innovation once you look for it.

The question going forward is this: Can inflation really destroy deflation? In my view, the competition between inflation and deflation is a sideshow. There may well be an epic battle between these two

---

* I am so grateful to Larry Lindsey, former Fed Governor and Chief Economic Advisor to George W. Bush, for this illuminating concept.

† Madhumita Venkatarmanan, 'Inspired by CERN, these lab instruments double as kitchen appliances' *Wired* magazine (UK Edition), December 2013.

‡ This new sport was introduced in 2003 but the momentum behind it has exploded since the financial crisis.

conflicting forces, these two demons, but there is a force that is capable of vanquishing the both. Innovation. Great innovations create growth and wealth and will help keep prices where they should be. Great innovation is going to come mainly from the quiet everyday acts of calculated risk-taking that brave individuals undertake all the time. The only question is whether the state will help these individuals or try to stand in their way as they forge the path forward. When I listen to people's life stories from recent years, full of heartbreak and loss and recovery and reinvention, I hear innovation.

Emerson and economics

When I see people protest at the breakdown of the social contract, I am encouraged that innovation applies in the field of politics as well. Social contracts around the world will need to better serve the interests of the citizens who agree to abide by them. Their renegotiation can only be a good thing for the world economy. Of course, there will be missteps and accidents. As an American, I know that it took several efforts to create the institutions and ideals that permit our social contract to bend and change without threatening the collapse of society. Let us not forget that America did not even manage to sort out the right model for a central bank until 1914 – and only after quite a few false starts. Many will argue the current model is still not right. The model may well be in need of review today, but the institution is strong enough to withstand a good hard look.

Serendipity

When I look for signals I see the opportunity to innovate, to adapt, to prepare, to create the life that I hope to have.

Serendipity will play its part.

Some will misinterpret the signals. Some will interpret them correctly but balance their own hubris badly and find themselves confronted by failure. Nonetheless, failure brings its own lessons and rewards. Chanel N°5, the classic perfume, was an epic mistake. The assistants of perfumer Ernest Beaux apparently misread his formula and added some ten times the required amount of aldehyde. When Coco Chanel chose from the many samples Beaux provided, she chose number 5, the one with the huge mistake. Not only has Chanel N°5 been a massive success, the use of aldehydes is mainstream in most perfumes today.

The stakes may be extremely high. I mentioned racing cars earlier, and I have witnessed terrible car accidents on the F1 circuit over the years. One involved a car driving straight over the top of another. I thought there was no chance the driver of the car underneath would survive. Instead, he jumped out, hopping mad. Such a moment makes me remember that it was the death of one of Formula One's greatest drivers, Ayrton Senna, that led the F1 authorities to commit to whatever was necessary to protect their drivers.* Many safety features and procedures resulted from that decision, including safety belts, fireproof face masks and clothing, chicanes and safety helmets. Some of these innovations were later applied to the general public. Senna paid with his life but left a legacy that has protected the many drivers who followed him. Yes, the edgeworker went over the edge. But in doing so he opened the door for safer driving. Striking a balance between safety and speed is essential both in race-car driving and when it comes to managing the world economy. Too much 'safety' (regulation) limits the speed of growth.

Failure is a fact of life that involves losses at every level: loss of confidence, vision, money, time, resources. The cutting edge of the world economy is a bloody business. So, if permitted, I would write a second letter to the Queen:

---

* Sid Watkins, *The Science of Safety: The Battle Against Unacceptable Risks in Motor Racing*, Haynes Manuals, 2000.

Her Majesty the Queen
Buckingham Palace
London sw1a 1aa

Madam,

I was moved by your question at the LSE in November 2008 and though unqualified to answer it myself, I hope that by bringing the concept of signals to attention, I can empower people to make better decisions about their economic future. The business of engaging in edgework, in reaching for something beyond our grasp, in building a future without knowing the outcome for sure, is a challenging task. But as you said in 1952 in your first BBC Christmas Broadcast, human beings are surely capable of adapting to change and building a new future. We would do well to remember your wise words:

> *Many grave problems and difficulties confront us all, but with a new faith in the old and splendid beliefs given us by our forefathers, and the strength to venture beyond the safeties of the past, I know we shall be worthy of our duty. Above all, we must keep alive that courageous spirit of adventure that is the finest quality of youth; and by youth I do not just mean those who are young in years; I mean too all those who are young in heart, no matter how old they may be . . .*
>
> *On this broad foundation let us set out to build a truer knowledge of ourselves and our fellow men, to work for tolerance and understanding among the nations and to use the tremendous forces of science and learning for the betterment of man's lot upon this Earth.**

---

* Andrew Pierce Read, 'The Queen asks why no one saw the credit crunch coming', *Daily Telegraph*, 5 November 2008. Full transcript in *The Daily Telegraph* online, 25 December 2012.

Yes, there has been loss. Yes, everyone should be aware of the effort to pass this loss on to us – the common man and woman. Everyone should be given a chance to prepare for the consequences. But this loss has also created the foundation for transformation. Perhaps we can all spend the coming years trying to imagine the impossible and the unexpected – a more dynamic economy than before, because that is what is most likely to actually happen.

It is my hope that by learning to interpret signals we can all, at the very least, become more flexible, more attuned to the dynamic nature of the world economy. With this knowledge we can then pursue the best personal vision that hubris and fear of nemesis will permit. In this way, the world economy of tomorrow will progress regardless of the damage it has caused in the past.

I believe the same signal can be interpreted in different ways by different people. That's the essence of a market. It's a place where all views (buyers and sellers) meet. But the really important point is that signals and their interpretation are personal. I may have seen the same signals as, say, Steve Jobs, but his skills, opportunities and his vision were different from mine. I would never have been able to build Apple even if we had entirely agreed on the signals that led him to believe that Apple could and would come to life. Then again, the signals I've noted, my skills, and the way I have balanced my hubris against the risk of nemesis have brought me to a different place. That's the key: the same signals are subject to different interpretations and different outcomes. The business of matching the external awareness of signals and the internal awareness of one's own skills and ability to manage risk is the key to managing, no matter what happens to the world economy.

Sincerely,

Pippa Malmgren

André Malraux, the French novelist, art theorist and Minister for Cultural Affairs, once said, 'Often the difference between a successful person and a failure is not that one has better abilities or ideas, but the courage that one has to bet on one's ideas, to take a calculated risk – and to act.' This is as true of those who are building the economy as it is of those who are addressing the policy infrastructure and the social contract. But which signals should be acted upon? We must all decide for ourselves.

In or out?

I have endeavoured to fulfil Henry James' exhortation that we must all 'try to be someone on whom nothing is lost', but have I explained what a person should 'do' about the signals the economy is sending? Should we be in or out of stocks? In or out of bonds? Buy or sell property? Should we invest in ourselves or in the economy? Should a person take the free money today and put it in risky assets that might pay off or might lose a fortune in the future?

The answer is that each one of us must make such decisions for ourselves based on our own skills, appetite for risk, our own level of hubris and fear of nemesis. There are many answers but only a few are right for you. Hopefully, everyone will make a different decision. The diversity of opinion and action is what will reinforce society's ability to withstand the sharp ebbs and flows of the world economy. It is the diversity of opinion about signals that gives strength to the economy. Some will be right, some will be wrong, but without edgework and calculated risk-taking there won't be an economy. No one has a monopoly on the right answer – not the Federal Reserve, not the White House or any equivalent, and not your neighbour. Instead, there is a range of opinions, which form a 'market'. A market is a clearing mechanism that efficiently matches buyers and sellers. This is a better approach than relying on the views of a few 'smart' people who happen to work at the top of government or at the top of businesses, whom we presume 'know' the answer. We can read and interpret signals for ourselves based on individual experience, skills and risk-taking inclinations.

The thread of the story

You, my reader, may or may not agree with my own conclusion – that without sufficient bread at the right price, a country and a family can become . . . well, toast. The vice-like grip of financial pain is spurring social unrest and innovation alike. Quantitative easing is creating qualitative squeezing and converting the peace dividend into a conflict premium. Social contracts all over the world are straining under these pressures, but new social contracts are being forged in their place, and these too are examples of innovation. It is worth considering the possibility that these new ideas might be an improvement on the old. The new social contracts may be better. For what it is worth, I don't think we will fix the ogre of deflation by unleashing the genie of inflation. Instead, we will have to contend with both demons. Redistributing the existing wealth is a circular game that drives down new wealth creation. The only productive way out is innovation. But, everyone must decipher the signals those demons are sending for themselves. Only then can everyone know what kind of edgework and calculated risk-taking each of us can safely undertake.

I have tried to weave together a picture of the world economy, connecting seemingly unrelated and even contradictory pieces of information that actually come together to form patterns. There are endless, easily observable signals that illuminate these patterns on the landscape of the world economy. One need not be an economist or an expert at algorithms to detect and discuss them. In fact, a little common sense might be a welcome addition to the usual conversation about economics.

Signals from close to home are important. I was in a lively Twitter exchange just before Christmas 2013, when the news that big-brand chocolate companies – including Mars, Cadbury and Rowntree – would be selling their Christmas collection chocolates for the same price as the previous year but with somewhere between two to eleven fewer pieces in the box.* When Toblerone tried to widen the spaces between their famous triangles and reduce the amount of chocolate in 2016, people were so outraged it was dubbed Tobleronegate.† Shrinkflation strategies like this diminish the public's willingness to swallow what policymakers say. The credibility of official inflation statistics is being called into question by citizens everywhere. I write this eyeing the Hershey's Kiss on my desk, which the company announced will cost 8 per cent more going forward. Chocolate is being called 'the new champagne' with good reason, due to the price increases and the supply shortages. Candy bars and their sizes may seem a small and insignificant signal. But, it is a signal that tells us the input costs of daily life are accelerating whether the official data reflects this or not.

The thread of the story travels from the central bankers, who are potentially 'pushing on a string', to textile workers in China and Bangladesh to couturiers and quilters and all those who are ripping up or re-stitching the fabric of social contracts. Loose ends are everywhere. Some threads of information clash. Some prices rise while others fall. But we can all feel that the warp and weft of the social fabric is under pressure. Open your eyes and you see that people are knitting together a new social contract. Witness the 'pussy hats' that symbolised political opposition in the International Woman's March in 2017. Those soft, pink hats signal that the social contract is being renegotiated before our eyes. Economics is not the only nor even the most important thread in this fabric. Culture, history, politics all play their part. But I hope I have imbued the thread of economics with some colour. Because economics is not grey nor boring. If anything, it is a shocking neon that flashes warnings all the time.

Both history and economics seem to be conspiring to demand

* 'Manufacturers reduce size of festive boxes of chocolates (but the price stays the same)', *Daily Mail*, 13 November 2013.
† Kate Taylor, 'Toblerone made a major change to save money and people are furious', *Business Insider*, 8 November 2016.

that everyone reconsiders what sort of social contract is desired and desirable. What is the right relationship and balance between the government and the citizens? What are the rights and responsibilities of the state versus those of the citizens? What social fabric do we want? This is the central question that the world economy is compelling everyone to address.

The liquidity problem continues to wash over the fabric of every day life. It matters that there is such a deep divide between those who think deflation is the biggest risk and those who think inflation is the biggest risk. Those who are quick to declare inflation dead somehow cannot see that they stand in the largest pool of liquidity ever known. An inflationist believes the pool that is filled with accelerant rather than innocuous water. A deflationist believes it is water that will drown out doubt and bring growth to life. There are those who are quick to declare that the accelerant will blow us all sky high and return us to the hyperinflation of earlier eras. But they underestimate the role of innovation in keeping prices down.

Either way, until the liquidity returns to normal levels, we will not be able to judge whether it has enhanced or damaged the fabric of society. Peggy Noonan, the famed American political writer, offered this: 'There are the protected and the unprotected. The protected make public policy. The unprotected live in it. The unprotected are starting to push back, powerfully. The protected are the accomplished, the secure, the successful – those who have power or access to it. They are protected from much of the roughness of the world. More to the point, they are protected *from the world they have created.*'* President Trump picked up on this sentiment at his inauguration when he said, 'The establishment protected itself, but not the citizens of our country. Their victories have not been your victories. Their triumphs have not been your triumphs.' Once again, the answer lies in the collective decisions

* Peggy Noon, 'Trump and the Rise of the Unprotected', *Wall Street Journal*, 25 February 2016.

we all make, that collective blanket of our own truths which may or may not cover the interests of all. Much depends on how everyday people and policymakers alike proceed and whether they proceed in a freshwater or saltwater direction.

Meanwhile, central banks have had to engage in QE precisely because governments are so deeply in debt that they are often incapable of sustaining military action or expenditure. This inability or unwillingness to respond invites other states to test the boundaries of territory and diplomacy, thus increasing the risk of geopolitical events.

But an even greater irony lies in the notion I have tried to explain here. Rightly or wrongly, there are those who believe the efforts by central banks to create inflation should be viewed as a hostile act since the consequences – higher food and energy prices and the attendant social unrest – fully justify reaching for such assets across borders. The logic is this: if you default on us (and inflation is a form of default), we are justified in protecting ourselves by any means. The end result is an endless circle where the solution to the debt problem provokes both greater complacency and greater risk of political and geopolitical stress. We find the thread of the story loops back on itself and creates a knotty problem that we will be tangling with for some time.

I can't help but think that the shrinkflation and zigzagging I see at the grocer's is somehow related to the near-misses between military airplanes and vessels I see reported in the press. How can we expect nations to defend their interests abroad if they are having to default on their citizens at home? How can nations enforce the global 'social contract' – the 'rules of the game' – abroad if the local social contract at home is itself fluid and changing?

It would be nice if nations could find ways to get along. But, interests can clash when prices move in one direction or another. If only a high degree of economic interconnectedness was sufficient glue to hold the common interests of nations together.

But we know for a fact that Britain and Germany were close trading partners one year before the First World War broke out. While I do not condone the military actions that I have written about here, I can see why many nations will use or see economics as an excuse to step into the realm of geopolitics and conflict. We can no longer assume that all national interests are aligned. As social contracts change, national interests must change too. No policymaker can afford to ignore the insight of George Bernard Shaw when he said, any 'nation that lets its duty get on to the opposite side of its interest is lost'.*

Some careful thought has to be put into managing the 'common wealth' of the world economy in ways that meet everybody's needs. Price stability is perhaps an even more valuable 'common wealth' commodity than we realise. It is worth fighting over price stability whether the fight occurs inside the Federal Reserve or between central banks or even among the general public. We should not have to learn the hard way that, for some, it may be worth fighting for militarily as well.

Meanwhile, it is a small miracle that workers in the industrialised world have accepted a lower standard of living so quietly – thus far. It is harder to expect emerging-market workers to silently accept a reduction in their standard of living. We cannot say, 'I am very sorry but you are no longer as competitive, so you can't have as much meat in your diet or anything else you aspire to for now. Let us know when you have a new business model'. We have to expect a reaction. People will not quietly tolerate the growing pain forever. They may feel that the culprit lies in the growing gap between the rich countries and the poor countries, or between the rich and the poor within nations. But the real issue is that we need more wealth generation all around. The solution is innovation: in business models, in entrepreneurial ventures, in diplomacy, in governance, in technology and in

* Bernard Shaw and Richard Burton, *The Man and the Mask*, Henry Holt, 1916.

personal goals. Only innovation can generate a greater alignment of interests between nations and among the people who inhabit them.

No one now needs to fall back on the excuse that 'the algorithm made me do it'. No one now needs to push all of the risks they can't quantify off the table into a box labelled 'black swans'. No doubt some risks belong in that category, but armed with an awareness of signals, it will be easier to see the things that can be seen. We can take comfort from the Nobel Prize-winning physicist, Niels Bohr, who reminds us that, 'Prediction is very difficult, especially about the future.' Nobody should feel bad about being unable to predict or forecast accurately. All that is asked is better preparedness for a range of possibilities.

It is heartening when Shakespeare reminds us that, 'All things are ready, if our mind be so.'*

The Gordian knot will be cut asunder not by unravelling the past, or even by correctly predicting the future, but by acts of creation, by the stitching together of something new, something more robust out of whatever it is we have to work with. What we have are different people with different skills, different talents, different goals, different interpretations of signals. Out of that rich mix will emerge a social fabric that serves better and is more robust than before. It is only through these quiet individual choices that anything can be done to rebalance societies and improve the balance between the rich and the poor, the haves and the have-nots, between governments and their citizens. It is not such a big leap to imagine that we will cook and sew and build and write and in many other ways simply innovate our way out of the current mess.

People can create something out of nothing and often do. So, whether you are saltwater or freshwater; an entrepreneur or intrapreneur; a high-flyer, 9-to-5-er or job-seeker; a plumber or a policymaker; a

---

* Spoken by King Henry: *Henry V*, Act IV, scene 3.

politician; a butcher, a baker, a candlestick maker; tinker, tailor, soldier, spy; someone who only speaks the language of math and algorithms or someone who only knows plain speaking; 'hardscrabble or high roller',* please join in the ongoing conversation about signals instead of leaving it to the economists and policymakers alone.

Your views are the key that unlocks the gift that is the economy of the future. No one can predict what this gift will look like, but its character depends on the nature of the decisions every individual makes today. Think of the world economy as a constant character test that demands an eccentric and edgy response, a calculated risk that can result in hurt (as opposed to injury) or fulfil hope. The edgework we choose to pursue, or not pursue, defines the character of the outcome.

The alternative is clear. If we lack the character to face the signals and we choose to avoid the edgework, we will once again hear people say the cause of the next crisis was 'principally a failure of the collective imagination' just as the members of the British Academy told the Queen regarding the last crisis.† I think we can dodge that bullet (remember what the Chinese say about wars being fought with silver bullets?). We just have to learn a new dance.

A new dance

We did not fight as much when there was enough cash to fund everyone's needs. But now that there isn't enough, we are fighting all around: amongst ourselves and with everybody else too. Now strategic security and economics are forced to dance together on a more challenging and uncertain geopolitical landscape, but the defence community does not easily recognise or accept its new dance partner: economics. Nor does the economics community easily accept its new dance partner: geopolitics. Of course the two have met before. In fact,

* I am grateful to Charles Blow for this elegant turn of phrase which he used in a *New York Times* Opinion article of 14 March 2014: 'We Can't Grow the Gap Away'. But, I would argue, we can innovate the gap away.
† From the British Academy letter to the Queen of 10 August 2009.

they are usually found hand in hand. But the Fall of the Berlin Wall made a star of economics and banished geopolitics to the side of the world stage. We think that separation is normal when it's probably an exception to the rule.

Today, the state is being outrun by the market and in response the state tries to control the market. This makes for an inelegant dance with a partner that has not been seen in a while and the memory of whom is uncomfortable. Is the dance led by the tune of deflation or inflation? Will the dance partners innovate or stagnate? Where do hubris and nemesis and even the ghost of Gollum linger, waiting for us to choose a path?

Perhaps knowing all this, and being better armed with an awareness of signals, we may all be better prepared to balance our hubris and nemesis and thereby take advantage of and better manage the diverse troubles and treasures the world economy inevitably brings. The character of your choices define what it will bring to you and to us all.

Index